CULTURE AND CUSTOMS OF IRAN

Iran. Cartography by Bookcomp, Inc.

CULTURE AND CUSTOMS
OF IRAN

Elton L. Daniel and Ali Akbar Mahdi

Culture and Customs of the Middle East

Greenwood Press
Westport, Connecticut • London

Library of Congress Cataloging-in-Publication Data

Daniel, Elton L.
   Culture and customs of Iran / Elton L. Daniel and Ali Akbar Mahdi.
     p. cm. — (Culture and customs of the Middle East, ISSN 1550–1310)
   Includes bibliographical references and index.
   ISBN 0–313–32053–5 (alk. paper)
   1. Iran—Civilization. 2. Iran—Intellectual life. 3. Iran—Social life and customs. I. Mahdi,
'Ali Akbar. II. Title.
   DS266.D265 2006
   955—dc22   2006022941

British Library Cataloguing in Publication Data is available.

Library of Congress Catalog Card Number: 2006022941
ISBN: 0–313–32053–5
ISSN: 1550–1310

First published in 2006

Greenwood Press, 88 Post Road West, Westport, CT 06881
An imprint of Greenwood Publishing Group, Inc.
www.greenwood.com

Printed in the United States of America

The paper used in this book complies with the
Permanent Paper Standard issued by the National
Information Standards Organization (Z39.48–1984).

10 9 8 7 6 5 4 3 2 1

Every reasonable effort has been made to trace the owners of copyright materials in this book, but in some
instances this has proven impossible. The authors and publisher will be glad to receive information leading
to a more complete acknowledgments in subsequent printings of the book and in the meantime extend
their apologies for any omissions.

Contents

Series Foreword   vii
Preface   ix
Chronology   xiii

1. Introduction: The Land and the People   1

2. Religions and Religious Life   37

3. Literature   65

4. Drama and Cinema   93

5. Architecture   119

6. Carpets   137

7. Food and Dining   149

8. Family, Women, and Gender Relations   157

9. Holidays, Festivals, and Annual Events   177

10. Music and Dance   189

Glossary   211
Selected Bibliography   215
Index   223

Series Foreword

At last! *Culture and Customs of the Middle East* fills a deep void in reference literature by providing substantial individual volumes on crucial countries in the explosive region. The series is available at a critical juncture, with, among other events, the recent war on Iraq, the continued wrangling by U.S. interests for control of regional oil resources, the quest for Palestinian independence, and the spread of religious fundamentalist violence and repression. The authoritative, objective, and engaging cultural overviews complement and balance the volley of news bites.

As with the other Culture and Customs series, the narrative focus is on contemporary culture and life, in a historical context. Each volume is written for students and general readers by a country expert. Contents include:

Chronology

Context, including land, people, and brief historical overview

Religion and world view

Literature

Media

Cinema

Art and architecture/housing

Cuisine and dress

Gender, marriage, and family

Social customs and lifestyle

Music and dance

Glossary

Bibliography

Index

Photos and country map

Preface

Greenwood's series on the culture and customs of different countries is a wonderful way of introducing the intricacies of various cultures to English-speaking readers. We are glad to have the opportunity to be a part of this series by exposing the rich and varied elements of Iranian society and culture. We have tried our best to provide an accurate presentation of various aspects of the cultures and customs of Iran. However, writing about the culture and customs of a multicultural society like Iran is not without its challenges. We believe it is important to acknowledge the challenges we faced and the extent of coverage we offer.

First, Iran has had a long and tumultuous history. The country has been invaded and influenced by foreign forces several times. These invasions often interrupted the social and economic life of the country, changed demographics and ethnic composition, and influenced the culture and customs practiced in daily life.

Second, ethnically, religiously, linguistically, and regionally speaking, Iran is a very diverse society, despite the fact that Persians make up the dominant ethnic group, the Persian language is the official language, and Shiism is the dominant religion. This diversity can hardly be described in simple categorizations. Cultural customs associated with the same event often take various forms in different regions among different ethnic, regional, and religious groups.

Third, culture is a dynamic phenomenon, subject to change and interpretation. The meaning and significance of an event and the customs associated with it vary for people of different religions, ethnicities, and social classes within the same society. When affected by the ideological and political trends in a specific period of social history, these interpretations may become controversial and contestable for various constituencies in the society.

Fourth, the series has a format that may work effectively with the culture and customs of some societies and less effectively with others. We definitely faced the challenge of incorporating into a predetermined number of pages the very long and varied history, culture, and customs of diverse groups that have lived in a country whose changing boundaries at different times have stretched as far as India and Egypt.

Fifth, each of us is trained in modern social sciences, one as a historian and the other as a sociologist, and we specialized in narrowly defined subjects within our fields. Yet, covering the culture and customs of Iran required us to write on such broad and different subjects as carpets, music, cinema, and architecture. This was not an easy task, but we have done our best to offer a general understanding of the description and history of elements associated with each subject without engaging in their specialized and controversial aspects.

Finally, despite our best efforts, the book does not cover all elements of Iranian culture. Our coverage of sports is limited to a few references to traditional athletic culture. Not being able to discuss diversity and the evolution of dress, we have tried to provide readers a sense of this diversity by three visuals. While major aspects of the arts are well covered, others, like painting, ceramics, and metalwork, are either mentioned casually or are not covered at all. To help our readers interested in topics not adequately covered, we have offered appropriate sources in our suggested readings.

A NOTE ON TRANSLITERATION AND PRONUNCIATION

As one would expect, most of the names and technical terms found in this book come from Persian and other languages that do not use the Latin script. The problem of how to present these in English for a general audience is a difficult one for which there is no entirely satisfactory solution. For Persian, we have attempted to use a systematic but simplified system of transliteration that will also give readers a general idea of how such words are pronounced. For other languages (including ancient Iranian languages), we have attempted to use whatever form of the name or terms that seems to us to be the most familiar and least confusing for readers.

The method of transliterating Persian needs some explanation to assist readers with pronunciation and other concerns. The Persian script is based on Arabic, a good deal of its vocabulary is of Arabic origin, and Arabic grammatical expressions (such as the definite article) are sometimes used.

Several consonants in the Arabic alphabet have distinct sounds in Arabic, but they are pronounced the same in Persian. Some of these consonants have no equivalent in English either and require the use of special diacritical marks to denote them in Latin script. We have generally treated these phonetically and do not distinguish, for example, between the initial *h* in the name Hasan and that in Hushang. We have, however, indicated the difference between the soft guttural *gh* and the hard guttural *q* (neither of which has an equivalent in English and both of which are often pronounced the same in Persian or even written interchangeably). We also use the symbol """ for the consonant *'ayn* (a kind of strong glottal stop in Arabic that has no English equivalent and is pronounced in Persian like a weak glottal stop if at all). The Arabic glottal stop, *hamzeh*, is not indicated except in a few cases where it is significant for orthography; in that case it is represented by an apostrophe (as in the name Ma'mun). For short vowels, we use *a, e,* and *o* (all pronounced about as one would expect in English), and for long vowels *â* (pronounced like the *a* in father), *i* (pronounced like *ee* in feet), and *u* (pronounced like *oo* in pool). The principles behind other conventions used in the transliteration system should be apparent to specialists but of no real concern to general readers.

Finally, there are some names and terms that have become so commonly used and accepted in English that it was not felt necessary to transliterate them fully or at all. These anglicized forms include a few names of people such as Khomeini and Khamenei; some cities and provinces such as Tehran, Isfahan, Kurdistan, and Azerbaijan; important religious sects such as the Sunnites and Isma'ilis; most dynasties, such as the Umayyads or Abbasids; and technical terms and titles such as Koran, Imam, shah. (Note, however, that terms like Imam and shah are transliterated as *emâm* and *shâh* when used as part of a name or in Persian phrases, etc.)

Chronology

ANCIENT IRAN

ca. 4000 B.C.	Bronze Age settlements (Sialk, Hasanlu, Hessar).
2400–1600 B.C.	Elamite Kingdom.
ca. 728–550 B.C.	The Median Kingdom.

ACHAEMENID PERIOD (550–330 B.C.)

ca. 550 B.C.	Cyrus the Great.
522–486 B.C.	Darius the Great.
331 B.C.	Alexander the Great defeats Darius III at Gaugamela.

SELEUCID AND PARTHIAN PERIOD (312 B.C.–A.D. 224)

312–281 B.C.	Seleucus Nicator founds Seleucid Kingdom.
ca. 238 B.C.	Revolt of Arsaces, king of Parthia.

THE SASANID PERIOD (A.D. 224–651)

A.D. 224	Ardashir defeats Parthians and founds Sasanid Dynasty.
A.D. 531–579	Khosrow I Anushirvan.
A.D. 637–642	Arab-Muslim armies defeat Sasanids at Qâdesiyeh and Nehâvand.
A.D. 651	Death of last Sasanid king.

CLASSICAL ISLAMIC PERIOD (A.D. 651–1040)

A.D. 747   Abbasid Revolution in Khorâsân.

A.D. 874–999   Samanid Dynasty in eastern Iran.

A.D. 932–1055   Buyid Dynasty in Western Iran.

A.D. 994–1040   Ghaznavid Dynasty in eastern Iran.

TURKO-MONGOL PERIOD (A.D. 1040–1501)

A.D. 1040   Battle of Dandânqân: Saljuq Turks in Khorâsân.

A.D. 1055   Saljuqs capture Baghdad.

A.D. 1219   Beginning of Mongol invasion.

A.D. 1256–1349   Mongol Il-khanid Dynasty.

A.D. 1380–1393   Conquests of Timur (Tamerlane).

SAFAVID AND EARLY MODERN PERIOD (A.D. 1501–1797)

A.D. 1501   Shah Esmâ'il founds Safavid Kingdom.

A.D. 1587–1629   Shah 'Abbâs the Great.

A.D. 1722   Afghan invasion and siege of Isfahan.

A.D. 1736–1747   Nâder Shah.

A.D. 1750–1779   Karim Khân Zand.

THE QÂJÂR PERIOD (A.D. 1797–1925)

A.D. 1797   Âghâ Mohammad Shah establishes Qâjâr rule.

A.D. 1804–1813   First Russo-Persian War.

A.D. 1826–1828   Second Russo-Persian War.

A.D. 1848   Amir Kabir as Prime Minister.

A.D. 1856–1857   Anglo-Persian War.

A.D. 1891   The Tobacco Protest.

A.D. 1896   Assassination of Nâser-od-Din Shah.

A.D. 1901   D'Arcy Concession for petroleum and gas.

A.D. 1905–1911   The Constitutional Revolution.

A.D. 1909   Formation of Anglo-Persian Oil Company.

A.D. 1921   Coup d'etat by Rezâ Khân and Ziâ-od-Din Tabâtabâi.

PAHLAVI IRAN (A.D. 1925–1979)

A.D. 1925	Constituent Assembly votes to establish monarchy under Rezâ Shah Pahlavi.
A.D. 1941	Allied occupation; abdication of Rezâ Shah.
A.D. 1951	Mohammad Mosaddeq becomes prime minister.
A.D. 1953	Mosaddeq overthrown in coup d'etat.
A.D. 1962	Inauguration of the White Revolution.
A.D. 1963	Religious protests; Âyatollâh Khomeini exiled.
A.D. 1967	Coronation of Mohammad-Rezâ Shah.
A.D. 1971	Celebration at Persepolis of 2,500 years of monarchy in Iran; Tehran agreement on oil prices.
A.D. 1978	Anti-Pahlavi riots and demonstrations leading to Black Friday massacre.
A.D. 1979	Mohammad-Rezâ Shah leaves Iran; Shâpur Bakhtiâr attempts and fails to establish a transitional government.

THE ISLAMIC REPUBLIC (A.D. 1979 TO PRESENT)

A.D. 1979	Return of Âyatollâh Khomeini to Iran; Mahdi Bâzargân appointed prime minister of a provisional government and resigns later in the year; Constitution of the Islamic Republic of Iran adopted; beginning of the U.S. embassy hostage crisis.
A.D. 1980	Bani Sadr elected president; beginning of Iran-Iraq War.
A.D. 1981	American embassy hostages released; Khomeini removes Bani Sadr from office; Mohammad-'Ali Rajâi elected as president in August and killed with several of his ministers in the same month; 'Ali Khamenei elected president.
A.D. 1983	Tudeh (Communist) Party banned; consolidation of clerical power com pleted.
A.D. 1988	Khomeini accepts cease-fire in Iran-Iraq War.
A.D. 1989	Âyatollâh Hosayn-'Ali Montazeri removed as heir to Khomeini; death of Khomeini; the constitution is revised and approved; election of 'Ali-Akbar Hâshemi Rafsanjâni as president.
A.D. 1997	Election of Mohammad Khâtami as president.
A.D. 2005	Election of Mahmud Ahmadinejâd as president.

1

Introduction: The Land and the People

GEOGRAPHY

Geography obviously has a significant impact on the development of society and culture anywhere in the world, but its effect is particularly dramatic in a country like Iran. It severely limits where people can live, makes transportation and communications between different areas of the country difficult, and has greatly affected the kinds of lifestyles that are possible.

First of all, Iran is, relatively speaking, a very large country. In its current borders, it has a total area (land and water surface combined) of about 636,000 square miles. It is now the seventeenth largest country in the world in physical size (falling from sixteenth after the breakup of the Soviet Union and the creation of Kazakhstan as an independent state). By way of comparison, it is about 10 percent larger than Alaska, more than double the size of Texas, or four times the size of California, but somewhat smaller than Mexico. While Iran's area is thus much less than that of a country like the United States or Canada or Russia, it is substantially greater than most of its regional neighbors—more than double the size of Turkey, Afghanistan, or Pakistan and quadruple that of Iraq, but less than that of Saudi Arabia.

The central core of the country consists of an almost uninterrupted expanse of salt and sand deserts stretching over 700 miles from the northwest to southeast. The desert basin in the north is known as the Dasht-e Kavir, an exceptionally desolate region of salt desert that runs for some 200 miles from east to west and almost 100 miles from north to south. Another area in the south, the Dasht-e Lut, includes a great sandy desert 100 miles long and 40 miles wide. These regions are not only barren but are also virtually impenetrable to anything but specialized forms of modern mechanized transport.

Flanking the desert basin are two equally imposing mountain chains, the Alborz and the Zagros. The Alborz chain forms a relatively compact crescent across the north of the country approximately 300 miles in length and an average of 60 miles in width. It is dominated by the majestic snow-covered volcanic peak of Mount Damâvand, the tallest mountain in Iran at an elevation of 18,628 feet. On the north side, the Alborz Mountains fall away precipitously from elevations of around 10,000 feet to the littoral of the Caspian Sea (about 25 feet below sea level). Because of this steep drop-off and the lack of many practicable passes, the Alborz Mountains make up a virtual wall that effectively blocks off the Caspian area from the rest of the country. The more complex Zagros chain consists of a broad band of parallel ranges, about 125 miles in width, running from the northwest to the southeast of the country. The mountains of the Zagros are not quite as lofty as those of the Alborz but are still quite impressive: the highest peak, Zardeh Kuh, rises to 14,920 feet. The Zagros also has more practicable passes, but the layout and direction of the individual ranges present considerable difficulties for crossing the mountains from east to west. In the south, the Zagros also descend fairly abruptly from about 2,000 feet to sea level at the Persian Gulf. This combination of mountains and a central plateau gives Iran a very high mean elevation. Most land is above 2,000 feet, and on the central plateau, where the most important cities are located, the average elevation is 4,000 feet.

In addition to the loftiness and ruggedness of the terrain, another important characteristic of the geography of Iran is its aridity. The average precipitation for the country as a whole is only 10 inches per year—not very much considering that a desert can be defined as a region receiving less than 6 inches of rain per year. Moreover, this precipitation is either seasonal, falling as snow in winter, or concentrated in a few specific areas, notably the Caspian-facing slopes of the Alborz and parts of the Zagros. Areas along the Caspian may receive 40 inches or more per year, and certain other mountain regions perhaps half that amount. Barely half of the country receives enough annual precipitation to exceed the marginal amount typical of a desert, and only 10 percent of the country can be considered arable.

Iran, despite its size, has little in the way of rivers or lakes. The only navigable river is the Kârun, which makes commercial shipping possible for a distance of about 70 miles. Some rivers, notably the Safid Rud and the Atrak, feed into the Caspian Sea; but they do not carry much water, are seasonal in flow, and are not practicable for navigation. The Aras (Araxes) River forms part of Iran's border in the northwest, and the Helmand, which drains southern Afghanistan, provides some water for irrigation in the southeast. A good many seasonal torrents carry run-off from the mountains to the central basin, where they eventually disappear into the desert. Perhaps the best-known of these inland rivers is the Zâyandeh Rud, which runs through the city of Isfahan before dissipating in the Gâv-khuni swamp. The largest lake is Urmia (about 1,800 square miles in area but no more than 50 feet deep); like most lakes in Iran, it has no outlet and is consequently very saline (comparable to the Dead Sea). In recent years, dams have been constructed on some of these rivers to provide electricity or increase reservoirs of water.

CLIMATE

The northernmost part of Iran lies at approximately latitude 40° north, about the same as Philadelphia in the United States, and its southernmost part around latitude 25° north, about as far south as Miami. The diversity of climate between Philadelphia and Miami, however, is not nearly as extreme as that to be found in Iran, which varies dramatically from region to region and according to elevation. On the plateau, aridity combined with high elevation produces a very rigorous continental-type climate, with great variation in temperature between seasons and even between day and night. At Tabriz (elevation 4,400 feet), in the northwest, the temperature falls as low as −13°F in winter and soars to 104°F in summer. At Mashhad (3,300 feet), in the northeast, it drops to −18°F in winter and rises to 108°F in summer. Other major cities are far enough south to avoid these extremes in winter. Tehran (3,800 feet), the capital, has an average yearly temperature of 64°F: winter brings a good deal of snow and average lows of 29°F in January; summer is extremely hot and dry, with an average high of 97°F in July. The extremes vary from a record low of 9°F in January to 108°F in July. Isfahan (5,150 feet), in the center of the plateau, has a yearly average of 62°F, with average lows of 29°F in January and highs of 95°F in July.

Of course, areas in the high elevations are extremely cold in winter, while some of those in the south can be blisteringly hot in summer—daily highs over 122°F are not uncommon in Irânshahr (2,200 feet). Spots in the Dasht-e Lut can claim to be among the hottest on earth, with temperatures often over 134°F and reported measurements as high as 156°F.

Off the plateau, the climatic regime is quite different. The Caspian areas are much more humid and also milder in temperature, rarely falling below freezing in winter in the lower elevations and with summer highs around 93°F. In the Khuzestân plains, the temperatures at Ahvâz range from highs of around 68°F in January to 118°F in July. The British traveler Percy Sykes noted that the temperature at nearby Shustar in June 1896 measured 129°F in the shade day after day.[1] Along the Persian Gulf, humidity hovers near 100 percent, and daily highs range from 68°F in winter to 106°F in summer.

POPULATION AND LANGUAGES

The demography of Iran is as diverse and complex as the geography. As of 2001, Iran was estimated to have 66,128,965 inhabitants, which would make it the sixteenth largest country in the world in terms of population. At first glance, this might suggest a fairly low density of population: Turkey, for example, has almost exactly the same number of people in a country half the size, giving it twice the population density of Iran (220 people per square mile as opposed to 103 in Iran). Indeed, the population density in Iran is about the same as that in Afghanistan, less than that in Iraq (135 per square mile), and a mere fraction of that in Pakistan (460 per square mile), Israel (732 per square mile), or Lebanon (902 per square mile). These statistics, however, are misleading unless one also takes into account another very important element in the geographical character of the country: over half of the land is made up of essentially uninhabitable mountains and deserts, so that the population is actually concentrated in a relatively small but diffuse area and is generally more dense in the north and west of the country.

All of this population is Iranian in the sense that the people are citizens of the nation-state of Iran. The population is also quite uniform in terms of religion: over 99 percent are followers of Islam, either Shi'ite Muslims (estimates range from 89 to 95 percent) or Sunni Muslims (4 to 10 percent). Language, however, is also a powerful or determining factor in individual and group identity, and the population of Iran is anything but homogeneous in that regard. Over two-thirds of the people speak languages or dialects belonging to what is known as the Iranian branch of the Indo-European family of languages. The Iranian languages are thus closely related to some languages spoken in India and more distantly related to Romance, Germanic, or Slavic languages. The most widely spoken of the Iranian languages is Modern (or New) Persian, which is the official and commonly understood language of the country. It is the mother-tongue, however, of only a slight majority of the population, and it is not mutually intelligible with other Iranian languages such as Kurdish or Baluchi. Turkic languages and dialects, which belong to the Ural-Altaic family and are unrelated to the Iranian languages, are spoken by some 26 percent of the population in Iran: by the now mostly sedentary and nontribal Azeri Turks, by the Qashqâi tribal confederation, and by the formerly nomadic or seminomadic tribes usually called Turkomans.

Some of these languages and dialects are only spoken and have no written form. The literary languages in Iran use the Arabic script, and they have been affected to varying degrees by Arabic vocabulary and even Arabic grammar. That is one reason foreigners sometimes assume that the languages are related, when in fact they belong to completely different language families. Arabic is a Semitic language, and only about 1 percent of the people in Iran are native speakers of Arabic, but the language is widely studied and understood due to its religious importance in Islam. It is only because of historical circumstances that languages like Persian or Azeri came to be written in Arabic script. Despite its widespread use, this script is really not well suited for writing Persian and is even less satisfactory for Turkic languages. Arabic has several consonants that do not occur in Persian or Turkish, and those languages have some consonants that do not occur in Arabic. The vowel structure in Arabic words is generally predictable since words are constructed according to standard forms, and the script has characters for only three long vowels (there are ways of indicating the short vowels, but these are not usually written). Turkish, on the other hand, has eight distinct vowels, and there are no rules for predicting what vowels will be used in Persian and Turkish words. The ambiguities in the script thus make learning to read those languages somewhat more difficult than might otherwise be the case.

CITIES, REGIONS, AND ETHNIC GROUPS

Contemporary Iran is divided into 28 provinces, but these are mostly artificial administrative divisions that are of little real consequence and subject to frequent changes. Geographical factors, however, have created a number of quite distinct regions in Iran, and their identity is often reinforced by ethnic and cultural differences as well.

The most fundamentally different regions of the country are the lowlands facing the Caspian Sea and the Persian Gulf. The Caspian region has three main components: Gilân, a broad plain in the west, with Rasht and the port of Anzali as major urban centers; Mâzandarân, a narrow, central strip of land between the Alborz and the Caspian, with Sâri as its major city; and Gorgân, another large plain to the east (now part of the province called Golestân, which includes the cities of Gorgân and Gonbad-e Qâbus). None of these areas are predominantly Persian speaking. Gorgân is a Turkic-speaking area inhabited by various Turkoman tribes such as the Yomut or Goklen, some of whom are still nomadic or seminomadic. Elsewhere in the Caspian region, people speak Gilaki or Mâzandarâni, both Iranian but non-Persian languages. Throughout much of this area, the climate is subtropical and humid, making possible the cultivation of crops such as rice and tea. Toward the mountains, the region is heavily forested. Gorgân is more arid, but cotton has become an important crop there. The sea and marshes are also important to the local economy and diet, with many popular seaside resorts and a supply of sturgeon and caviar. Traditional housing in this region is quite unique, too, with thatched-roof houses raised on stilts in Gilân and round felt tents for the Turkoman nomads in Gorgân. The areas facing the Persian Gulf include Khuzestân, an expansive plain along both sides of the Kârun River in the southwest, and the Tangsir, a narrow and sparsely populated coastal strip along the Gulf. Khuzestân has a mixed population, which includes a substantial number of Arabs. It is, of course, best known in modern times for its petroleum industry, which has made Ahvâz, Âbâdân, and Khorramshahr major industrial centers. The Tangsir, or Tangestân, consists mostly of sleepy, isolated fishing and pearling villages; people there speak their own peculiar dialect of Persian. In general, the Iranian coast of the Persian Gulf has very few good ports, the two main exceptions being Bushehr and Bandar-e 'Abbâs. In recent years, efforts have been made to build up islands like Kish or towns like Châhbahâr as free-trade zones.

In northwest Iran, Azerbaijan gets a fair amount of rainfall and has many pasturelands and relatively fertile mountain valleys that have always been attractive to nomadic groups seeking places to graze their animals. Many Turkoman tribes thus occupied this area in the centuries before and after the Mongol conquest, and most of the population of this area still speak a Turkic language. Because of its location, Azerbaijan has also been an important avenue of trade from the Iranian plateau to Anatolia and the Caucasus. In many ways, the cultural and economic ties of Azerbaijan have been closer to areas of the Caucasus than to the plateau. The major city of Azerbaijan, and one which has played a particularly important role in Iranian history in recent centuries, is Tabriz. The region is also home to Assyrian and Armenian Christian communities, especially in the area around Urmia, the great salt lake. To the south, in the mountainous areas of western Iran, live several non-Persian speaking ethnic minorities, the most important being the Kurds and the Lurs.

At the opposite, southeastern, corner of Iran are Sistân and Baluchestân. They are lumped together in one administrative province today, but they really form quite distinct subregions that extend beyond Iran's contemporary political borders into Afghanistan and Pakistan, respectively. Both are generally sandy desert areas: very hot, very dry, subject to violent windstorms, and thinly populated. Sistân would be one of the most inhospitable environments on earth were it not for the waters of the Helmand River, which end in a kind of large oasis in Iranian Sistân around the town of Zâbol. In earlier times, dams and other irrigation projects made extensive agriculture possible, and the region was much more prosperous than it is today. The Helmand also provided an important artery for trade. The people of Sistân have traditionally been fiercely independent in spirit and proud of their regional identity. Baluchestân is the area south of the city of Zâhedân, running between the Jaz

Muriân desert and the Pakistani border. It is peppered with small mountain villages and groups of nomadic or seminomadic pastoralists. The origins of the Baluch people are obscure, but their language is an Iranian one, close to some of the ancient languages of Iran and quite different from modern Persian. This whole region is one of the poorest in Iran, and its economy has not been helped in recent years by an influx of thousands of refugees from Afghanistan. It is also one of the most difficult areas for the central government to control and has a reputation for lawlessness, especially the smuggling of drugs and other goods, that makes it something like the "Wild, Wild East" of Iran.

Among other important regions, mention must be made of Fârs and Khorâsân. Fârs is the mountainous region of south-central Iran and is in many ways the historical and cultural heartland of Iran. One of the earliest advanced civilizations in Iran began there, two great Iranian empires originated there, several of Iran's most famous archaeological and artistic sites are located there, and many of Iran's greatest writers and poets lived there. The capital, Shiraz, is among the most attractive cities in Iran, a place whose reputation conjures up the images of roses, nightingales, gardens, ambrosial wine, heavenly poetry, and relaxed living that seem so quintessentially (or stereotypically) Iranian. It is not without reason that among foreigners, since the time of the ancient Greeks, the name of this region, Persia, has been applied to the whole of Iran.

If Fârs is the heartland of Iran, Khorâsân is its shield, its main frontier province. The mountains of northeastern Iran do not pose quite the barrier to movement as do those of the north and west. While Iran has occasionally been invaded from the west, it has been under an almost constant threat of attack or invasion by the nomads of central Asia. The fortified villages and garrison cities of Khorâsân have had the historical task of resisting that pressure and have suffered the most from failures to do so. Today, the Iranian province of Khorâsân is only a remnant of what was once a much larger territory and an important bastion of Iranian culture. On the other hand, now that the external threat has ebbed, the economy of the area is reviving, and its population is increasing at a faster rate than that of other parts of Iran. Its major city, Mashhad, now has over 2 million inhabitants (up from 240,000 in 1956). Mashhad is also a spiritual center of Iran, since one of the most important religious shrines is located there and is visited by about 12 million pilgrims each year.

Central Iran consists of the plateau and great desert basin, on the periphery of which are scattered the other major cities of Iran: Qazvin, Hamadân, Qom, Isfahan, Yazd, Kermân, Birjand, Semnân, and so forth. This represents the dominant, Persian-speaking core of the country and is thus, along with Fârs and Khorâsân, the area one is most likely to have in mind when trying to describe the culture and customs of Iran. In recent times, these cities have all been overshadowed by the capital, Tehran. Since the eighteenth century, it has grown from a small village at the foothills of the Alborz Mountains to a sprawling metropolis of 12 million people. It dominates every aspect of the political, economic, and cultural life of the country—even the vernacular language of Iran, which foreigners have encountered and taken to calling *Fârsi* is most often really just the Tehrâni dialect of Persian. Compared with other major cities, though, Tehran is an upstart in terms of its historical heritage and a rather drab, ordinary, and faceless modern city in appearance. The most glamorous city is easily Isfahan, which was the capital of Iran in the sixteenth century, when it was adorned with a multitude of beautiful and impressive mosques, parks, and palaces.

OUTLINE OF IRANIAN HISTORY
Ancient Iran

The area occupied by the modern country of Iran was home to simple semiagrarian cultures as early as 13,000 B.C. Conditions on the plateau, how-ever, were not well suited for the development of the kind of advanced agri-cultural societies that appeared in other parts of the Fertile Crescent. Without any great rivers to exploit, that had to await the development, at an uncertain but late date, of a satisfactory method of irrigation, now known as the *kariz* or *qanât* system (a network of underground channels to carry water by grav-ity feed from highland water tables to fields at lower elevations). In some areas, agriculture was thus eclipsed by pastoralism (herding cattle, probably on a nomadic basis, to graze on the meager natural vegetation) or by trading societies supplying the great cities of Mesopotamia and the Indus with raw materials such as metal. It was only along the Kârun River in the southwest that geographic factors were conducive to the rise of an early civilization. This area was really just an extension of the Mesopotamian plain and was under the influence of Mesopotamian culture, but it came to be occupied by a people, the Elamites, who definitely had their roots on the plateau. They formed a kingdom in approximately 2700 B.C. and became a major power during the period 1500–1100 B.C., when they even managed briefly to defeat and sack Babylon.

Although the Elamites thus founded the first known civilization in Iran, they were not ethnically "Iranian": that is, they spoke a unique language that cannot be connected with any other particular group of languages. It was at about the time when their kingdom was at its peak that people calling themselves Aryans (from a word probably meaning "noble") and speaking languages belonging to the Iranian group moved onto the Iranian plateau. The process of migrations or invasions that separated these Iranians from the closely related Indo-Aryans (who moved into the Indus Valley) and brought them onto the plateau is difficult to trace and highly controversial among specialists. It is clear enough, though, that Iranian tribes had reached the Zagros by the beginning of the first millennium B.C. One of these tribal groups, the Medes, was under attack by the Assyrians from 881–788 B.C. In response, the Medes eventually organized themselves into a kingdom with a capital at Ecbatana (modern Hamadân in the central Zagros). Under King Cyaxares (625–584 B.C.), the Medes allied with Babylon to crush the Assyrians. They subsequently expanded into Asia Minor (modern Turkey), where, after an indecisive war with the Lydians, they negotiated a border along the Halys River.

The Persian (Achaemenid) Empire

The Medes had also established a kind of alliance with another Iranian tribal group, the Persians. The Persians had settled in the southern areas of the Zagros, the old homeland of the Elamites, and their rulers styled themselves "kings of Anshan" (a former Elamite stronghold). Presumably to strengthen the bonds between the two people, the Median king Astyages married one of his daughters, Mandane, to the Persian king Cambyses I (600–559 B.C.). Mandane gave birth to a son who would become one of the most celebrated rulers of all antiquity: Cyrus the Great. In 549 B.C., Cyrus led a successful revolt against his grandfather Astyages, who was deposed, and created a unified Persian-Median empire with himself as "great king, king of kings, king of the lands." He then asserted his authority over the Iranian tribes to the east, defeated King Croesus of Lydia and annexed his kingdom (ca. 547 B.C.), took over the Greek city-states of Ionia, and occupied Babylon (539 B.C.). The rest of his life was mostly spent in attempting to pacify eastern Iran and defend its borders; he apparently died in 530 B.C. fighting off nomads from central Asia. Cyrus was a master of diplomacy and propaganda who ruled his empire, the largest the world had seen, with a light hand; he is reputed to have dealt magnanimously with defeated rivals and to have followed a policy of allowing subject peoples to retain their local religion and customs (the most famous example being the Jews who were released from captivity in Babylon and encouraged to rebuild the Temple in Jerusalem).

The empire founded by Cyrus is known either as the Persian Empire, after the Persian people and the name of their homeland (Persis, the modern province of Fârs), or the Achaemenid Empire, after Achaemenes, the reputed ancestor of the dynasty. Already impressive at the time of Cyrus' death, this empire was further expanded by his son Cambyses (530–522 B.C.), who conquered Egypt, and in many ways was perfected by Darius the Great (522–486 B.C.), a (perhaps distant) kinsman who took over the throne as the result of a murky palace coup. Darius proved to be an extremely successful ruler. He put down numerous attempted rebellions, defended the frontiers against the threat of nomadic invasions, and created the sophisticated system of communication and administration necessary to hold together such a vast empire. Among the many achievements of his reign were the system of organizing the empire into administrative units known as *satrapies*, the Royal Road and postal service linking the capital and the provinces, a canal linking the Nile and the Red Sea, the introduction of coinage, promulgation of a new law code, standardization of weights and measures, reorganization of the army and creation of the elite guard known as the Immortals, and the adoption of a script for writing the Old Persian language.

Unfortunately, Darius is most often remembered, at least among non-Iranians, for initiating the unsuccessful and ultimately disastrous series of wars between the Persians and the Greeks. The landing of Persian forces that the Athenians repulsed at the Battle of Marathon (490 B.C.) was, to Darius, probably little more than a punitive raid that went awry. The invasion of Greece under his son Xerxes (486–465 B.C.) was a more serious affair and one that had more far-reaching consequences. After defeating the Spartans at Thermopylae and sacking Athens, Xerxes' campaign also ended in failure at the great naval battle of Salamis in 480 B.C. and on land at Plataea the following year. The ensuing struggle between the Greeks and Persians culminated in the invasion and destruction of the Persian Empire (334–330 B.C.) by Alexander the Great and a period of Greek rule under the Seleucids. After the Greek interlude, two more great Iranian empires eventually arose, the Parthians and the Sasanids.

Parthians and Sasanids

The Parthians emerged around 238 B.C. as a coalition of tribes in eastern Iran led by a king named Arsaces (hence the dynasty is also referred to as the Arsacids). They moved into western Iran during the reign of their king, Mithridates I (171–138 B.C.). Their empire lasted longer than any other Iranian empire, but it is the least well understood because of a lack of historical sources from that period. Although the Parthians were quite partial to Greek culture (calling themselves Hellenophiles on their coinage), they were relentlessly anti-Roman in their foreign policy; it is the history of their wars, as recorded by Roman sources, that makes up most of what is known about them. Their most famous battle was with the Roman general Crassus, whose forces were annihilated at Carrhae in 53 B.C.

The Sasanid Dynasty was established as the result of an epic and somewhat mysterious adventure that recalls in some ways the rise of Cyrus. Around A.D. 224, Ardashir, the leader of a priestly family in the province of Persia (Persis; Fârs), overthrew and killed the Parthian governor. He then exploited a dispute over the accession to the Parthian throne and, by A.D. 228, defeated the Parthian king Artabanus V. Through a tireless series of military campaigns, Ardashir and his successors effectively recreated the borders of the Persian Empire as it had existed under the Achaemenids; the early Sasanid rulers were consequently preoccupied with the task of defending those borders against the Romans and Byzantines in the West and the Hephthalites and other nomads in the East, as well as beating back occasional challenges to their rule by Arsacid pretenders. The dynasty reached its peak under Khosrow I Anushirvan, known as the Just (A.D. 531–79), and Khosrow II Parviz, the Victorious (A.D. 591–628). Khosrow I suppressed a major socioreligious uprising (the Mazdakites), reorganized the fiscal and administrative structure of the empire, promoted a cultural revival, and gave refuge to pagan Greek philosophers fleeing oppression by the Christian Byzantine rulers. Khosrow II, who also had to put down a major rebellion by a general from a Parthian family, supposedly dreamed of becoming ruler of the world, an ambition symbolized by keeping two empty thrones below his own for the kings of Byzantium and China whom he hoped to make his vassals. He hardly posed much of a threat to China, but he did engage in a major war with the Byzantines, capturing Jerusalem in A.D. 614, occupying Egypt in A.D. 616, and reaching the Bosphorus in A.D. 617. Nonetheless, this adventure ended in disaster as the empire's finances were exhausted, the Arab subjects in Mesopotamia rebelled, and the Byzantines mounted a counteroffensive which threatened the Sasanid capital in A.D. 627. The next year, Khosrow II was deposed and executed by members of his own family, plunging Iran into chaos and setting the stage for the invasion and destruction of the empire by the armies of Islam.

The "Iranian National History"

The preceding summary reflects the way pre-Islamic Iranian history has been understood by modern and non-Iranian historians. In Iran itself after the Sasanid period, historical memory of the Achaemenids was almost totally lost, that of the Parthians largely forgotten, and only that of the Sasanids preserved in recognizable form until fairly recently. Instead, most Iranians would have been familiar with what has been called the "Iranian national history,"[2] a semilegendary and epic narrative of events from the creation of the world to the Islamic conquest. In this sense, Iran actually has not one but two ancient histories, and for many generations of Iranians it was this national history that was accepted as real. Since this is primarily a book on Iranian culture and customs, and since the national history has played such a vital role in shaping Iranian culture and sensibilities, it is worth giving a synopsis of it here.

According to the national history, the earliest rulers, rather like the great sages of Chinese tradition, were universal sovereigns who lived for fantastically long periods of time, developed agriculture and domesticated animals, introduced the various arts and crafts, and laid the foundations of civilization. The first of these monarchs, and in some versions of the story also the first human being, was Kayumars. He and his descendants, Hushang and Tahmuras, battled the primordial demons that afflicted the world and taught men how to use fire, dress in animal skins, plant trees, dig canals, and so on. Hushang also established the formal traditions of kingship and thus founded the dynasty of kings known as the Pishdâdiân, "the first to dispense justice." Tahmuras was followed by Jamshid, a proud king who invented the implements of war, organized society into four social classes based on profession, constructed great palaces, taught men how to weave textiles, began to use perfume and jewels, and established the New Year holiday. Toward the end of his reign, however, he turned haughty and ungrateful toward God; as punishment, an "Arab" usurper appeared—Zahhâk, who stirred up a rebellion and had Jamshid killed. Although he had been divinely sent to chastise Jamshid for his pride, Zahhâk was transformed into an instrument of the devil (Ahriman or Eblis); disguised as a cook, the devil had kissed Zahhâk on his shoulders, causing snakes to grow from them that had to be fed on the brains of children. This bloody tyranny was brought to an end by a revolt proclaimed by Kâveh, a brave blacksmith of royal lineage; Kâveh's apron became the banner of the rebellion and the symbol of the Iranian national struggle against the forces of evil. Zahhâk was eventually defeated and imprisoned deep in the volcanic caldera of Mount Damâvand, where he would suffer torment until the end of time.

The new king, Fereydun, eventually decided to divide his kingdom into three parts to be assigned to his three sons: the west to Salm (the oldest), the east to Tur, and the central, favored land of Iran to Iraj (the youngest). Salm and Tur were jealous and conspired to murder Iraj, sending his head to the horrified but helpless Fereydun. Iraj was eventually avenged by his son Manuchehr, who challenged his uncles to combat, killed them, and succeeded Fereydun as king. Among the Iranian noblemen who gave allegiance to Manuchehr was Sâm, a prince of Sistân. Sâm's son, Zâl, was born with white hair, an ominous portent which caused Sâm to expose the baby on a mountain. However, Zâl was discovered, nurtured, and protected by a great bird, the Simorg, until he was reconciled with his father. Later, Zâl sought to marry the beautiful Rudâbeh, daughter of the king of Kâbol. King Manuchehr, however, opposed their marriage since Rudâbeh was also descended from Zahhâk, and he almost went to war with Sâm to prevent their union before finally agreeing to it. Manuchehr's fears did prove unfounded since the marriage of Zâl and Rudâbeh led to the birth of Iran's greatest champion, Rostam, a hero who saved Iran from disaster in the turbulent years after the death of Manuchehr and repeatedly fended off attacks from the eastern lands of Turân and its king, Afrâsiâb.

Faced with the weakness of the last of the Pishdâdiân kings, Zâl convened a council of nobles to pick a new ruler; Rostam was sent on a mission into the Alborz Mountains to bring back another of Manuchehr's descendants, Kay Qobâd, who founded a new dynasty of kings known as the Kayâniâns and who distinguished himself in combat with Afrâsiâb. Unfortunately, his successor, Kay Kâvus, was utterly incompetent and had to be saved by Rostam from one near disaster after another. Kâvus even managed to drive his own son, Siâvosh, over to the side of the Turanians, who then treacherously murdered him. The wife of Siâvosh, daughter of Afrâsiâb, survived and gave birth to Kay Khosrow; Khosrow returned to Iran, deposed Kâvus, and launched a war of revenge against the Turanians. After the defeat of Afrâsiâb, Khosrow abdicated, to be followed by two relatively mediocre kings, Lohrâsp and Goshtâsp, during whose reigns the prophet Zoroaster supposedly appeared. Goshtâsp was overshadowed by his son Esfandiâr, who championed the new religion and fought off attacks by the Turanians. Jealous and suspicious of Esfandiâr, Goshtâsp once had him imprisoned and later ordered him for no good reason to go and arrest Rostam. In that tragic era, Rostam fought and killed Esfandiâr; Rostam himself was killed in a trap set by his wicked brother Shagad; and Esfandiâr's son, Bahman, killed Zâl and exterminated his family. Bahman's son Dârâb, abandoned by his mother in a basket set afloat on a river, was found and raised by a commoner but was eventually recognized and installed as king. He married the daughter of Filfus, a king of Greece, but sent her back because he was offended by her bad breath. Pregnant, she gave birth to Eskandar, who later quarreled with the new king. Dârâb's other son, Dârâ, defeated him and made himself the ruler of Iran, bringing the Kayâniân Dynasty to an end. Eskandar proved to be an impressive philosopher-king who accomplished many astonishing feats. After his death, the succession was disputed, and the world was in turmoil under various regional rulers and the petty Ashkâniân kings until Ardashir emerged to found the Sasanid Dynasty.

Versions of this national history were disseminated over the centuries by popular bards *(gosân)*, who recited stirring stories based on it as a kind of popular entertainment; by medieval historians, who sometimes explored its inconsistencies or sought to identify its heroes with other historical individuals; and by court poets, who added their own flourishes to the basic outline. Without doubt, what became the most widely appreciated, eloquent, and aesthetically attractive presentation of the story was the long epic poem by Abo'l-Qâsem Ferdowsi (ca. A.D. 940–1020) known as the *Shâh-nâmeh* (Book of Kings). While following the general structure outlined above, Ferdowsi also added many details and additional stories for dramatic effect: Rudâbeh, like Rapunzel, lowers down her long hair so Rostam can climb up to her in her castle; Rostam fathers a son by a Turanian princess but does not know of his birth and later kills him in combat; the daughter of a man named Haft-vâd finds a magic worm in an apple that brings great wealth and power to Haftvâd and his town, but which is then destroyed by Ardashir, founder of the Sasanid Dynasty.

Some elements of the national history can be traced back to material in the oldest Iranian myths and beyond that to the common mythology of the Indo-Europeans: Fereydun and Zahhâk, for example, correspond to the ancient Iranian hero Thraetaona and the evil dragon Azhi Dahâka that he imprisoned; there are many parallels between the stories of the deeds of Ros-tam and those of the labors of Hercules. Other details can be attributed to folklore, local legends, or the embellishments of individual authors. Parts of the narrative do reflect historical facts: despite the legendary embellishments, Dârâ, Filfus, and Eskandar are recognizable as Darius III, Philip of Macedon, and Alexander the Great. From the last of the Kayâniân kings onward, the national history thus draws closer and closer to conventional accounts of pre-Islamic Iranian history, and with the establishment of the Sasanids, the two are virtually indistinguishable.

Whatever the sources, though, the national history as a whole conveys many ideas that are generally regarded as fundamental to an understanding of Iranian culture: the stark emphasis on the struggle between good and evil in the world; the role of Iran itself as the most favored land and center of civilization; or the theme of continuing assault on Iran by hostile and envious powers to the west and east. Above all, the twin ideals of a just, charismatic monarchy and a rigid social order are viewed as necessary for human prosperity and national survival. Especially in Ferdowsi's version of the national history, the concept of righteous kingship is exalted, but alongside it there is the issue of what to do about rulers who are foolish or oppressive (and there are a good many of them) and the need to stand up for what is right. At the same time, the desire for a directed, stable, orderly society is emphasized.

That concept is brought home with great clarity in a famous story about the Sasanid king Bahrâm Gur: Displeased that the people of a village had not greeted him properly, he wished that the village would be destroyed. His priest accomplished this by telling the people that the social hierarchy was abolished; instead of having a headman, there would be complete equality among the men, women, and children of the village. At first the people were overjoyed with their newfound liberty, but they soon fell to fighting each other and neglecting their work, so that within a year the village was in ruins. Only when the office of headman was reinstituted did the village recover.

From the Islamic Conquest to the Regional Dynasties

The decline in Sasanid power following the deposition of Khosrow II was dramatic and caused by many factors, ranging from the financial and military exhaustion that resulted from the wars with Byzantium to bloody disputes over the succession to the throne to continuing popular unrest. Just when it appeared stability might be restored with the accession of Yazdgerd III in A.D. 634, a grave new threat appeared from an unexpected direction. Newly unified by the Prophet Mohammad and the religion of Islam, the Arabs of the Hejâz and the Bedouin of the Arabian Peninsula joined forces with other tribes and disaffected groups in the Iranian-ruled areas of Mesopotamia to thwart the Sasanid revival. After a period of skirmishing, a decisive pitched battle took place over a period of four days in A.D. 636 at a place known as Qâdesiyeh (near modern Kufa in Iraq). The Iranian general—named, ironically, Rostam—was killed, the Iranian army was routed, and the fabled Banner of Kâveh fell into the hands of the Arabs. Since the Sasanid capital was not far away, it was promptly captured and its vast treasures were looted by the conquerors. The Sasanids never recovered from this disaster, and, after the failure of a last-ditch stand at the Battle of Nehâvand (A.D. 642), virtually the whole of Iran was occupied; Yazdgerd was murdered by one of his vassals in A.D. 652 in central Asia, apparently on his way to seek help from China against the Arabs. For more than a century, Iran would be little more than a set of provinces in the Islamic Empire of the caliphs of Medina, Damascus, and Baghdad.

Of all the foreign invasions of Iran, that of the Muslim Arabs was arguably the most disruptive and far-reaching in its effects. It entailed not only military defeat, the destruction of the ancient regime, and political subjection, but also led to colonization by some Arab settlers and considerable social and cultural change, most obviously in the collapse of Zoroastrianism as the national religion and the spread of Islam as the dominant faith in Iran (to be discussed in more detail in the next chapter). However, the perception that all this amounts to a major discontinuity in Iranian history should not be exaggerated. Some areas of Iran, especially in the rugged Alborz area, remained autonomous under local dynasties, even after accepting Islam. Elsewhere, Iranians played an increasingly important role in political affairs: The revolution which overthrew the Umayyad Dynasty of caliphs and established the Abbasid Dynasty began in Iran under the command of an Iranian leader, Abu Moslem Khorâsâni, and with the support of much of the Iranian population. Thereafter, Iranians served in the highest echelons of the Abbasid administrative, military, and scholarly elites. Iranians also had had long practice at incorporating aspects of the culture of their non-Iranian neighbors while retaining their own identity, and this continued to be the case. Iranians distinguished themselves in virtually every field of learning and culture: law, theology, philosophy, medicine, astronomy, and even Arabic literature and philology—some of the first Arabic grammarians were of Iranian ancestry, and one of the first and most skilled practitioners of formal Arabic literary prose was an Iranian, Ebn al-Moqaffa'. At the same time, many aspects of the ancient Iranian culture, such as the New Year festival, survived and were even adopted by non-Iranian people. Most important, and contrary to what happened in most other areas conquered by the Muslim Arabs, the general population in Iran did not accept the language of the conquerors; they adopted the Arabic script and borrowed a good deal of Arabic vocabulary, but the common language, spoken at first and then used as a literary language, became New Persian, a tongue based on the ancient Iranian languages.

Not surprisingly, the attitude of Iranians over the years regarding these developments has thus been highly ambivalent: They were often rankled by the fact that the humiliation of imperial Iran had come at the hands of people it had held in the lowest esteem, the so-called lizard-eating nomads of the desert. On the other hand, they embraced the new religion and took great pride in Iranian contributions to the development of a new, cosmopolitan Islamic civilization.

With the weakening of the power of the Abbasid caliphs from the late ninth century onward, more areas of Iran became essentially independent, under the rule of hereditary dynasties of Iranian origin. In A.D. 861, for example, a coppersmith (saffâr) named Ya'qub-e Lays, took command of a kind of popular militia (the ayyârân) in Sistân. An effective and popular leader, Ya'qub raided non-Islamic areas on the frontier with India, defeated the pro-Abbasid governor of Khorâsân, and forced the caliph to recognize him as governor of the provinces Kermân, Fârs, and Khuzestân. In A.D. 876, he invaded Iraq and briefly threatened Baghdad itself. The dynasty he founded, the Saffarids, remained a power in southwestern Iran until A.D. 1003. In addition to being militantly anti-Abbasid in his politics, Ya'qub also championed Iranian culture. He himself did not understand Arabic and consequently had his poets praise him in the Persian language. In contrast, the Samanid Dynasty, which ruled in Khorâsân and central Asia (ca. A.D. 874–999), professed to be governing on behalf of the Abbasid caliphs and supported Arabic scholarship. They resisted the expansion of the Saffarids and adopted an aggressive policy to defend against the Turkish nomads on their frontier, supplying Turkish slaves to the caliphs. Yet they too acted as independent rulers, were proud of their Iranian identity (claiming descent from Bahrâm Chubin), and promoted the revival of Persian as a literary language by sponsoring translations of famous Arabic works into Persian. Another dynasty of Iranian origin, the Buyids, came to power in western Iran (ca. A.D. 932–1055), conquered Baghdad, and ruled as de facto masters of the Abbasid caliphs.

The Turko-Mongol Era

At least at the political level, the Iranian revival was cut short by the arrival of the Turks. The Turkish nomads of central Asia, identified in the popular mind with the Turanians of the national history, had been a threat on Iran's northeastern frontier for several centuries but had been decisively defeated by the Samanids in A.D. 893. Many of the Turks then began to be brought into the Iranian and Islamic world as slaves, to be trained and used primarily as soldiers. As the Samanid Dynasty lost power, some of these slave-troops, led by their commanders, founded their own independent emirate (known as the Ghaznavids) in eastern Iran and Afghanistan. Other Turkish tribes were converted to Islam, often by itinerant mystics (Sufis), and some of them began to migrate into Iran. In A.D. 1040, the Turkish confederation known as the Saljuqs crushed the Ghaznavids at the Battle of Dandânqân; by A.D. 1055, they had reached Baghdad and deposed the last of the Buyids. The Saljuq chieftain took the title of sultan and claimed to be acting as the temporal agent and protector of the Abbasid caliphate; various territories of the Saljuq Empire were entrusted to direct rule by other members of the family, army officers, and slave-commanders. Some of these eventually broke away to found their own autonomous dynasties; among them were the descendants of a Turkish slave who had been appointed governor of Kh^vârazm (a province near the Aral Sea). He and his successors took the title Kh^vârazm-shâh, expanded their territory to the east and west, and, in A.D. 1194, defeated the last of the Saljuq sultans. For more than a century, Turkish warlords thus ruled virtually the whole of Iran, and Turks dominated political and military affairs.

The next great incursion by non-Iranian people into Iran was far more catastrophic in its effects. In A.D. 1219, Genghis and the Mongol armies attacked the lands of the Kh^{v}ârazm-shâh 'Alâ-od-Din Mohammad. Apparently provoked by the execution of some Mongol emissaries, this invasion had the character of a war of revenge: 'Alâ-od-Din was defeated and chased all across Iran before finally dying on an island in the Caspian. Eastern and northern Iran suffered immensely in the course of this war, with formerly great cities like Marw, Herât, Tus, and Nishâpur reduced to ruins and much of their population massacred or deported. There was a respite after the death of Genghis in A.D. 1227, while the Mongols were preoccupied with other matters, but the campaigns resumed after Genghis' grandson Hulâgu was commissioned in A.D. 1251 to expand the area under Mongol control and to suppress the efforts then underway by the Isma'ili religious sect and the Abbasid caliph to organize resistance to the Mongols. Hulâgu crossed into Iran in A.D. 1256, forced the submission of various petty rulers, destroyed the Isma'ili strongholds, and, in A.D. 1258, captured Baghdad and executed the caliph. The Il-khanids, the dynasty founded by Hulâgu, ruled Iran until A.D. 1335. The Il-khanids were not only ethnically different from the Iranian population, just as the Saljuqs had been, they were also different in religion (favoring Christianity and Buddhism rather than Islam) and tended to look at the people they had conquered with a mixture of disdain and distrust, seeing them as fit only to be exploited like chattel. In general, the Mongols in Iran resisted any cultural assimilation, imposed exorbitant taxes, neglected both agriculture and the traditional system of trade and commerce, and frequently warred with their Muslim neighbors. An attempt in A.D. 1294 to impose the use of paper currency created a fiscal crisis and political upheaval. This ended with the accession in A.D. 1295 of Ghâzân Khân, who declared himself a Muslim and, with the assistance of capable Iranian ministers such as Rashid-od-Din, introduced a number of measures to revive the economy and ameliorate conditions for the subject peoples. When the last of the Il-khanids, Abu Sa'id, died in A.D. 1335, there was no obvious successor to the throne, and the country quickly broke up again into a number of petty principalities ruled by various Turko-Mongol warlords.

A semblance of unity was restored to Iran when its territory was incorporated into the vast empire of the last great Mongol conqueror, Timur Lang (Tamerlane; A.D. 1336–1404). Timur had started out as little more than an adventuresome if talented mercenary with a dubious claim of descent from Genghis, a militant Islamic religious fervor bordering on fanaticism, and an apparently limitless ambition to conquer as his chief assets. In A.D. 1369, with only a small band of followers, he was able to capture Balkh and proclaim himself ruler; by A.D. 1380, he had made himself master of all that part of central Asia known as Transoxiana. He then immediately began a series of campaigns into Iran (A.D. 1380–88) which added Khorâsân, Sistân, Gorgân,

Mâzandarân, Azerbaijan, and Fârs to his realm—only part of a process of empire-building which soon extended to Iraq, Asia Minor, Russia, and India. In Iran, as elsewhere, Timur's ferocity was unrestrained, as exemplified by his massacre of prisoners in Sistân in A.D. 1384, his reported slaughter of 70,000 people at Isfahan in A.D. 1387, and his treacherous murder of most of the surviving members of the Mozaffarid family (former rulers of Shiraz) in A.D. 1393. Although Timur wanted the vast empire he had created to remain united, it fragmented after his death as his sons and grandsons, whom he had established as governors of various provinces, struggled for parts of it. The bulk of the territory, including almost all of Iran, eventually was ruled by Timur's fourth son, Shâh Rokh (A.D. 1377–1447).

The situation in northwestern Iran was more complicated. It had come under the rule of Mirânshâh, Timur's third son, but his authority was contested by other Timurids and by rival tribes. Even in the days of Timur, the confederation of Turkish tribes known as the Black Sheep (Qara Qoyunlu), which had formerly ruled the area, had proved troublesome. In A.D. 1408, the Black Sheep leader, Qara Yusof, defeated and killed Mirânshâh. As Shâh Rokh moved into western Iran in A.D. 1419, he prepared to attack Qara Yusof, but the latter died before a battle could be engaged. Despite a victory over the Black Sheep army in A.D. 1421, the hold of the Timurids over the region was very tenuous, and Shâh Rokh rather prudently chose to allow Qara Yusof's descendants to continue to rule as his nominal vassals. Under Jahân Shâh (r. A.D. 1439–67), the Black Sheep principality became a major regional power. Even as the Black Sheep were threatening to eclipse the Timurids, they themselves were coming under attack by another Turkish tribal confederation, the White Sheep (Âq Qoyunlu), led by their ambitious chieftain, Uzun Hasan. Unable to expand to the west because of the rise of the Ottoman Empire, the White Sheep directed their energy eastward against the Black Sheep and the Timurids. In A.D. 1467, Uzun Hasan ambushed Jahân Shâh and took over the Black Sheep capital and territories. Two years later, the Timurid ruler Abu Sa'id attempted to invade the White Sheep principality but was captured and executed.

For more than four centuries, Iran was thus under the domination of various Turko-Mongol conquerors and rulers. The area suffered much devastation as the result of invasions and warfare. The ethnic makeup of the population was changed considerably by the arrival and settlement of large numbers of Turkomans and, to a lesser degree, Mongols. The fact that so many of these newcomers were tribally organized and nomadic pastoralists also affected the socioeconomic as well as the political balance within this area. Nonetheless, this did not result in anything like the Turkification of Iran, nor did it prevent the continued development of an Iranian culture based on the Persian language. This somewhat paradoxical outcome can be explained by several factors. From the very beginning, the Turko-Mongol military elites were heavily reliant on an Iranian bureaucracy to administer their principalities, and able ministers like the famous Nezâm-ol-Molk under the Saljuqs or Rashid-od-Din under the Mongols influenced state policies and practices in many ways. Moreover, the Samanid system for training Turkish slaves had instilled in them a deep respect for Islamic and Iranian culture. Subsequently, the Turks, and the Mongols after them, also came to accept the norms of this civilization, especially in art and literature, and could even be said to have further stimulated its revival. Even a ruthless warmonger like Timur had a desire to be seen as a glorious and pious king; throughout the Turko-Mongol period, rulers continued to promote trade, to patronize favored religious leaders, to encourage the production of art and literature (especially works of history), and to beautify their capitals. It was thus during this period that a number of famous Iranian poets and scholars lived and when cities such as Isfahan, Tabriz, and Mashhad acquired some of their most impressive architectural jewels.

From the Safavids to the Qâjârs

The Turko-Mongol rulers of Iran generally derived their power from tribal confederations that were notoriously fractious and undisciplined. Their principalities also tended to be patrimonial in nature; that is, territories and resources were shared among members of the ruling family and their retainers, with the head of the family as at least a nominal overlord. In terms of sentiments of loyalty and commonality of interests, the gulf between the ruling elites and the subject peoples was very great. All this made it difficult for any of the Turko-Mongols to construct a state that would be both centralized and durable, and virtually impossible to create anything resembling a unified nation. Instead, the characteristics of the period were incessant warfare, skirmishing among contenders for authority, and political instability. This changed dramatically with the rise of the Safavids (A.D. 1501–1722), under whose rule Iran began to take on the shape and character of the country we recognize today.

What might well be called the Safavid revolution took place against the background of the struggles of the Timurids, Black Sheep, and White Sheep in northwestern Iran. The eponym of the dynasty was a certain Safi-od-Din (A.D. 1252–1334), the spiritual leader of a Sufi religious order based at Ardabil. Gradually, and through a process that is still not well understood by modern historians, this order became increasingly esoteric in its religious teachings as well as militant and political in its objectives, carrying out a propaganda

mission (*da'vat*) to bring about rule by Safi-od-Din's descendants. The movement was particularly successful in winning the support of dissident Turkish
tribes in Azerbaijan, so much so that the Black Sheep ruler Jahân Shâh threatened to destroy Ardabil. During the Black Sheep ascendancy, the Safavids
had allied with the White Sheep; but once the White Sheep were in power,
they, too, felt endangered by the Safavids, turned against them, and arrested
the leading members of the family in A.D. 1494. One Safavid, the seven-year-
old Esmâ'il, somehow made his way to Gilân, where he was given refuge by
a sympathetic local ruler.

In A.D. 1499, Esmâ'il returned to Ardabil, and thousands of Turkish war-
riors from many different tribes rallied to his side. Known as *qezelbâsh* ("red
hats") because of the symbolic headgear they wore, they were enthusiastic
supporters of the religious ideology of the Safavid order, which at that time
apparently included the belief that Esmâ'il was an infallible incarnation of
the divinity and could make them invincible in battle. In A.D. 1501, Esmâ'il's
forces defeated a much larger White Sheep army at the Battle of Sharur,
a victory that gave the Safavids control of Azerbaijan. Esmâ'il immediately
entered Tabriz, proclaimed himself ruler with the ancient Iranian title of shah
(king), and declared Imami Shi'ism as the official religion. By A.D. 1510, he
had conquered the whole of Iran and was giving every indication that he
wanted to expand his territory still further. He had also made two powerful
enemies in the Ozbek Turks to the east and the Ottoman Turks to the west.
A Safavid attempt to cross the Oxus was repelled by the Ozbeks in A.D. 1512,
and in A.D. 1514 the Ottomans soundly defeated Esmâ'il at the Battle of
Chaldirân. These defeats ended whatever ambitions Esmâ'il may have had
to restore a Timurid-style empire and shattered the *qezelbâsh* faith in the
Safavid ruler as godlike and invincible. They did not, however, threaten the
existence of the Safavid state itself; if anything, they accelerated the process of
its acquiring its own distinctive territorial and cultural identity.

After Esmâ'il's death in A.D. 1524, his young son Tahmâsp faced the problems of fending off foreign enemies and controlling the *qezelbâsh* army without the charismatic authority enjoyed by earlier Safavid leaders (although
the prestige of the family was still great since it claimed descent from a
Shi'ite Imam). Among other things, Tahmâsp sought alliances with foreign
powers in Europe and India, moved his capital from Tabriz to the safer location of Qazvin, signed a peace treaty with the Ottomans, and resisted Ozbek
attacks. He made a conspicuous effort to cultivate the favor of Shi'ite religious scholars; even though this inevitably meant giving up some of his own
claim to religious authority, it helped assure the support of this important
and influential element in society. He also began the process of building up
a corps of slave-troops (*gholâm*) composed of recruits from the non-Muslim

population of the Caucasus (Circassians, Armenians, and Georgians) as a counterweight to the military might of the *qezelbâsh*. Tahmâsp's strategies were not entirely successful, but they at least enabled him to keep his throne for some 52 years. Once he died (poisoned by the mother of one of his sons in a conspiracy to bring her child to the throne), the power struggle among the *qezelbâsh, gholâm,* Persian (Tâjik), and court factions came into the open. The next 12 years were marked by internal conflicts and defeats at the hands of Ottomans and Ozbeks. In A.D. 1588, in the course of a civil war, one of the *qezelbâsh* commanders installed the young Safavid prince ʿAbbâs as shah. ʿAbbâs soon managed to eliminate his former patron and initiated an array of policies that carried the power of the monarch and Safavid Iran to an unprecedented level. Among other things, he expanded the *gholâm* forces and began to entrust them with high military posts and administrative duties; he also created a salaried standing army, including riflemen and artillery units, that would be under his command rather than that of *qezelbâsh* tribal officers. This was financed by reorganizing the system of fiscal administration so that the revenue from certain provinces went directly to the crown rather than being used by the tribal forces based in them. The revitalized Safavid army was able to push back the Ozbeks in A.D. 1598, recapture territory from the Ottomans in A.D. 1607, and force the Ottomans out of Iraq in A.D. 1624. ʿAbbâs also stimulated the Safavid economy by opening contacts with European countries and encouraging Armenian merchants to settle in a suburb of his new capital, Isfahan.

Unfortunately, the successors of Shah ʿAbbâs the Great lacked his skills and energy, and Safavid Iran began a slow but steady decline. Harem intrigues, oppressive taxation, neglect of the army, and an increasingly xenophobic and religiously intolerant atmosphere all played a role in weakening the state. In A.D. 1722, a fairly small band of Ghilzai Afghans led by Mir Mahmud crossed into Iran, marched almost unopposed to Isfahan, and besieged the city. With the capital on the point of starvation, Shah Soltân-Hosayn had little choice but to surrender and yield his crown to the Afghan commander.

Just as the Afghans had lacked the strength to capture Isfahan outright, they also lacked the ability to hold together the territory they had acquired. Opposition to the Afghan occupation rallied under one of the surviving Safavid princes (39 members of the family had been murdered by Mir Mahmud), Tahmâsp II, who was assisted by a particularly capable leader of the Afshâr tribe of Turkomans, Nâder-qoli Khân. With the help of Nâder and his forces, Tahmâsp recovered control of Khorâsân and defeated the Afghan army in three successive battles (A.D. 1729–30); he was also able to push back the Ottoman Turks, who had taken advantage of the turmoil in Iran to seize Azerbaijan and Iraq. Tahmâsp had thus recovered most of the Safavid

Kingdom by allowing Nâder to act as his "sultan," but in A.D. 1731 he made the mistake of attempting to lead an army himself against the Ottomans and was soundly defeated. This gave Nâder the opportunity to depose Tahmâsp.

At first, Nâder acted as regent for Tahmâsp's infant son, but in A.D. 1736, at a carefully orchestrated assembly of notables (modeled on the Mongol *kuriltay*), he proposed to retire and asked the assembly to decide who should be shah. The assembly proclaimed that he himself should become ruler; feigning reluctance, Nâder agreed to accept on condition that the assembly accept his new religious policy of restoring Sunni Islam in Iran. The abandonment of Shi'ism was necessary as the linchpin of a peace treaty he wanted to conclude with the Sunni Ottomans and was probably intended also as a way of diminishing the religious prestige of the Safavid house and of making Nâder a more attractive figure to the Sunni populations of areas he was planning to conquer. As shah, Nâder's career was in many ways phenomenal: he took the Ghilzai stronghold of Qandahâr (A.D. 1738), invaded Moghul India and captured Delhi (A.D. 1739), conquered Kh^vârazm (A.D. 1740), set out to recover formerly Safavid territories in the Caucasus and Caspian littoral that had been overrun by the Russians (A.D. 1741), and renewed the war with the Ottomans (A.D. 1743). At the same time, Nâder's religious policy and exorbitant taxes fueled discontent in Iran itself; there was an attempt to assassinate him in A.D. 1741, and there were numerous revolts aimed at bringing about a Safavid restoration. Nâder became ever crueler and more erratic in his behavior and was finally murdered in A.D. 1747 by some of his own officers who feared he was about to have them executed.

The Afsharid Dynasty founded by Nâder Shah became after his death nothing more than a short-lived regional power in eastern Iran with no rulers of any distinction. Authority over the rest of Iran was contested by various rivals, mostly defectors from the Afshârid army, of whom the most important proved to be Karim Khân, a soldier from an Iranian tribal group known as the Zand. Nâder had deported the Zand from their homeland in the central Zagros to Khorâsân in A.D. 1732; Karim Khân led them back after Nâder's death. By political skill even more than military prowess, Karim Khân had made himself master of all Iran except Khorâsân by A.D. 1765. However, Karim Khân never took the title shah for himself. From A.D. 1751 to 1759, he had acted as *vakil* (agent) for the Safavid pretender Esmâ'il III; in A.D. 1759, he deposed Esmâ'il because of the latter's gross incompetence and ingratitude. Karim Khân thereafter described his position as *vakil-or-ra'âyâ* (agent on behalf of the people). In fact, Karim Khân does seem to have conducted himself in the spirit of someone who felt he had been entrusted with the welfare of the people. He rarely engaged in military adventures or used harsh measures against opponents; he concentrated on developing agriculture, trade, and commercial activities. Most of his time was spent in Shiraz, which served as his capital and which he beautified with many famous buildings. His reign (A.D. 1750–79) is remembered by Iranians as a period of exceptional peace, prosperity, and justice.

Among the groups most hostile towards Karim Khân had been the tribal confederation of the Qâjârs, another of the Turkoman *qezelbâsh* elements in the earlier Safavid army. Their chief, Mohammad-Hosayn Khân, had besieged Shiraz in A.D. 1758 only to be outdone by Karim Khân, who had denuded the countryside of provisions and bribed elements of the Qâjâr army into deserting. After this defeat, Mohammad-Hosayn Khân had been murdered by the leader of a rival branch of the Qâjâr tribe. Karim Khân held Mohammad-Hosayn Khân's oldest son, Âghâ Mohammad Khân, as a kind of hostage, albeit a very well-treated one, at his court. Much earlier (in A.D. 1747), the five-year-old Âghâ Mohammad had been captured and castrated by the Afshârid 'Âdel Shâh. There is little doubt Âghâ Mohammad was seething with rage at both this indignity and his captivity in Shiraz, despite Karim Khân's kind treatment of him, and that he channeled this anger into a relentless and ruthless drive for power. He escaped from Shiraz after Karim Khân's death, returned to his tribal homeland near the southeastern shores of the Caspian, asserted his leadership over the Qâjâr tribe, and took advantage of succession disputes among the Zand to expand his tribal lands at their expense. By A.D. 1789, he was in control of the north of Iran and made Tehran his capital. In A.D. 1792, he took Shiraz (thanks to the treachery of the city's governor) and chased the last of the Zand rulers, Lotf-'Ali Khân, to Kermân. When that city fell in A.D. 1794, the whole population is said to have been enslaved, blinded, or killed. He was crowned as shah in A.D. 1796 and set out to recover Khorâsân and to expel Russian forces from the Caucasus. While preparing to invade Georgia in A.D. 1797, Âghâ Mohammad was murdered by three of his servants, perhaps as part of a plot by one of his generals. He had, however, had the foresight to make elaborate arrangements for the succession in the event of his death, and his nephew ascended the throne as Fath-'Ali Shah (A.D. 1797–1834).

Qâjâr Iran

The early Qâjâr rulers saw themselves as the heirs to the Safavid legacy, in much the same way as the Safavids served as heirs to the Timurids. Left to themselves, they would probably have sought to re-create that heritage as much as possible, both territorially and culturally. Âghâ Mohammad Shah had demanded the cession of lands in central Asia and Afghanistan and adopted an aggressive policy in the Caucasus. Fath-'Ali Shah likewise attempted to restore the Safavid frontier in the Caucasus, reopened the war with the Ottomans, put down a revolt in Khorâsân, and attempted to assert his authority over Herât (as did his successors, Mohammad Shah in 1837 and Nâser-od-Din Shah in 1856). The Qâjârs could not hope to emulate the personal religious charisma of the Safavid monarchs, but they staunchly supported Shi'ism and cultivated the favor of Shi'ite religious leaders. They also actively promoted a revival of the arts and literature.

What made the Qâjâr period fundamentally different was Iran's troubled encounter with European powers and European culture. This certainly had precedents going back for centuries: the overtures between the crusaders and the Mongols; the mission of the Castilian Ruy Gonzalez di Clavijo to Tamerlane; the efforts of Caterino Zeno of Venice and the White Sheep ruler Uzun Hasan to forge an anti-Ottoman alliance; or the English embassies of the Sherley brothers and Dodmore Cotton to the court of Shah 'Abbâs the Great. When the Qâjârs got swept up in the complicated geopolitical machinations of the era of the French Revolution, however, the relative military and economic relationship was entirely to their disadvantage.

Napoleon first approached the Qâjârs, aiming to use Iran as a threat against the British in India and the Russians in the Caucasus; the Qâjârs were receptive, in the hope of recovering their Caucasian principalities. This was undone by the Convention of Tilsit (1807), as the French and Russians then became allies; Britain was consequently able to make its own alliance with Iran and sent a military mission to help the Qâjâr prince 'Abbâs Mirzâ reform the Qâjâr army and conduct the campaign against the Russians (although not too vigorously after Britain and Russia once more allied against the French). The end result was that Russia defeated the Iranian armies in the Caucasus, and Iran had to accept the Treaty of Golestân (1813), mediated by Britain, by which it ceded almost all its territories in the Caucasus and gave up its right to maintain a navy on the Caspian. A second war with Russia in 1826 ended in defeat, and by the Treaty of Torkmânchay (1828), Iran was compelled to pay a large indemnity, give up more territory north of the Aras River, and make many other concessions to Russia, such as most-favored-nation trading status. When the Qâjârs attempted to compensate for these losses by moving on Herât, they were consistently blocked by the British, who wanted to guard the lines of communication and defense to India.

The Russians thus came to feel that they had vital interests in the north of Iran, while the British were primarily concerned with their influence in the south of Iran. For the rest of the century, the British and the Russians continued to work to promote their respective positions in Iran, while not coming into overt conflict with each other, and to exclude other countries from any significant role there. This culminated in the notorious Anglo-Russian

Agreement of 1907. The document's pledge "to respect the integrity and independence of Persia" was nothing more than a platitude; in fact, it recognized
a sphere of influence in northern Iran where Russia would have a free hand to
do much as it pleased, and a corresponding sphere of influence was assigned
to Britain in the south.

Since Britain and Russia were anxious not to become embroiled in a military
confrontation over Iran and did not seek to colonize the country outright, the
main vehicle for expanding their influence by proxy was by encouraging commercial and other activities in Iran by their nationals—constructing a tele-
graph line, establishing banks, extending loans, building factories, setting up
shipping companies, obtaining concessions to exploit the natural resources of
the country, and even taking over aspects of its military, police, and administrative functions. Sometimes an entrepreneur from one country would push
too far, so the other would block the enterprise. This happened in the case
of the Reuter Concession in 1872, whereby Nâser-od-Din Shah gave a British subject a monopoly over the development of railroads, mining, and a
national bank, all to be financed by running the customs service. Russian
pressure forced its cancellation. Another proposed concession in 1891, which
would have given a monopoly over the tobacco trade in Iran to a British subject, aroused not only Russian opposition but popular outrage and a boycott
of tobacco products. The Tobacco Protest movement that brought about the
cancellation of the concession is generally regarded as the first example of
effective mass mobilization and national resistance to imperialism in Iran.

Of all these economic ventures, the most momentous was undoubtedly the
granting in 1901 of the right to exploit gas and petroleum resources in the
south of Iran to William Knox D'Arcy. After initial difficulties, oil was struck
in 1908 at the Masjed-e Solaymân site near Ahvâz, a development which led
to the formation of the Anglo-Persian Oil Company. Since the British navy
was in the process of converting from coal to oil, a source of petroleum so
near the Persian Gulf was seen as a major asset; in 1914, the British government itself took a controlling interest in the company. Wealth from oil would
of course play a vital role in the future economic development of Iran, but it
also gave Britain an incentive to make protection of its oil interests in Iran a
major priority of its foreign policy.

Throughout the nineteenth century, the rulers of Qâjâr Iran faced enormous obstacles—poverty, military weakness, political factionalism, and corruption as well as domination by Britain and Russia—to any program of
reform and modernization that might have made the country truly strong
and independent. Nonetheless, much significant progress was made toward
laying the foundations for a modern nation-state during this period. One
burst of reform took place under the dynamic prime minister Amir Kabir

(1848–51), who sought to strengthen the army, improve the administrative and fiscal practices of the government, stimulate agriculture and industry, regularize the legal system, and introduce new educational institutions (notably the renowned military and technical school, Dâr-ol-Fonun). Unfortunately, Amir Kabir's enemies at court and in the bureaucracy manipulated the young and insecure Nâser-od-Din Shah into dismissing Amir Kabir from office and then had him murdered. Many Iranians gradually came to see the introduction of a constitutional system of government as the best guarantee against such arbitrary and irresponsible actions and the basis for a genuine national revival, and a number of political societies (*anjoman*s) were formed to work toward that end.

The Constitutional Revolution and World War I

In 1906, popular protests which had begun over the treatment of some merchants by the governor of Tehran grew in size until a group of several thousand merchants, artisans, religious leaders, students, and intellectuals took refuge (a customary right to sanctuary known as *bast*) on the grounds of the British legation, where they began to organize political demonstrations. They articulated as their main demand the election of a national assembly (Majles), and this was approved by Mozaffar-od-Din Shah. Mozaffar-od-Din died shortly thereafter, in January 1907, and the new ruler, Mohammad-'Ali Shah, was much less sympathetic to this Constitutional Revolution. Divisions also began to appear among the constitutionalists themselves, with some favoring a secular system based on the concept of popular sovereignty, and others a more conservative system that would have given religious leaders a veto over legislation deemed un-Islamic. In 1908, Mohammad-'Ali Shah, backed by the Russian-officered Cossack Brigade, staged a coup; the Majles was attacked, and prominent constitutionalists were killed, arrested, or forced to flee. Supporters of the constitution rallied in Tabriz, which held out against a siege by royalist forces, and in other parts of the country. In 1909, Russian forces intervened to break the siege of Tabriz, and pro-constitutionalist forces advanced on Tehran from Gilân in the north and Fârs in the south. A special assembly then deposed Mohammad-'Ali Shah, who was sent into exile in Russia, and put his son Ahmad Shah on the throne. The Second Majles proved much too independent-minded for either the Russians or the British. The imperial powers were particularly irritated that the Majles turned to an American, Morgan Shuster, for help in solving the country's financial crisis, and that Shuster proved to be both effective and willing to put Iran's interests ahead of those of Russia and Britain. With British approval, Russia issued an ultimatum in 1911 demanding Shuster's dismissal, invaded the country, dissolved the Majles, and crushed the remaining pockets of constitutionalist resistance.

World War I added to the troubles in Iran. Even though Iran was not a party to the war, it was caught between the opposing forces. The Russians maintained troops in Qazvin and the north, and the British moved in troops to protect their oil installations in the south. German agents were active in the country and stirred up tribal revolts against the British, and their Ottoman allies warred vigorously with the Russians in Azerbaijan and pressured the British in Khuzestân. Economic crisis and food shortages caused much hardship for the Iranian population. Ethnic minorities in Kurdistan, Azerbaijan, and Gilân looked for an opportunity to gain provincial autonomy or even independence.

The end of the war, with the collapse of Russia and the Bolshevik Revolution, left Britain as the dominant power in Iran. The British government moved quickly to pressure Iran into accepting an agreement that would have turned the country into a virtual British protectorate. Rumors about the Anglo-Persian Agreement of 1919 galvanized resistance to it in Iran and alarmed foreign powers, notably the new Soviet regime, which did not want to see Iran become a base for counterrevolution. Defeated White Russians had taken refuge in Iran, and it appeared that the Russian officers of the Cossack Brigade and, to some extent, British forces were collaborating with them. Elements of the Red Army occupied Anzali in 1920, pushing the British and Cossack Brigade back to Qazvin; the Soviets announced they would not leave Iran as long as British troops were there. To avoid drawing the Soviets further in, to dampen political unrest, and to deal with problems elsewhere in their empire, the British decided to abandon the Anglo-Persian Agreement and withdraw their forces from Iran, while hoping to leave behind a viable and pro-British government. They also decided to remove the remaining Russian officers from the Cossack Brigade, which would be placed under the command of an outstanding Iranian officer, Colonel Rezâ Khân.

Pahlavi Iran

On February 21, 1921, Rezâ Khân, backed by the Cossack Brigade, staged a coup d'etat. He occupied Tehran, declared martial law, and installed a pro-British politician, Sayyid Ziâ-od-Din Tabâtabâi as prime minister. Rezâ Khân became commander of the army and minister of war. Tabâtabâi proved to be a disaster as prime minister. He made enemies on every side and alienated Rezâ Khân; he was forced to resign in May 1921 and fled the country. Rezâ Khân, on the other hand, proved to be a dynamic leader and the de facto ruler of the country. He expanded and reorganized the army, put down separatist revolts in the provinces, and brought in another American advisor to sort out the country's finances. In 1923, Ahmad Shah named Rezâ Khân as prime minister and then promptly left for a European vacation, never to return. Inspired by the example of Mustafa Kemal in Turkey, there was increasing talk of making Iran a republic, with Rezâ Khân as president. Conservative and religious elements (perhaps prodded by Rezâ himself) objected to the idea of a republic as un-Islamic. In 1925, the Majles deposed Ahmad Shah and amended the constitution to transfer the monarchy to Rezâ Khân and his descendants; he crowned himself in a ceremony in 1926.

In accordance with a law regulating personal names, Rezâ Khân had adopted the family name of Pahlavi, and he was thus now Rezâ Shah of the Pahlavi Dynasty. The word itself was the name of a language of ancient Iran, and choosing it symbolized the Iranian nationalism that was the hallmark of Rezâ Shah's policies. He was remarkably effective in breaking the power of the great tribal groups, in crushing any tendency toward provincial or ethnic separatism, and in building up the institutions of a centralized nation-state. He implemented many measures to instill a sense of pride and unity and national identity, ranging from encouraging the study of Iranian antiquities to regulating the kind of clothes people could wear to demanding that foreigners call the country Iran instead of Persia. In addition to nationalist policies, Rezâ Shah leaned toward the secularization of society, particularly after his visit with Mustafa Kemal Ataturk in 1934. Of his various reforms, the introduction of civil law and courts, the state control of education, and the emancipation of women struck most clearly at the traditional role of religion in Iranian society. Although he never pushed as hard in any of these areas as Ataturk had done in Turkey, the changes were enough to earn him the animosity of many religious leaders. They were too overawed by him, however, to make much trouble; as he is supposed to have said, it was easy to control the clergy simply by bribing the corrupt and beating the rest.

In foreign policy, Rezâ Shah dealt firmly if cautiously in his relations with the Soviet Union and Great Britain. Iranians tend to believe that Britain organized the coup which brought Rezâ Khân to power and that Rezâ Shah was essentially a British puppet; nonetheless, he was quite bold in taking action at British expense. In defiance of British demands, he had suppressed the efforts of the Arab Shaykh Khaz'al to gain autonomy in Khuzestân in 1924; in 1932 he cancelled the British oil concession and forced a renegotiation of its terms under the auspices of the League of Nations; in 1940, taking advantage of wartime conditions, he extracted higher royalty payments from the Anglo-Iranian Oil Company (the name of the company had been changed in accordance with Rezâ Shah's insistence on the use of the name *Iran* rather than *Persia* for his country). Rezâ Shah also succeeded in improving and strengthening Iran's ties with its regional neighbors, and he continued the Iranian policy of seeking close relations with a third Western power to offset the influence of the Russians and the British. For a number of reasons, economic and cultural, that power turned out to be Nazi Germany. After Hitler invaded the Soviet Union in 1941, the USSR joined Britain in claiming that the rise of German influence in Iran was intolerable; this was mostly a pretext for aggression since the Allies needed control of Iran to facilitate their defense against the German advance and to secure the unimpeded movement of lend-lease equipment from the Persian Gulf to the Soviet Union. In August 1941, the Soviets invaded Iran from the north, and the British attacked by sea in the Persian Gulf. Iranian resistance collapsed after three days; a few weeks later, Rezâ Shah abdicated in the hope of preserving the throne for his son Mohammad-Rezâ Pahlavi. Since the Allies could not find anyone else they could agree on as a successor, they accepted this arrangement. Rezâ Shah died in exile in 1944.

By the terms of the Tripartite Treaty (1942) and the Tehran Declaration (1943), the Allies were obligated to maintain the sovereignty and territorial integrity of Iran, to withdraw their forces after the war, and to contribute to the economic reconstruction of the country. The Soviets, however, built up the Communist (Tudeh) Party in Iran, backed separatist movements among the Kurds and in Azerbaijan, and actually increased the number of their troops in Iran. The United States was a signatory to the Tehran Declaration and thus a party to its commitments; its efforts to bring about the withdrawal of Soviet forces from Iran constituted an opening round in the Cold War and marked the beginning of America's protracted, convoluted, and ultimately disastrous involvement in Iranian affairs.

In 1949, a group of liberal, nationalistic Iranians led by Mohammad Mosaddeq, a politician renowned for his honesty and integrity, formed an organization called the National Front and began to agitate for terminating the agreement with the Anglo-Iranian Oil Company and nationalizing the company. A bill to that effect was passed in 1951, and the Majles asked Mohammad-Rezâ Shah to appoint Mosaddeq as the prime minister to implement the measure. This enraged the British government, which used any number of means to try to prevent or overturn the nationalization. After military threats, legal actions, and a boycott of Iranian oil, the British succeeded in winning the support of the Eisenhower administration for a covert operation to overthrow Mosaddeq. This conspiracy was facilitated by the internal conditions in Iran, where Mosaddeq faced economic problems caused by the loss of oil revenue and growing political divisions. Already at odds with royalists because of his perceived hostility toward the monarchy, he was also caught between the conflicting interests of the Communists and the conservative religious groups—they supported Mosaddeq on the nationalization of oil but were naturally at odds with each other on everything else. The foreign intelligence agents in Iran, directed by a CIA operative, did everything possible to split the religious elements from Mosaddeq and align them with the royalists, even sending out agents disguised as Communists to threaten religious leaders and stir up violent demonstrations. One of their hardest tasks proved to be convincing the shah to collaborate in the plot; he was finally persuaded in August 1953 to exercise his authority to dismiss Mosaddeq as prime minister. When Mosaddeq refused to accept the dismissal, the shah fled the country and crowds of demonstrators clamored for the abolition of the monarchy. They were sometimes incited to violence, it seems, by agents provocateurs in order to alarm the conservatives and arouse fears of a Communist takeover. A few days later, a massive pro-royalist demonstration, organized and funded by the conspirators, rushed through Tehran; units of the army surrounded Mosaddeq in his house and arrested him when he tried to escape. Mohammad-Rezâ Shah then returned in triumph to Iran.

From 1953 onward, political life in Iran was increasingly and, before long, thoroughly controlled by the shah himself, who almost always adopted policies attuned to expectations of what would be most pleasing to the presidential administrations in Washington. In the 1960s, the Kennedy era, he was concerned to show himself as a progressive and enlightened ruler. His so-called Revolution of the Shah and the People, also known as the White Revolution, promised land reform, economic reform, improvements in education, programs for health care and increased rates of literacy (especially in rural areas), and voting rights for women. It delivered somewhat less than all that but was still radical enough in its effects to alienate religious leaders and arouse protest demonstrations, which were violently suppressed in 1963 and 1964. One of the chief instigators of this opposition was an *âyatollâh* (a high-ranking member of the clergy), Ruhollâh Khomeini, who was briefly imprisoned and finally sent into exile. In the 1970s, the Nixon era, the shah sought to portray himself as a strong and reliable regional ally capable of maintaining order and stability in the Persian Gulf area. Through OPEC, he was able to lead the drive to raise oil prices, and then, with his vastly increased revenues, he was able to purchase an impressive arsenal of advanced military hardware from the United States and elsewhere. Economically, too, he claimed that he was building a great civilization *(tamaddon-e bozorg)* and that Iran would take its place as an advanced industrial nation alongside countries like Germany or Japan. He also became even more ruthlessly autocratic and insensitive to the country's cultural values, crushing any political dissent and on at least one occasion openly mocking the abilities of his people. He could be both megalomaniacal and contemptuous of Islamic religious concerns, exalting the country's pre-Islamic history, holding an opulent celebration at Persepolis of 2500 years of monarchy in Iran, introducing a new imperial calendar in place of the Islamic calendar, and enacting laws that contradicted Islamic teachings.

Revolutionary Iran

To some degree, Mohammad-Rezâ Shah's failings were masked by the progressive nature of some of his reforms (improving the status of women, for example) and by the undeniable explosion of wealth brought about by the oil boom. Under the surface, however, there was growing opposition on both the Marxist left and the religious right of the political spectrum. Among the elite and middle classes, too, there was anger and frustration that the economic advances in Iran were not paralleled by greater opportunities for political expression and participation. After 1976, an economic downturn coupled with rising expectations for political liberalization stimulated dissent. Hopes that the Carter administration, which had proclaimed its concern for human rights, would pressure the shah to become less autocratic were dashed when Carter visited Tehran in late 1977 and praised the shah extravagantly for what Carter called his "enlightened leadership." Not long after, a slanderous attack on Khomeini in the state-controlled press touched off mass demonstrations among religious students in Qom that soon spread throughout Iran. By fall, the various opposition groups had united under the leadership of the exiled Khomeini and pledged to keep up their strikes and demonstrations until the shah was forced to abdicate. The shah was both ineffective and inconsistent in dealing with the unrest, whether because of problems deriving from his terminal illness, his hope that Washington would tell him what to do, or darker conspiracies against him, is impossible to say. To his credit, he did steadfastly avoid turning the full weight of his military on the crowds; of course, the rank and file might have refused to obey if he had given such orders. By the end of 1978, it was obvious that the shah's position was hopeless; he left Iran for a so-called vacation in January 1979, after entrusting a regency government to Shâhpur Bakhtiâr.

Bakhtiâr was promptly expelled from the National Front for agreeing to take office at the shah's request. The Iranian military disintegrated, and crowds, now armed with looted weapons, took control of the streets. Unable to prevent the return in February 1979 of Khomeini, who was welcomed by millions of enthusiastic supporters, the Bakhtiâr government collapsed, and Bakhtiâr fled the country. Khomeini appointed Mahdi Bâzargân as prime minister, who in turn put together a cabinet of reassuringly liberal, secular, and nationalist figures. In March, a plebiscite was held on whether the monarchy should be replaced by an Islamic Republic. It was approved by 98 percent of the voters, and work began on drafting a new constitution.

Two things soon became apparent: First, the Bâzargân provisional government had no effective authority over the multitude of armed gangs and *komiteh*s (committees) that had sprung up in every neighborhood; they had tasted power and liked it, as evidenced by their increasingly bloody dispensation of revolutionary justice. Second, those who had thought Khomeini and the religious leadership were just symbolic figureheads of the revolution without a political agenda of their own could not have been more wrong. Inexorably and remorselessly, the revolutionary clerics built up their own militias and organizations, made sure that their interests were incorporated into the new constitution, and eliminated one competing faction after another. Tactically, the takeover of the American embassy in November 1979 and holding hostage its personnel for 444 days served these objectives since political dissent could be stifled in the name of maintaining national unity during the crisis. In particular, criticism of the controversial constitution, which placed ultimate authority in the hands of Khomeini as supreme religious leader (in accordance with his doctrine of clerical authority, known as *velâyat-e faqih*), was drowned out by the hostage crisis; the constitution was approved overwhelmingly in a referendum in December 1979.

In September 1980, Iraq attacked and invaded Iran, beginning a war that would last for eight years and inflict untold devastation on both countries. After its initial advances, the Iraqi offensive faltered, and in spring 1982 the Iranians mounted a successful counteroffensive that drove the Iraqi forces almost completely out of Iran. The Iraqi leader, Saddam Hussein, had indicated a willingness to end the war, but Khomeini saw an opportunity to topple Saddam and thereby perhaps make possible a pro-Iranian Shi'ite regime in Iraq. The Iranians thus set impossibly high demands for a peace settlement and then carried the war into Iraq. By 1983, much to the alarm of the Arab states of the Persian Gulf as well as Western governments, it appeared that Iraq might collapse. This was averted by the massive supply of funds, military equipment, and intelligence information to Iraq by governments (including France, the United States, and the Soviet Union) opposed to any spillover of the Iranian Revolution. Thus bolstered, the Iraqis stepped up air raids on Iran, used chemical weapons to stop Iranian human-wave attacks, fired missiles at Iranian cities, and attacked Iranian shipping and oil installations. In November 1986, news of secret arms deals between Iran and the United States, with Israel as an intermediary, became public. This highly embarrassed the Reagan administration, which had been urging other countries not to ship weapons to Iran as well as professing its support of Arab countries against the supposed threat to them from Iran. The United States then abandoned any effort to seek a rapprochement with Iran and sided more or less openly with Iraq by protecting the shipping of neutral countries trading with Iraq, clearing Iranian mines from the Persian Gulf, and occasionally attacking Iranian vessels and oil installations; an American warship also shot down a civilian Iranian airliner in July 1988. Diplomatically isolated and exhausted financially and militarily, Iran finally accepted U.N. Resolution 598 calling for an end to the war.

What the Iranian government called the "imposed war" with Iraq, like the hostage crisis, had made it very awkward for anyone in Iran to criticize or oppose the policies of the Khomeini regime. Against the backdrop of the war, a faction of the clergy, organized as the Islamic Republican Party (IRP) and backed by Khomeini, consolidated its grip on power and eliminated secular rivals as well as more moderate or dissident clerics. Militias and paramilitary groups loyal to the IRP were created in order to combat both Iraq and domestic opponents. The first elected president, Abo'l-Hasan Bani Sadr, was driven from office. Former revolutionary officials such as Sâdeq Qotbzâdeh were accused of crimes and executed. The military and bureaucracy were purged. Universities were closed down for two years as part of a cultural revolution. The Tudeh Party was destroyed, and the vestiges of the National Front reduced to impotence. The Mojâhedin-e Khalq, a leftist group, continued to carry on a low-level guerilla campaign against the Islamic regime, but its credibility suffered because of its willingness to work with Iraq and other hostile governments.

The end of the war with Iraq, followed by the death of Khomeini in June 1989, brought many suppressed differences over economic and social policies out into the open. A midranking cleric and former president, 'Ali Khamenei, was selected to succeed Khomeini as *faqih,* the ultimate source of authority in Iran. Khamenei kept a rather low profile at first, but when he exerted himself he consistently came down on the side of conservative religious policies and a militantly anti-American and anti-Israeli foreign policy. The new president, 'Ali-Akbar Hâshemi Rafsanjâni, was essentially a pragmatist who sought to rebuild the economy and improve ties with Middle Eastern and European countries. His economic policies, however, were undermined by slumping oil prices; they also conflicted with constitutional barriers to foreign investment, threatened to disrupt the system of welfare and largesse that kept the poorer social classes (the *mostaz'afin,* or "oppressed") loyal to the clerical regime, and were plagued by accusations of corruption and inefficiency. Relations with European countries were complicated by the controversy over Khomeini's earlier religious ruling calling for the execution of the author Salman Rushdie as an apostate. At the same time, many Iranians, especially women and young people (in a country with an increasingly young population), were restive over the restrictions placed on their behavior by the mores of a highly traditional religious regime as well as worried over the deteriorating economy and lack of prospects for jobs.

The vigorously contested presidential election of 1997 represented a major upheaval in the politics of the Islamic Republic of Iran. The candidate clearly preferred by the religious establishment was defeated, and Mohammad Khâtami, regarded as an amiable, moderate, and progressive cleric, won in a landslide (69 percent of a record turnout of voters). Subsequent elections more than confirmed overwhelming popular support for Khâtami and a policy of reform and liberalization. The constitutional system in Iran, however, made it very difficult for Khâtami, even with the backing of a Majles dominated by his supporters, to translate his promises about a "civil society" and a "dialogue of civilizations" into reality. His conservative opponents, usually supported by Khamenei, controlled the judiciary and the Council of Guardians; they could thus use the courts to harass opponents and the Council to veto legislation they disliked. They could also stir up controversies (such as one over the trial of a German man accused of kissing an Iranian woman in Mashhad) that made it more difficult to improve relations with European countries. Hanging over everything, too, was the threat of violence from the paramilitary organizations and vigilantes, expressed in the wrecking of the offices of reformist newspapers and a string of gruesome murders of political opponents. The position of Khâtami and the reformists in Iran was also made much more difficult by George W. Bush's labeling of Iran as part of a so-called axis of evil, the entrenchment of American forces in countries bordering Iran, and demands that Iran cease its supposed efforts to develop bomb-making nuclear technology: all this renewed fears of an external threat to the country, and the reformists could be tarred as advocates of rapprochement with the American "Great Satan." As for the reformist agenda itself, well into Khâtami's second term, it was difficult to point to any but the most minor changes in the character of life in the Islamic Republic. Moreover, the election as president in June 2005 of Mahmud Ahmadinejâd, an archconservative layman (widely assumed to be acting on Khamenei's behalf, in part to keep Rafsanjâni from returning to office), appeared to mark the collapse of the reformist and pragmatist movements in Iranian politics. The great unknown in Iran's future, apart from the distinct possibility of foreign aggression, is how long the tension between the competing visions of the country and its culture can persist without either being resolved or erupting in another revolution.

NOTES

1. Percy Sykes, *A History of Persia*, 3rd ed. (London: Macmillan and Co., 1951), 1:10.

2. See Ehsan Yarshater, "Iranian National History," in *Cambridge History of Iran* (Cambridge: Cambridge University Press, 1983), vol. III, bk. 1, pp. 359–477.

2

Religions and Religious Life

Western theorists of the political and social sciences have typically held that increasing secularism is an inevitable feature of modern nation-states. Some states may be openly hostile to any expression of religion as a factor in public affairs; others tend to reduce religious life to the realm of nothing more than individual, discretionary, personal behavior in a few compartmentalized areas of activity to which the state is indifferent. The Iranian Revolution of 1979–80 demonstrated beyond question that Iran, despite fifty years of secularizing reform under the Pahlavi regime, would not conform to this model. The Islamic Republic of Iran is as thoroughly a theocratic state as one could imagine apart from the Vatican or a Tibet under the Dalai Lama. The constitution itself confirms that all sovereignty belongs to God, recognizes the Twelver (*Esnâ 'ashari;* also called Ja'fari or *Emâmi*/Imami) school of Shi'ite Islam as the official religion, specifies that the state exists in order to promote a favorable environment for religion, vests the highest executive authority in representatives of the Shi'ite *'olamâ* (professional religious scholars), and requires that "all civil, penal, financial, economic, administrative, cultural, military, political, and other laws and regulations must be based on Islamic criteria."

There is thus virtually no aspect of the culture and customs of Iran—be it law, social customs, festivals and holidays, art, architecture, or even dress and diet—that lacks a religious dimension of some kind, and these will be examined as appropriate in other chapters of this book. The purpose of this chapter is to survey the development of key religious ideas, practices, and institutions that have played an important role throughout Iranian history, with a particular emphasis on those specific to its main contemporary religion, Shi'ite Islam.

ISLAM AND IRAN

The basic features of the religion of Islam are well known, and as they are common to Muslims in a variety of countries around the world as well as to those in Iran, they need only be summarized briefly here.

The two absolutely essential doctrines of Islam, on which all others are based, are encapsulated in what is known as the *shahâdeh,* or profession of faith: "I testify that there is no god but God; I testify that Mohammad is the prophet of God." The first clause of this profession of faith expresses belief in an austere, uncompromising monotheism. God is a supreme, eternal, transcendent being, creator and sustainer of the universe and all that it encompasses. The second attests to the belief that this God has revealed knowledge of Himself and His will to mankind through a series of prophets, and the last of these apostles or "messengers" *(rasuls)* was Mohammad, who lived in Mecca and then Medina in the Arabian peninsula (ca. 570–632). The revelations received by Mohammad were eventually collected together in a scriptural text, the Koran *(al-Qor'ân* in Arabic), which represents, quite literally, the word of God to mankind in its purest and final form.

Islam itself means "submission" to God and His will. The Koran emphasizes over and over the majesty of God, the beneficence that He has shown to human beings in particular, the acts of obedience and gratitude that creatures owe in return to their Creator, and the rewards that await the faithful at the end of time. These ideas are enunciated with perhaps the greatest eloquence in the "Chapter of Light" *(surat-on-nur)* of the Koran, where the transcendental sublimity of God is compared the light of a lamp in a niche: "God is the light of the heavens and the earth. The parable of His light is if there were a niche and within it a lamp, the lamp enclosed in glass, the glass as it were a brilliant star. Lit from a blessed tree, an olive neither of the east nor of the west, whose oil is well- nigh luminous, though fire scarce touched it. Light upon light; God doth guide whom He will to His light. God sets forth parables for men, and God knows all things."[1] God has dominion over all the earth; it is He who heaps clouds together and causes rain to fall from them, and He who causes night and day to alternate. All creatures celebrate and praise Him in their own way, by "birds with wings outspread" and throughout the day by men who are not distracted by trade and commerce in houses of worship. For those who submit to God and obey the Prophet, who do not compromise their monotheism, who establish prayer and practice charity, there will be recompense in this world and the next: "God has promised to those among you who believe and work righteous deeds that He will certainly grant them in the land inheritance as He granted it to those before them; that he will establish in authority their religion, the one which He has chosen for them; and that He will transform them from the state of fear in which they live to one of security and peace."[2]

As the last of the prophets and the founder of the Islamic community, Mohammad himself played a special role in teaching Muslims the meaning of the Koran and the requirements God had imposed on them. Especially in terms of law and ritual, many details of the religion are not drawn directly from the Koran but are based on the examples or instructions of the Prophet as handed down in reports known as hadith. All of this traditional information about the practices of the Prophet collectively constitutes the Sunna, a comprehensive guide to conduct must likely to be pleasing to God. The Koran and the Sunna together form the basis for the Shari'a, the whole body of rules and regulations that determine how Muslims should live and worship. Part of what is described in the Shari'a has to do with the well-known ritual aspects of Islam: daily prayers, fasting during daylight hours of the month of Ramadan (pronounced Ramazân in Persian), pilgrimage to Mecca once in a lifetime for those who are able to do so, charitable contributions, the rules of ritual purity and ablutions, etc. In theory, it also governs a wide range of matters pertaining to law and the regulation of daily law: marriage, inheritance, contracts and business dealings, torts and penal law, sexual behavior, deportment, dress, permitted and forbidden foods and drinks, etc. It is this aspect of the Shari'a that has become controversial in modern times, especially as the more or less secularized governments of nation states have laid claim to authority over these same areas of conduct. In the case of Iran, the Islamic revolution promised to harmonize state and Shari'a, but if anything the debate over the continued relevance of the Shari'a and the extent to which it is binding on individual behavior has intensified.

Sunnism and Shi'ism

Despite the common elements which hold it together, Islam is not and never has been an absolutely monolithic or homogeneous religion. Over the course of its history, it has given rise to many schools of thought and sectarian divisions as well as esoteric and mystical movements like Sufism. Very real and significant divisions exist among Muslims today, just as they do among Jews, Christians, or Buddhists. Of these, the two most important branches of contemporary Islam are usually referred to in English as Sunnism and Shiism (and their adherents as Sunnites and Shi'ites). A common misconception, based on these names, is that the difference between these two sects has to do with acceptance of the Sunna. Although Sunnites and Shi'ites do disagree on numerous technical points of doctrine, ritual, and law, they both emphatically believe they are following the Sunna, and in general they do not have major disagreement about the basic principles and rituals of Islam. They use the same text of the Koran, believe in the same notion of God, venerate the same prophet, perform the same number of daily prayers (albeit with minor differences in the ritual), pray in the same direction and to the same God, fast the same number of days, etc. The fundamental divergence with Sunnism developed not over following the Sunna, but over questions of legitimate authority and leadership in Islam.

Shi'ism is itself a rather generic label applied to a number of related but distinct movements within Islam. At the heart of all of them, however, one finds the principle of "partisanship" in the sense of (1) veneration of the *ahl-ol-bayt*, the "People of the House" (i.e., the family of the Prophet), and (2) allegiance to certain members of the *ahl-ol-bayt* as Imam (*emâm*), the Shi'ite term for the supreme leader of the Muslim community. Sunnite Muslims also have great respect for the person of Mohammad, his family, and his descendants (known as *sharif*s or sayyids), and in earlier historical periods they also recognized a series of caliphs as actual or at least nominal leaders in Muslim affairs. The Shi'ite conceptions of the *ahl-ol-bayt* and the Imamate are nonetheless unique in several respects.

First of all, the Shi'ites have a very restrictive view of how membership in the *ahl-ol-bayt* is constituted. Sunnites, for example, have generally understood the *ahl-ol-bayt* to include all of Mohammad's wives (he had about fifteen and as many as nine at one time); Shi'ites reject this and in fact regard one of those wives, 'Âesheh, as an inveterate enemy of the true *ahl-ol-bayt*. They believe that Mohammad himself defined the *ahl-ol-bayt* on an occasion when he spread his cloak around himself; his daughter, Fâtemeh; his cousin and son-in-law, 'Ali b. Abi Tâleb; and his grandchildren, Hasan and Hosayn, while reciting a verse from the Koran: "God wishes to remove defilement from you, People of the House, and to purify you completely."[3] Mohammad, as a young orphan, had been cared for by 'Ali's father Abu Tâleb. Mohammad later reciprocated by virtually adopting 'Ali, and 'Ali had married Mohammad's daughter Fâtemeh. Fâtemeh was the only one of Mohammad's offspring to survive long enough to have children; thus, Mohammad's bloodline lived on exclusively through the children of 'Ali and Fâtemeh. Membership in the *ahl-ol-bayt* is limited to these five people, the *ahl-ol-kesâ* ("People of the Cloak"), and their descendants. Their special charisma is attested by the Koranic verse speaking of their "purification," and the obligation of other Muslims to bless them, to show affection for them, and to confer certain material benefits upon them is confirmed by other verses that emphasize the importance and sanctity of the "close of kin."

On the issue of leadership of the Muslim community, most Sunnites essentially accepted as legitimate the various individuals and dynasties that held the office of caliph, while attributing a special aura of sanctity to the first four caliphs, known as the *Râshedun* ("Rightly Guided"). In accordance with the historical precedents, they eventually adopted the theory that membership in the Prophet's tribe, Qoraysh, was one of the criteria of eligibility for the office, which could be obtained through election or designation. Other Muslims took a more restrictive view and questioned the legitimacy of some of those who acted as caliphs. Some early groups associated with the Shi'ites were apparently willing to extend the right to rule to members of the Prophet's clan, the Banu Hâshim (which would have included the Abbasid caliphs as descendants of the Prophet's uncle 'Abbâs), or to the Tâlebid branch of that clan (i.e., 'Ali's brothers or his children by wives other than Fâtemeh). For the Shi'ites proper, however, eligibility for the Imamate was the exclusive prerogative of the *ahl-ol-bayt* and usually conferred through express designation by a previous Imam.

The term Shi'ism is derived from the Arabic word *shi'a*, meaning sect, faction, or party, and the earliest Shi'ites were the "partisans" or "devotees" of 'Ali. After Mohammad died, they expected 'Ali to become the head of the Muslim community. In their view, 'Ali was distinguished as the first male convert to Islam, a brave warrior, and an exemplary Muslim; moreover, he had been explicitly designated by Mohammad to be his successor in an oration delivered at a place called Ghadir Khomm. Instead, the Prophet's clear and express will had been frustrated by the machinations of a faction which repeatedly conspired to exclude 'Ali from power and give the caliphate to others, none of whom had any tie of blood kinship with Mohammad. 'Ali was passed over for the office three times, but he did eventually become caliph in the wake of a rebellion that had led to the murder of the third caliph, 'Osmân, in 656. His authority was immediately contested by 'Osmân's relatives (especially Mo'âvieh, the governor of Syria and leader of the Umayyad clan) as well as others. A conspiracy among members of a dissident faction resulted in 'Ali's assassination in 661.

'Ali's son Hasan yielded his claim to rule to Mo'âvieh, first of the Umayyad caliphs, in a negotiated settlement. Hasan then withdrew to Medina, where he lived quietly until around 670, when, according to the Shi'ites, he was treacherously murdered at the instigation of Mo'âvieh. After Mo'âvieh's death in 680, the Shi'ites of Kufa in Iraq invited Hasan's younger brother Hosayn to lead a revolt against the umayyads. Despite the improbability of success and premonitions of his death, Hosayn set out for Iraq with his family and a small band of supporters. During the first days of the Islamic month of Moharram, they were surrounded by an umayyad army at a place called

Karbalâ. Abandoned by the Kufans and cut off from water, Hosayn and his followers suffered terribly. They made their last stand on the tenth day of the month of Moharram, called 'Âshurâ, and were annihilated.

Hosayn was the last to fall, after being repeatedly wounded; he was then beheaded and his corpse trampled by horses. The 72 martyrs included not only Hosayn but his son, 'Ali-Akbar; his nephew, Qâsem, a handsome young man killed mere hours after his wedding; and his brother, 'Abbâs, the epitome of bravery and chivalry. Only one male member of Hosayn's family survived the bloodbath, his young son 'Ali-Asghar Zayn-ol-'Âbedin (d. ca. 712), who was lying sick in his tent.

For Sunnites, these were essentially historical incidents—more tragic evidence of the evil and oppression spawned by conflict and competition within the Muslim community. They represent much more than that in Shi'ism. Psychologically, morally, and spiritually, as well as historically, the events culminating at Karbalâ were decisive in the formation of Shi'ite thought and culture.

After Karbalâ, the Shi'ite movement continued to be pulled back and forth between the contrasting models of the apolitical passivity of Hasan, who was willing to yield his rights to avoid bloodshed and harm to the community, and the militant activism of Hosayn, who was willing to face certain death to stand up against injustice. This was reflected in the most immediate problem, the question of leadership given the loss of so many members of the *ahl-ol-bayt.* The Shi'ites began to split into subsects over questions related to which individual had been designated or should be accepted as Imam, how actively that individual should seek the political power that was rightfully his, and the nature and extent of his religious authority. One group broke away to recognize the Imamate of Zayd, son of 'Ali Zayn-ol-'Âbedin, who led a revolt against the Umayyad caliphs in 740. The Zaydis had no dynastic principle or concept of designation in their theory of the Imamate; they held that any male descendant of Hasan or Hosayn could be Imam as long as he had the highest degree of religious knowledge and, like Hosayn, he declared and actively pursued his claim to the office against oppressive and unqualified rulers. Despite this emphasis on political activism, the Zaydis were quite moderate in other respects and barely distinguishable from Sunnites. More radical Shi'ites, known as *gholât* ("extremists"), recognized various other individuals as Imam, often as leaders of very militant chiliastic movements. They were noted for their tendency to attribute almost divine qualities to the Imam, for dispensing with the need to conform to the usual ritual and legal requirements of Islam, and for their belief in unusual doctrines such as reincarnation.

The mainstream of the Shi'ites, however, recognized as the fifth and sixth Imams Mohammad Bâqer (d. 731) and Ja'far Sâdeq (d. 765). Neither of them advocated any violence or made any attempt to seize political power, and both concentrated on the development of a distinctly Shi'ite school of religious law. Ja'far Sâdeq was particularly important as an architect of Shi'ite jurisprudence, and many Shi'ites consequently describe themselves as "Ja'fari" in their legal orientation.

Another major division among the Shi'ites developed when they disagreed over the succession to Ja'far Sâdeq. One group recognized his oldest son, Esmâ'il, as the seventh Imam (even though Esmâ'il had apparently predeceased Ja'far). These Isma'ili or Sabi'a ("Sevener") Shi'ites developed their own highly esoteric doctrinal system and eventually established the Fatimid caliphate in North Africa and Egypt (909–1171). Other Shi'ites recognized the Imamate of Ja'far's youngest son, Musâ Kâzem (d. 799). He was succeeded by the eighth Imam, Ali Rezâ, whom the Abbasid caliph Ma'mun proposed to make his heir but who died in 818 (poisoned, according to the usual view of the Shi'ites) before this could come to pass. He was buried near the grave of Ma'mun's father, the caliph Hârun-or-Rashid, and the religious shrine which grew up around his tomb formed the nucleus of the city of Mashhad and is today the most important religious monument in Iran. Imam Rezâ was succeeded by Mohammad Javâd (d. 835), 'Ali Hâdi (d. 868), and Hasan 'Askari (d. 874).

The Shi'ites continued to splinter into different factions during this period, and some claimed that Hasan 'Askari had died childless, thus leaving no successor. One important group, however, insisted that Hasan had a young son, Mohammad, whom he had concealed in order to protect him from his enemies. This Twelfth Imam remained in "occultation" (*ghaybat*) and communicated with his followers only through a few "emissaries" until 941, the year of the "greater occultation," when he cut off all contact with the world. The Shi'ites who recognize his Imamate are thus often called the Twelvers (*Esnâ-ash'ariyeh*). In their belief, the Twelfth or Hidden Imam, the Imam of the Age (*Emâm-e Zamân*), did not die; he remains alive but in concealment even now and will ultimately emerge again as the Qâ'em ("the One who Arises") and the Mahdi (Messiah), who is destined to spread Islam throughout the world and usher in the utopian era that precedes that end of the world. Consequently, the Imami Shi'ites fervently pray for the imminent return of Mohammad Montazar ("the Expected One"): "Manifest to us, O God, Thy Representative, the descendant of the daughter of Thy Prophet, the namesake of Thy Apostle, that he may overthrow all that is vain and worthless and establish the truth for those who are worthy...O God, be merciful to the helpless, and take away grief and sorrow from this people by granting his presence, and hasten his appearance."[4]

Most Sunnites emphasize that Mohammad, while a prophet and an exemplary moral figure, was ultimately a human being without the kind of supernatural or godlike qualities Christians attribute to Jesus. Similarly, individual Muslims like ʿAli or Hosayn might be regarded as exceptional, but only in terms of their piety and virtue. Sunnis also recognized the need for a successor to Mohammad, as exemplified in the institution of the caliphate, but they generally limited the scope of this office to political, economic, military, and legal affairs; religious authority came to be vested in the community and its religious scholars. Shiʿite groups went well beyond this, as the concept of the Hidden Imam makes quite evident. The Shiʿites not only accorded a special political, moral, and legal status to certain members of the *ahl-ol-bayt,* they also often gave them a spiritual quality unlike that of any ordinary mortal. In the case of the Imami Shiʿites, for example, Mohammad, Fâtemeh, and the Twelve Imams constitute the "Fourteen Infallibles" (known in Persian as the *Châhârdah Maʾsum*), and both Imami religious scholars and popular religion ascribe the most extraordinary characteristics to them. They were created before the world itself out of a pure substance, either light or a heavenly clay, and are superior to all other created beings. They were born without physical blemish, and their births were accompanied by miraculous happenings and portents, as were their deaths. They themselves could work miracles; some spoke the language of animals, revivified dead trees, raised the dead, turned stones into gold, and so forth. They were all absolutely sinless and fundamentally incapable of sinning or making a mistake. The historical record of them is but a pale indication of their spiritual and cosmic significance; in particular, the willing death of Hosayn in his struggle against evil was a sacrificial and redemptive act of the utmost importance. The Imamate was neither a temporal office nor an elective one like the caliphate: God was required by His benevolence to place a supreme guide in the world for the benefit of mankind, and the world could not exist for a moment without the presence of such an Imam. The Imams are the "proofs" or "lights" of God, the guardians of creation, and God's direct representatives on earth. They, and they alone, have the special and secret knowledge (*ʿelm*) necessary to understand the Koran, and indeed any aspect of religion, completely and perfectly. That, along with their intrinsic inability to sin make them infallible guides in all religious matters, and the faithful are thus absolutely obliged to recognize and obey the Imam in order to attain salvation.

SHIʿISM IN IRAN AND THE SHIʿITE "CLERGY"

As noted in the previous chapter, Islam came to Iran in the wake of the Arab conquests of the seventh century. Until the sixteenth century, the Iranian lands, or at least their major urban centers, were predominately Sunnite in orientation. A very large number of the most influential figures in the history of

Sunnism and Sufism—and some of the most aggressive anti-Shi'ite rulers and ideologues—either lived in this region or were of Iranian background. When the first Safavid ruler, Shah Esmâ'il, proclaimed Shi'ism the official state religion in 1501, his intentions, consciously calculated or not, were probably inspired more by pragmatic politics than by religion as such—legitimizing his rule by virtue of his claim to descent from Imam Musâ Kâzem, finding a bond to link his Turkoman supporters and his Persian-speaking subjects, providing a rationale for resistance to his Sunnite Ottoman and Ozbek neighbors. It was also something of a bold gamble, since it was supposedly almost impossible to find a Shi'ite book or a Shi'ite religious scholar in Iran, and Esmâ'il had to import much of his new religious elite from Shi'ite communities abroad, such as those in Iraq or Lebanon, and impose his new orthodoxy at the point of a sword. Yet within a couple of generations, the Iranian population had become overwhelmingly and enthusiastically Imami Shi'ite in religious identity, and in ways that Shâh Esmâ'il could not have anticipated and probably would have regretted. How was it possible for such a rapid and radical transformation to take place?

First of all, the religious discontinuity was probably not nearly as dramatic or as startling as it might appear, especially since the basic idea of veneration of the family of the Prophet had become deeply embedded in virtually all forms of Islam. Moreover, a specifically Shi'ite presence in Iran extended well back into pre-Safavid times, and all the major sectarian divisions of Shi'ism—Zaydi, Isma'ili, Imami, and Gholât—had exerted varying degrees of influence there. At the beginning of the eighth century, members of the *ahl-ol-bayt* and their supporters, fleeing from hostile rulers, began to seek refuge in remote parts of Iran and founded Shi'ite communities there. Among these early bastions of Shi'ism was Qom, settled by a Shi'ite Arab tribe in 712. The sister of Imam Rezâ, Fâtemeh Ma'sumeh ("The Pure"), fell ill while traveling across Iran to visit her brother and died and was buried in Qom in 816. Imam Rezâ reportedly said that anyone who visited her tomb would go to heaven, and this made Qom a major shrine city for Shi'ites. The city was further distinguished by the school of Shi'ite religious scholarship which developed there. Shi'ism also flourished in the Caspian region, where people invited a descendant of Imam Hasan, Hasan b. Zayd, to become their leader in 864. He founded a line of Zaydi Imams who ruled periodically in the area down to 1126, and Zaydi missionaries successfully proselytized the non-Muslim population still found there. The Buyid dynasty had its origin in this same region, and the Buyid rulers promoted a somewhat nebulous form of Shi'ism, probably Imami, in the areas they conquered. Isma'ili missionaries were also active throughout Iran, and there is evidence that a major dynasty in eastern Iran, the Samanids, briefly considered espousing the Isma'ili cause. Other

Iranian Isma'ilis received training and support for their missionary activities from the newly established Fatimid caliphate in Egypt. Under the leadership of Hasan-e Sabbâh (fl. 1071–1124), they established a network of effectively autonomous Isma'ili communities linked to a central stronghold at the castle of Alamut in northwestern Iran. However, they also broke with the Fatimids in 1094 over the succession to the caliph Mostanser, supporting the (losing) cause of his son Nezâr. Hasan-e Sabbâh helped formulate the new Nezâri Isma'ili doctrine, which emphasized his role as the agent of the missing Imam Nezâr and a subsequent line of Nezâri Imams at Alamut. The Nezâris were a potent force in Iran until their fortresses were finally destroyed by Hulâgu in 1256. Although hostile to the Nezâris, the Mongol Il-khanids supported the more apolitical Imami Shi'ites as useful allies in internal policies and against rival Sunni powers. After the Il-khanids' conversion to Islam, at least one of their rulers, Oljeytu Khodâbandeh, tried to promote Shi'ism as the state religion. Some of the Timurids were also supportive, or at least tolerant, of Shi'ism; Gowharshâd, the wife of Shâh Rokh, funded the construction of the magnificent mosque adjacent to the shrine of Imam Rezâ (on the pulpit of which, Shi'ites believe, the Twelfth Imam will sit on Judgment Day). And, of course, the Shi'ism of the *qezelbâsh* era that preceded Safavid rule was clearly rooted in the Gholât ideology that had produced numerous, if episodic and generally unsuccessful, rebellions in Islamic Iran. The promotion of Shi'ism as an official religion thus had a good deal of historical heritage behind it.

Second, Shi'ism proved to be a form of Islam very well attuned to deeply rooted features of Iranian culture. It is true, as most modern scholars emphasize, that Shi'ism was not an Iranian innovation or some Iranized form of Islam; it originated among Arabs and continued to have a strong Arab constituency in areas far beyond Iran. Nonetheless, certain features of Shi'ism as it developed had definite parallels with pre-Islamic Iranian religious culture or appealed in other ways to converts and believers of Iranian background. These included its emphasis on legitimism (the divinely sanctioned authority of a charismatic household); its messianic and millenarian message; its rejection of fatalism in favor of the free choice of individuals to resist evil and oppression in the world; and its promise of ultimate justice and salvation for the faithful. Concepts of the holy family of the "People of the Cloak" and the "Fourteen Infallibles" as preexistent beings of light and critical elements of creation immediately bring to mind the Zoroastrian idea of the "Bounteous Immortals" (Amesha Spenta); the function of the Hidden Imam in Islamic eschatology is not unlike that of the Savior (Saoshyant) in Zoroastrianism; the cult of mourning for the fallen Imam Hosayn is reminiscent of the ancient Iranian ceremonies of lamentation for the murdered prince Siâvosh. Iranians figured prominently in stories about early supporters of the Imams, and many historical anecdotes emphasized how the Imams insisted on the equality of the Iranian converts with Arab Muslims. Perhaps the best example to illustrate how Iranian and Shi'ite traditions could be fused was the claim that Imam 'Ali had married his son Hosayn to Bibi Shahrbânu, daughter of the last Sasanid king of Iran: She was thought to be the mother of 'Ali Zayn-ol-'Âbedin, who survived the slaughter at Karbalâ, and thus all of the subsequent Imams were of royal Iranian lineage as well as members of the *ahl-ol-bayt*.

Finally, under Safavid patronage, Shi'ite religious scholars diligently and systematically laid a solid intellectual and institutional foundation for the religion. The Shi'ism they constructed in Iran was most definitely not the *qezelbâsh* Shi'ism of the early Safavids that virtually deified the Safavid leader; that was neither credible, given the calamitous Ottoman defeat of Shah Esmâ'il at Chaldirân, nor in accordance with the doctrine of the exclusive claim of the Hidden Imam to legitimate authority. The Shi'ism that developed in Iran was a form of Imami Shi'ism that had much more in common with the traditional Shi'ism of Iraq and Lebanon than the radical notions of the *qezelbâsh*. At first, the Imami Shi'ite religious scholars were of course dependent on the Safavid shahs to establish themselves, and they continued to profess support for the Safavid shahs on the basis of their claim to kinship with the *ahl-ol-bayt* and their demonstrated devotion to the religion. Their ultimate loyalty, however, was to Shi'ism rather to the Safavid house, and that was painfully apparent by the end of the Safavid period.

At the same time, these scholars managed to work out amongst themselves what the accepted form of Shi'ism would be and to suppress its internal divisions and external rivals. The basic problem was this: If the Hidden Imam is in occultation, and genuine authority is his rather than that of any king or temporal ruler, who is responsible for giving guidance to the Shi'ite community? One group, the Akhbâris, argued that the Imams had already provided definitive answers to anything one really needed to know, and it was sufficient just to study and to follow the "reports" (*akhbâr*) of their words (rather like the way some Christians think any individual can discover anything he needs to know by studying the Bible alone). Another, the Shaykhis, claimed that even in the absence of the Imam there was always one "perfect Shi'ite" who could speak for the Imam (and God), so believers just needed to seek him out and follow his guidance. Looking for religious instruction from charismatic individuals was also possible among the Sufis in Iran. Although Shi'ism and Sufism were fundamentally incompatible as religious systems, some Iranian Sufis had been trying to reconcile the two by portraying the Imams as superb mystics. The authority of the Safavids themselves had originally been based on their function as the charismatic guide (*pir*) of a Sufi order, and a few such Sufi orders continued to be active in the Safavid and post-Safavid era.

All of these schools of thought were effectively crushed, however, by what is known as the Osuli school of Imami Shi'ism. The Osulis were quite clear that no one—no Sufi guru, no monarch however distinguished, no "perfect" Shi'ite—could even remotely approach the authority and legitimacy that belonged exclusively to the Imam. In his absence, no point of doctrine or practice could be regarded as absolutely established; it was certainly not acceptable for individuals to try to make individual judgments based on their own reading just of traditional reports handed down from earlier Imams. Instead, religious issues had to be constantly re-examined by serious scholars using serious methods of rational analysis and jurisprudence (*osul-ol-feqh,* hence the name Osulis). Only after such a program of rigorous study and training could a scholar offer guidance to other Shi'ites on religious practices, legal matters, and whatever other questions they might have. The most expert of the scholars were entitled to use their considered judgment (*ejtehâd,* a person qualified to give such an opinion is known as a *mojtahed*) to give a best-guess solution to novel problems, and it was acceptable for a Shi'ite to follow it as if it had come from the Imam himself. In theory, this gave Shi'ites the potential to rework constantly the details of their religion in the light of changing circumstances, but in practice it tied them to a highly conservative, technical, and legalistic form of the religion in which precedents accepted as established by earlier authorities were rarely overturned.

The triumph of the Osulis was the work of several great *mojtaheds,* foremost among them Mohammad-Bâqer Majlesi (1627–1698), who was able to produce both voluminous and highly technical works on Shi'ism in Arabic to buttress Osuli ideology and a number of accessible, readable manuals in Persian that helped disseminate and popularize Shi'ite doctrine. The system elaborated by Majlesi combined elements of several strands of earlier Shi'ite thought: the glorification of the Imams rooted in popular faith and imamology, the insistence that all aspects of religion are subject to demonstration by rational proofs, and the overriding importance of the Ja'fari school of jurisprudence. Majlesi also preached obedience to the Safavid shahs but exercised such influence over them that he was the de facto ruler for many years. Probably not since the days of the Zoroastrian high priest Kartir, who dominated several Sasanid shahs, had a religious official held such power and influence. One of the results of Kartir's establishment of a form of Zoroastrianism as a state religion had been the creation of what was in effect a Zoroastrian "church," and the outcome of Majlesi's doctrines and policies was much the same for Shi'ism in Iran.

As Muslims often like to point out, there is no priesthood in Islam nor any doctrinal basis for one to exist. There are no sacraments to be administered, no mysteries restricted to initiates, and no rites that lay believers are not theoretically capable of performing for themselves. As long as one has such a priestly function in mind, it is thus very misleading to speak of a "clergy" in Iran or any other Muslim country. Nonetheless, it is recognized that some individuals do have a greater degree of piety or a better mastery of religious knowledge than others, and there is a tendency among the masses to follow the lead of those recognized as religious scholars (the 'olamâ). They are trusted to know the details of how a ritual should be performed, or that a marriage contract or business arrangement or distribution of an inheritance is consistent with the requirements of Islamic law. Shi'ites are expected to choose one of these *mojtahed*s as their *marjâ'* (reference) and follow his advice on controversial or emergent questions. In the case of Shi'ite Iran, there are many other ways in which the 'olamâ have come to hold a position in society that could well be described as that of a clergy or even a religious aristocracy: They are referred to by a special term, *ruhâniân* ("those concerned with spiritual matters"), that sets them apart from the rest of the population. To be accepted as a qualified member of this class, they have to be confirmed, not exactly by a successive laying on of hands but by the granting of an "authorization" (*ejâzeh*) from a teacher, an established authority who has himself received such permission to carry out religious teaching and activities from a preceding authority. (In the contemporary religious schools which have developed in Iran, this authorization is now obtained through a rigorous process of tests and exams.) These clerics are distinguished by the special dress they are entitled to wear, typically slippers, a tunic and cloak (*qabâ* and *'abâ*), and a turban (*'ammâmeh*, black for those who are descendents of the Prophet Mohammad, the sayyids; white for others). They tend to be a very tight-knit group, with carefully arranged inter-marriages among the families and positions (like that of the leadership of a mosque) handed down in an almost hereditary fashion. They have a clearly defined hierarchy and the institutions and funding to sustain it through endowments, fees collected for providing individual religious services, and the right to collect the tithe (*sahm-e emâm*) that would otherwise belong to the Hidden Imam. In these respects, they certainly have most of the institutional aspects of a "clergy" or even a "priesthood."

It is obvious that the very nature of Osuli Shi'ism requires some means of determining exactly who is qualified to be a *mojtahed* and providing an educational framework in which those qualifications can be acquired. This is provided through what has come to be known as the "pool of religious knowledge" (*howzeh-ye 'elmiyeh*), a network of religious colleges or seminaries, the *madraseh*s, and the circles of students gathered around distinguished teachers that make them up. The *madraseh* was a venerable Islamic institution for higher education, typically funded by endowments from rulers or wealthy patrons to support the study of religious law. (In some contemporary Muslim countries, however, the term has also come to be applied to much simpler elementary schools that do not teach much more than Koran recitation.) Safavid dignitaries established a number of important Shi'ite *madrasehs* at Isfahan; later rulers promoted the Fayziyeh seminary at Qom. During the nineteenth century, many Shi'ites preferred to study and teach outside Iran, especially at Najaf and other Shi'ite shrine cities in Iraq. In 1920, a circle of Shi'ite scholars led by 'Abd-ol-Karim Hâeri-Yazdi revived the Howzeh-ye 'Elmiyeh in Qom, with a curriculum adjusted to meet the specific needs of Shi'ism at the time. Although the Pahlavi rulers generally tended to limit the role of religion and to supplant traditional religious education with state-supported secular schools at all levels from primary grades to university (even establishing a Faculty of Theology at the University of Tehran), Hâeri-Yazdi and his colleagues succeeded in preserving the independence of the seminary at Qom and made it into one of the most prestigious centers of Shi'ite learning in the world. Although the number of students enrolling at Fayziyeh and several other seminaries which emerged in Qom and other major cities, especially in Mashhad, fluctuated during the Pahlavi reign, it had dwindled to somewhat less than two thousand toward the end of regime. Seminaries and their programs revived dramatically after the Islamic Revolution. Today, there are more than 40,000 students from 91 countries enrolled at Qom, utilizing modernized systems of instruction and the latest technology including computers.

The traditional program of study and methods of instruction at Qom in their idealized form have been well described by the anthropologist Michael Fisher: "There are no grades, so students study only for learning's sake. Students who do not study are not flunked out, but neither are they elevated by bribery or favoritism. For each there is a place according to his capacity and inclination ... Students study with teachers of their own choice. There is thus never a disciplinary problem or a problem of lack of respect for teachers ... Teachers do not pontificate; rather all teaching is on a dialectic principle of argument and counterargument in which students are encouraged to participate insofar as they have the preparation to do so."[5]

Originally, anyone who received an *ejâzeh* might be considered a *mojtahed,* but over time a more elaborate hierarchy has developed. At the base are the *tâlebs,* students or seminarians, who are supported by grants from the schools or teachers and can remain in the classes indefinitely. The less talented, after completing the basic curriculum, become *mollâs* or *âkhunds* and typically take over the running of a small community or village mosque. A somewhat more advanced scholar is recognized as a *hojjat-ol-eslâm* ("Proof of Islam"). Those who go on to become still more distinguished teachers and who publish certain technical works on Islamic law are recognized as an *âyatollâh* ("sign of God"), roughly the equivalent of *mojtahed* in its original sense of someone entitled to use *ejtehâd* in juridical matters. There has long been a tendency in the Shi'ite community to take this system to its logical conclusion and recognize one *mojtahed* as the prime authority to be followed, the *marjâ'-e taqlid*. As *âyatollâh*s proliferated, even that term become diluted; in recent times, it has not been uncommon for there to be five or more active *marjâ'-e taqlids*.

The recently introduced concept of *velâyat-e faqih*, rule by one supreme scholar of religious jurisprudence overseeing all matters of the Shi'ite community, has only partially restored the notion of a head of the Shi'ite hierarchy. It was Khomeini who gave life to this concept and engineered its incorporation into the constitution of the Islamic Republic in 1980. It was a novel and controversial concept from the beginning, and several prominent religious leaders actually opposed it. There has never been any obligation on Shi'ites outside Iran to accept the leadership of such a *faqih*. Moreover, as the office has developed since Khomeini's death, it really reflects more a mastery of politics than religion: the current *faqih*, 'Ali Khamenei, was a mere *hojjat-ol-eslam* before his appointment, and even Khomeini was at most one *marjâ'* amongst several equals in terms of religious authority. The resultant tension between political and religious authority has posed something of a crisis for the clergy and for Iranian society as a whole that has yet to be resolved. Most secular Iranians, and even many of those with strong commitment to their religion, consider the system as anachronistic, paternalistic, and undemocratic. Much political criticism and opposition in the Islamic Republic in the past decade has been focused on resisting the enormous authority vested in the person of *vali-e faqih*. Hosayn-'Ali Montazeri, a prominent *marjâ'* and once a champion of Khomeini's idea, has become a major critic of the concept that he himself helped to develop and enshrine in the constitution. Immediately after the establishment of the Islamic Republic, Montazeri was designated as the successor to Khomeini. As the idea of *velâyat-e faqih* came to be implemented and its shortcomings became apparent throughout the 1980s, Montazeri began criticizing its ill-effects, thus alienating himself from Khomeini, who remained a staunch supporter of the concept to the end of his life. In 1988, Khomeini forced Montazeri to resign his position and arranged some changes to the constitution. The revised constitution, which was submitted for public approval after Khomeini's death, eliminated status as a *marjâ'* as a requirement of *velâyat-e faqih* and gave the position more authority in the form of *velâyat-e motlaqeh-e faqih* ("the absolute authority of the supreme jurist"). The Council of Experts (Majles-e Khebrehgân) then promoted Khamenei to *âyatollâh* and elected him as the new *vâli-e faqih*. For

criticizing the expansive powers of Khamenei, Montazeri was placed under
house arrest and constant surveillance.

Shi'ite Religious Culture

Given the radically different views of Sunnism and Shi'ism on matters
of history and doctrine, it might be assumed that there would also be a vast
and unbridgeable gap between them in terms of practices as well. In fact,
they have a good deal in common. Shi'ite law closely resembles some of the
most conservative and traditional schools of Sunnite law, and variations in
matters pertaining to the basic rituals are also very minor (though the differences are taken quite seriously). In the case of ritual prayer, for example, the
Shi'ites have a slightly different wording of the call to prayer, can combine
some of the five daily prayers rather than spreading them out more widely
over the course of the day, and use a few different postures and phrases
during the course of the prayer. The most serious dispute has been over a
question related to the ritual purification required to perform the prayer, the
Sunni practice known as *al-mash 'alâ'l-khoffayn,* wiping the shoes in lieu of
than washing the feet when renewing an ablution. This custom, which the
Caliph 'Omar had authorized, is emphatically rejected by Shi'ites. Shi'ites
in general tend to be much stricter on matters of ritual purity than is the
case with most Sunnites nowadays. For example, some types of physical
contact with a non-Muslim or something a non-Muslim has used have traditionally been regarded as involving a ritual pollution, and this can create
some embarrassing situations for non-Muslims in Iran in encounters with
extremely strict and pious Shi'ites (being barred from visiting mosques, being
prohibited from using public water cups, having the dishes one has used
smashed, and so on).

In terms of family law, there are some substantial differences between
Sunnism and Shi'ism that are relatively important in terms of their significance for Iranian customs and culture. In the laws of inheritance, for example,
Shi'ism takes a more restrictive view of the inheritance rights of agnates (the
'asabeh, basically the uncles and male cousins in an extended family). This is
usually explained as the result of the need to emphasize that Mohammad's
only legitimate heirs were 'Ali and Fâtemeh. There is also an important difference in marriage law. Shi'ism recognizes as valid what is called *mot'eh*
("enjoyment") marriage. In this form of marriage, the key difference is that
the contract specifies the length of time the marriage will last, which could
be anything from a few hours to many years. At the expiration date, the
marriage is automatically dissolved and the woman receives the amount of
money stipulated as a kind of dowry in the contract. It appears that this type

of temporary marriage was generally accepted in the early Islamic period, but Sunni religious scholars gradually restricted and eventually abolished it. It is still recognized as legal, and even meritorious, in Shi'ite law. It has been practiced extensively in Shi'ite Iran, where both the contract and the woman who engages in such a marriage are usually called *sigheh* ("formula"). For example, it was not uncommon for a man who went on a trip and was away from home for an extended period of time to contract a temporary marriage; in places like Mashhad, a popular pilgrimage destination, a virtual industry of providing temporary marriages developed. Women who accepted such marriages, however, were often seen as somewhat disreputable and stigmatized socially; they were unlikely ever to have a regular marriage because of the strong preference for a virgin bride in such cases.

In recent years, the practice of temporary marriage has become controversial. Its defenders see it as a perfectly valid and moral form of marriage that protects by legal contract the rights of all parties involved and that affords a means of livelihood to women who would otherwise be destitute. Its critics see it as a thinly disguised form of legalized prostitution that exploits women made vulnerable by social prejudices against those who have been divorced or are otherwise disadvantaged. It was one of the traditional customs that the secularizing and modernizing reformers of the Pahlavi era hoped to abolish. After the Islamic Revolution of 1979–80, however, its legitimacy in Shi'ite Islam was reaffirmed. Some clerics, such as Rafsanjâni, even went so far as to tout its advantages as a progressive means of dealing with contemporary gender problems by providing a legal framework that could accommodate things such as teenage dating or trial marriages (the contract could include clauses restricting conjugal rights or the like) and freer socialization (by establishing a token marriage between families so the females would not have to be veiled or secluded during visits with each other). Charitable organizations in the Islamic Republic have established agencies for promoting this type of marriage and have even developed Web sites to encourage and facilitate them.[6]

Law and ritual, however important they may be to the clerics and their supporters, constitute only one small facet of Shi'ism's contribution to Iranian religious and cultural life. One could argue that the whole Iranian worldview is inextricably linked to its Shi'ite religious orientation. At the same time, it is important to remember that the understanding of the religion varies greatly from one individual to another, that religious practices are often affected by factors such as class and social status, and that there is no really homogeneous or entirely consistent religious attitude. Peasants and herdsmen, for example, are much less likely to be concerned about the ritualistic aspects of the religion than merchants in the bazaar. Ordinary people often accept folk beliefs (such as the existence of malevolent spirits, jinn, or the efficacy of religious amulets) that would be frowned on as mere superstition by clerics.[7] The characteristically Shi'ite belief in free will and the sufferings of the Imams co-exist, in both the popular religion and to an extent the formal religion, with the notion that events are predestined and that somehow God rewards the good and punishes the evil in this world as well as the next. In just one small village, the anthropologist Reinhold Loeffler found an "amazing variety" of religious views: "Islam can take the form of a bland legalism or a consuming devotion to the good of others; an ideology legitimizing established status and power or a critical theology challenging this very status and power; a devotive quietism or fervent zealotism; a dynamic political activism or self-absorbed mysticism; a virtuoso religiosity or humble trust in God's compassion; a rigid fundamentalism or reformist modernism; a ritualism steeped in folklore and magic or a scriptural purism."[8] It is not possible in the space available here to discuss in any exhaustive or systematic way the many aspects of this religious culture, nor to try to separate those which are particularly Iranian from those which are commonly found throughout the Middle East or Islamic world.

There are, however, a number of important cultural practices, sometimes combined with ideas from popular or folk religion, that do set Shi'ism as practiced in Iran apart from the usual forms of Sunnite Islam. At the top of the list would be the dramatic and impressive ceremonies of mourning during the first 10 days of the month of Moharram that commemorate the death of Imam Hosayn at Karbalâ. These will be discussed in detail in the chapter on festivals and holidays. Closely related to this aspect of what has often been called a cult of martyrdom and lamentation in Iranian Shi'ism, however, is the phenomenon known as *rowzeh-kh'âni*. This refers to the recitation of stories about the sufferings of the Imams and other Shi'ite personalities. Originally, most of these stories were taken from a book by a popular preacher, Hosayn Vâ'ez Kâshefi, entitled "Garden of the Martyrs" (*Rowzat-osh-shohadâ*); hence the term "garden-reading" (*rowzeh kh'âni*). The recitations are typically performed by members of the clergy who have a particular skill at the highly emotional oratory and prodigious display of weeping that should accompany the stories. The popularity of this practice has increased over the years, and it has developed to go beyond just readings from Kâshefi's book to a larger repertoire of topics. The recitations can also be given throughout the year, rather than just during Moharram, and in private gatherings as well as public venues. Many well-to-do traditional families have a monthly *rowzeh* in their homes during which women gather and several clerics come and recite the stories of Karbalâ and Hosayn's suffering for a fee. At the end of each speech given in public prayers, whether in a mosque or a special place for that purpose (the *takiyeh*), clerics devote some time to recitation of *rowzeh*. In recent years, it has not been uncommon for political and ethical themes to be worked into the recitations, and the performances of famous reciters may be recorded and distributed. In the past twenty years, by utilizing modern audio technology and musical instruments, reciters have been able to produce highly effective *rowzeh* cassette tapes for the mass market.

The concept of "pilgrimage" in Iranian Shi'ism also has some unique aspects. This is not just confined to the ritual pilgrimage to Mecca (*hajj* as it is for Sunnites); it also includes visits to the tombs of Imams and other shrines (*ziârat*). Throughout the Islamic world, folk religion often attributes a holy charisma or blessing (*barakat*) to the burial sites of important religious personalities. It is believed that pious visits to such sacred places in effect transfer some of the blessing to the visitor and may lead to prayers and requests (sometimes left behind in the form of notes or ribbons tied to the shrine) being granted. Formal Sunni Islam tends to be suspicious of such practices—which in fact often do seem to represent survivals of pre-Islamic customs[9]—and conservative schools such as the Wahhabis of Saudi Arabia absolutely reject them. Iranian Shi'ism, however, embraces the visitation of various shrines (generally known as *emâmzâdehs*) and has even held that visiting some of them is superior to pilgrimage to Mecca in winning the favor of the Imams and their intercession for the believer. The Safavids enthusiastically promoted pilgrimages to places such as the tomb of their eponym Safi-od-Din in Ardabil (as it was claimed he was the descendant of an Imam) and the shrine of Imam Rezâ. Shah 'Abbâs the Great himself set such an example of piety by traveling on foot to Mashhad and humbly cleaning and sweeping the area around the Imam's tomb. The motivation of the Safavids may have been largely political (to enhance the aura of legitimacy around the dynasty and to deal with the obstacles the hostility of the Ottomans had created for Shi'ites wanting to go on *hajj* to Mecca), but the concept of *ziârat* clearly had much deeper foundations in the religion of the people. As a recent religious authority put it, the shrines are places "where divine favor and blessing occur, where mercy and grace descend; they are a refuge for the distressed, a shelter for the despondent, a haven for the oppressed, and a place of consolation for weary hearts, and will ever remain so until resurrection."[10] In earlier historical periods, this was almost literally true, since such shrines were recognized as a place of refuge (*bast*), where members of the political opposition wanted by the authorities, or even criminals at times, could take sanctuary and be immune to arrest for a while.

Some important centers of Shi'ite pilgrimage are found outside the borders of contemporary Iran. Foremost among these places are the 'Atabât or "sacred thresholds" in Iraq: the tomb of Imam 'Ali at Najaf, the tombs of Imam Hosayn and other martyrs at Karbalâ, the tombs of Musâ Kâzem and Mohammad Taqi at Kâzemayn near Baghdad, and the tombs of

'Ali Naqi and Hasan 'Askari (as well as a spot where the Twelfth Imam is supposed to have disappeared) at Samarra. The tombs of other Imams and Fâtemeh are in the Baqi' cemetery in Medina, but their funerary monuments were destroyed by the Saudis. In Syria, Iranians regularly visit the tomb of Zaynab in the suburbs of Damascus and the Maqâm-e Hosayn in Aleppo (one of the places where Hosayn's head was supposedly kept for a while after he was killed at Karbalâ). In Iran itself, there are well over a thousand *emâmzâdeh*s, of varying degrees of importance and ranging from very simple monuments to very grand sanctuary complexes. The most eminent of them is the Âstân-e Qods, the great sanctuary surrounding the tomb of Imam Rezâ in Mashhad (visiting it entitles one to be known by the honorific *mashhadi*/colloquial *mashdi,* just as pilgrims to Mecca are called *hâji*). Other very popular pilgrimage sites include the shrines of Shâh 'Abd-ol-'Azim near Tehran, Emâmzâdeh Dâud in northwest Tehran, and Shâh Cherâgh in Shiraz. The colossal tomb of Âyatollâh Khomeini recently constructed in the Behesht-e Zahrâ cemetery has also become something of a pilgrimage center for religious people.

The ritual aspect of *ziârat* typically involves circumambulating the tomb (*zarih,* which is often covered by beautiful grillwork, sometimes gold plated), and reciting special prayers for its occupant. The pilgrim may also touch or rub the *zarih,* in hope of receiving a vision, and they leave money, gifts, and written pleas near it. The funds donated at the *zarih*s constitute an important revenue source for the religious endowment in charge of each *emâmzâdeh.* Some people, especially those with a terminal illness, may sleep by the tomb for a short period in hope of a cure.

In addition to giving the visitors the prospect of pleasing the Imams and perhaps solving their personal problems, visits to the *emâmzâdeh*s can also serve as the occasion for a festive excursion and relaxation, almost like a form of recreation. That is especially true for women, whose opportunities for such activities have traditionally been so constricted. A delightful, if fictional, depiction of such a family visit to a simple country *emâmzâdeh* can be found in the recent film *Rang-e khodâ* "Color of Paradise" by Majid Majidi. Many travelers to pre-modern Iran have left descriptions of such practices, including this one of the visit to the shrine of Bibi Shahrbânu:

With the exception of *sayyids* (descendants of the prophet) and of boys who have not reached the age of puberty, men must never enter the sacred enclosure (*haram*) under any pretext, but must be content merely to chant the special litany (*ziaret-name*) in the courtyard and then go away after they have made an invocation (*do'a*) or a vow (*nadzr*). Women may enter the *haram,* read the *ziaret-name,* kiss the grille of the tomb, make a vow or invocation and then light candles, sacrifice a sheep or give money to the administrator (*motavalli*). They may sit in the courtyard and drink tea.[11]

It may be noted that the Bibi Shahrbânu shrine, although famous, is located on the top of a rough hill and thus not visited as often as other *emâmzâdeh*s. There is a folk belief that men who enter the Bibi Shahrbânu shrine will be turned into a stone. One of the authors of this book, however, used to play as a young boy near this shrine and entered it on a dare from his playmates, and he can testify there was no such effect.

Finally, mention should be made of the Shi'ite practice of *taqiyeh* or "prudent dissimulation" (also known as *ketmân,* "keeping secret"). This is the idea that one can, indeed must, conceal one's true religious knowledge or sentiments from one's enemies, especially if expressing those beliefs is likely to result in physical harm or death. Although this might seem curiously at odds with the glorification of martyrdom that runs throughout Shi'ism, it has long been a fundamental doctrine of the religion. The Koran enjoined Mohammad himself to use such caution in dealing with unbelievers; some of his early followers are said to have employed caution and deception to avoid being killed; and it is believed that the Imams and their followers regularly resorted to *taqiyeh* to escape persecution. In Safavid times, Mohammad-Baqer Majlesi exhorted Shi'ites to use *taqiyeh* by appearing to conform to Sunnism when they went on pilgrimage to Mecca or visited shrines or mosques outside Iran where Sunnites were likely to be around and might object to their presence—a challenge often confronting Shi'ite pilgrims to holy sites in Arabia during Hajj ceremonies each year. In those days, the danger of assault or death for Shi'ites was quite real; *taqiyeh* was literally necessary for the survival of the faith, and no one should thus be blamed for appearing to have compromised his convictions. There has been much debate about the continued use of *taqiyeh* in modern times, as physical threats to the Shi'ite minority have largely evaporated and Muslims find an increasing need for solidarity against external threats. At least in its religious dimension, there is now the widespread belief that *taqiyeh* is unneeded and should be discouraged except in the rare instances where there is a direct, immediate, and extremely serious danger to be eluded. Far from being unwilling to discuss their beliefs, Shi'ites have become eager to share and propagate them to any receptive audience. However, it can be argued that the practice of *taqiyeh* has become such an ingrained aspect of Iranian culture that is no longer related exclusively to religion and is not in abatement. Iranians are often wary of the intentions of foreigners or people outside their own trusted circle of family and acquaintances and consequently reticent to reveal their true feelings to them. Sometimes, that tends to result in the use of a certain amount of deception or prevarication in personal interactions. This is quite understandable given the Iranian historical experience with hostile outside powers and the odd mix in Iranian culture of intense socio-economic competitiveness with a polite concern to avoid doing or saying anything that might give offense to someone (a custom known as *ta'arof*).

MINORITY RELIGIONS IN IRAN

Although the number of non-Muslims in contemporary Iran is quite small, well under one percent of the population, the religions they represent are of considerable interest for both historical and cultural reasons. Zoroastrianism, for example, preceded Islam as the national religion of Iran and has greatly influenced both Iranian culture and the development of other world religions. The economic, and at times political, importance of Christians and Jews in Iran has been much more than their numbers might suggest. Thus some attention should be given here to the place of these minority religions in Iranian life and culture.

The secular orientation of the Pahlavi regime afforded religious minorities in Iran unprecedented freedoms and opportunities, in many ways effectively removing religion as a component of Iranian nationality. With the advent of the Islamic Republic, the country returned to the traditional model of treating certain non-Muslims in an Islamic state as *zemmis*, "protected" or "tolerated" citizens. To be accorded this status, the non-Muslim must be a follower of one of the revealed religions (*ahl-ol-ketâb*, "people of the book"). These are recognized explicitly by Article 13 of the constitution of the Islamic Republic as the religions of Zoroastrianism, Christianity, and Judaism. Citizens of these faiths are guaranteed the freedom to practice their religious rites and ceremonies, to receive religious instruction, to follow certain aspects of their religious law in personal affairs, and to elect representatives of the minority communities to the Iranian parliament (Majles). The government is obliged to treat them justly and to respect their human rights so long as they "refrain from engaging in conspiracy or activity against Islam and the Islamic Republic of Iran" (Article 14). In practice, however, a number of subtle forms of discrimination make it difficult for non-Muslims to be fully integrated into Iranian society, and certain political offices are reserved for Muslims only.

The Case of Bahaism

Ironically, there is no place in the system just described for what is in fact the single largest non-Muslim religion in Iran, Bahaism. Before the revolution, as many as half a million Iranians were members of this faith; today, officially, the religion does not exist in Iran even though the actual membership totals around 300,000. The reasons for this anomaly are complex and need some historical background to understand. Contemporary Bahaism is a successful missionary religion that has founded Spiritual Assemblies in well over a hundred countries and has its headquarters at the Universal House of Justice in Haifa, Israel; its core message emphasizes pacifism and the brotherhood of mankind. The origins of the religion, however, go back to a very specifically Iranian and Shi'ite background in the movement known as Babism. In 1844, a certain Sayyid 'Ali-Mohammad Shirâzi announced that he was the "gate" (bâb) to the Twelfth Imam and gathered a group of eighteen disciples to spread his message throughout the Shi'ite world. Shirâzi and the Babi movement drew strength from the ideas of the Shaykhi school of Shi'ism and widespread expectations that the return of the Hidden Imam was imminent as well as from the growing social unease in the country as a whole. The radical nature of Babism was underscored by the fact that one of its most prominent missionaries was a remarkable woman, Qorrat-ol-'Ayn, who considered herself an incarnation of Fâtemeh and preached unveiled before male audiences. Moreover, Shirâzi claimed in 1848 that he himself was the Imam and the existing laws of Islam were abolished. The Shi'ite clergy was alarmed at the spread of what it saw as a dangerous and seditious heresy, and the Qâjâr government felt obliged to suppress the movement. Consequently, Shirâzi was arrested, brought before an inquisition, and executed in 1850. After some of his followers attempted to assassinate the shah in 1852, the movement was ruthlessly suppressed. One branch, the Azalis (named for its leader Sobh-e Azal), continued to operate more or less covertly in an essentially Iranian and Shi'ite milieu. The Azalis were quite active during the period of the Constitutional Revolution, but their numbers eventually dwindled. The other branch of the movement, the Bahais (named for its leader Bahâollâh), moved outside Iran, transformed the teachings of the movement dramatically, and proselytized internationally as well as in Iran.

Babis and Azalis might be regarded as marginally acceptable heretics on the fringes of Shi'ism. Bahaism, however, presents itself as a new world religion which will replace Islam. From the point of view of the Shi'ite clergy, this is intolerable; Bahaism is a "misguided sect" that has no legitimate claim to be one of the acceptable revealed religions. Non-Muslims who convert to it are not entitled to zemmi status, and Muslim converts are guilty of apostasy—a capital offense in traditional Islamic law. This hostility towards Bahaism on religious grounds has been compounded by the suspicion that its members might be disloyal to Iran and potential spies (since the Bahai headquarters are in Israel) and by the perception that they received privileged treatment during the Pahlavi period. Although Iranian Bahais have often been subjected to harassment and persecution, they could generally practice their religion openly prior to the Islamic Revolution and, when politically feasible, Mohammad-Rezâ Pahlavi did his best to shield their community from harm.

The teaching and practice of the faith, however, is forbidden in the Islamic Republic: Bahai buildings have been destroyed or confiscated; individuals cannot declare a Bahai identity on government documents; Bahai marriages are not recognized officially; and known Bahais are barred from government employment, admission to universities, etc. Presumably to intimidate the community, a number of Bahais (perhaps several hundred) have been imprisoned or executed.

Christians and Jews

Judaism and Christianity in Iran are represented by small but significant religious communities that can also be regarded, to some extent, as distinct ethnic groups. Jews have lived in Iran since ancient times, and Iran has a special place in Jewish history and the development of Judaism: Cyrus the Great, who liberated the Jews from the Babylonian captivity and authorized the rebuilding of the Temple, was called by Isaiah the "anointed of the lord"; Queen Esther and Mordechai supposedly lived at the court of an Iranian king (their tombs are still believed to be in Hamadân, home to one of the country's largest Jewish communities). The Jews did not always enjoy the special favor given them in Achaemenid times, but the community flourished and become so thoroughly assimilated—speaking Persian and adopting Iranian customs—as to be recognizably different from other Iranians only in their religious identity. Unlike many other Jews in the Middle East, Iranian Jews had little interest in emigrating to Israel, which enjoyed friendly relations with Pahlavi Iran. Prior to the Revolution of 1979–80 there were about 80,000 Jews in Iran; the number has since dropped to less than 20,000. This exodus was not due to persecution so much as the fear of persecution: The rights of Jews, like those of other non-Muslims, were spelled out in the new constitution and have been generally respected (although they, like other non-Muslims, are subject to subtle forms of discrimination).

The militantly anti-Zionist policies of the Islamic Republic, however, created a very tense and uncomfortable situation for Jews, who were vulnerable to accusations of collaboration with an enemy state. This led in fact to something of a crisis for the Jewish community in 1999, when thirteen Jews from Isfahan and Shiraz were arrested, charged with spying for Israel, and, despite harsh international criticism of their trials, sentenced to prison or execution (the sentences were later commuted and all the prisoners eventually released).

Christianity also has a long, but rather complicated, history in Iran. According to Christian tradition, contacts with Iran began with the visit of the Three Wise Men (*Magi;* Iranian priests) to Bethlehem and continued through the first century with the visits of various apostles to spread Christianity in the east. By the third century, Christianity was flourishing throughout the Sasanid empire and organized into what could be called an officially recognized "Persian Church." Once Christianity became the official religion of the Late Roman/Byzantine empire, Sasanid Iran's main enemy, Christians were suspected of being a potentially subversive fifth column in the country and sometimes subjected to severe persecution. The doctrinal intolerance of the Western church, however, drove many Christian dissidents, especially Nestorians, to seek refuge in Iran, where they were welcomed and encouraged to propagate their faith. From the fifth century onwards, the "Persian Church" was essentially independent from the West in administration and Nestorian in doctrine. After the rise of Islam, the presence of Christianity in Iran gradually eroded. The main surviving remnant of this ancient Christian community in Iran is now found among the people generally known as "Assyrians." There are approximately 60,000 Assyrians in Iran, concentrated in the area around Lake Urmia. A little less than half of them still belong to the Ancient Church of the East, which rejects all of the Orthodox Church Councils except for the Council of Nicaea and follows the quasi-Nestorian theology of Theodore of Mopsuestia (d. 428). Half are Eastern Catholics ("Chaldeans"), who broke away from the Ancient Church of the East in the sixteenth century. They also have a liturgy in Syriac but are in communion with Rome and accept the theology of the Catholic Church. The remaining Assyrians, two or three thousand in number, are converts to Protestantism. Armenians make up the other, and by far the largest, group of Christians in contemporary Iran (numbering well over a quarter million). When Armenia was under Safavid rule, Shah 'Abbâs forced as many as 300,000 Armenians to relocate to New Julfa, a suburb of his capital at Isfahan; it remains the spiritual and cultural center of Armenian Christianity in Iran.

Zoroastrianism

Zoroastrians make up one of the smallest religious minorities in contemporary Iran, numbering only about 32,000 (as of 1986). That is, of course, rather ironic, since Zoroastrianism can claim to be the oldest and most authentically Iranian religion of all. It is also somewhat misleading, since the cultural influence of Zoroastrianism in Iran has been much stronger and persists in many ways despite the decline of the religion as such. This will be seen, for example, in the discussion of Iranian festivals and holidays in a subsequent chapter of this book.

The pagan Aryans, who later moved into Iran and India, apparently believed in a pantheon of anthropomorphized gods and goddesses who represented either human activities (such as warfare or herding cattle), natural phenomena (such as storms or fire), or celestial beings and the order of the universe (the moon, sun, bright stars, etc.). At some time, often said to have been in the seventh century B.C. although there are many reasons to suspect a much earlier date (ca. 1200 B.C.), this religion was dramatically reformed by the prophet Zoroaster. A priest of the ancient religion himself, Zoroaster was disturbed by both some of its practices, such as the ritual slaughter of cattle, and the unethical actions attributed to the deities in its mythology. Harassed and persecuted for ten years, he finally received a revelation which formed the basis for his new religion and subsequently succeeded in converting an Iranian king, Vishtaspa, to the faith. Put as simply as possible, Zoroaster taught through his hymns (the *Gathas*) a form of dualism: Ahura Mazda (later known as Ohrmazd), god of creation, seeks to promote the good; Angra Mainyu (later Ahriman), god of destruction, promotes evil. In the course of the struggle between these eternal, "twin," divinities, Ahura Mazda brought into being the seven Bounteous Immortals (Amesha Spenta), guardians of beneficial forces who create in turn other protective spirits or angels, as well as the material universe and all the good things that it provides. All the good or "praiseworthy" divinities and spirits assist Ahura Mazda in his struggle against the evil Angra Mainyu and his minions. Human beings play a key role in this cosmic drama, as they combine both spiritual and material qualities and are endowed with free will to choose between doing good or evil. Pious Zoroastrians of course choose to do good; they will be rewarded at the end of time, after the appearance of a savior (the Saoshyant) and the final defeat of Angra Mainyu, by admission to paradise, while all evil-doers will be destroyed.

The doctrines of Zoroastrianism are brilliantly original and provocative; there is not much doubt that they have exerted considerable influence on other religions, whether monotheistic, like Judaism and Christianity and Shi'ite Islam, or dualistic, like Manichaenism. Yet it has never been a missionary religion, even though some of Zoroaster's original teachings imply that it was meant to be a world faith. Instead, it became and has remained an Iranian national religion, to which conversion by non-Iranians is essentially impossible.

This nationalistic aspect of the religion has proved to be both a great strength and a fatal weakness. A form of the Zoroastrian religion was clearly being promoted as the official state religion of Iran during Achaemenid times, at least from the time of Darius onwards, and another, known as Zurvanism, was in effect the national church under the Sasanids. By late Sasanid times, however, the religion not only faced competition from other faiths such as Christianity and Manichaeism, it was also riven by internal doctrinal and especially social conflicts. The destruction of the Sasanid monarchy by the

Arab conquests removed its chief prop of support. Mass conversion to Islam followed fairly rapidly, although Zoroastrianism persisted in the countryside and certain areas for quite some time. In modern times, the cities of Yazd and Kermân have been the main bastions of the remaining Zoroastrian community. Outside Iran, although small pockets of Zoroastrians can be found in Europe and North America, the largest community is that of Iranian Zoroastrians who migrated to India.

The fundamental beliefs of the Zoroastrian or "Mazda worshipping" religion have also been accompanied by the development of a specific set of practices that have persisted throughout much of its history. Membership in the Zoroastrian community is signified by the wearing of a ritual girdle (*kusti*), a cord wrapped three times around the waist (symbolizing the commitment to good thoughts, words, and deeds) and knotted at the front and back over a white inner shirt. Young men and women first put this on as a kind of initiation rite when they are teenagers and then wear it for the rest of their lives. Celebration of seven ritual and communal feasts (*gahambars*) throughout the year serve both to commemorate the good things brought into existence by Ahura Mazda and the Bounteous Immortals and to promote the solidarity and social harmony of the Zoroastrian community. Strict rules for maintaining cleanliness and ritual purity are maintained, so as neither to pollute the good creations of Ahura Mazda such as water, earth, and fire nor to be polluted by the noxious creations of Angra Mainyu. Formal worship typically consists of reciting five daily prayers and, for the priesthood, the maintenance of sacred fires, symbol of light and Ahura Mazda, at special temples. Among the unusual aspects of the traditional religion were such practices as the encouragement of marriage between close relatives (*khvaetvadatha,* marriage with a child or sibling, such as brother-sister marriage, was regarded as highly desirable) and the exposure of the dead in open structures (known as *dakhmas*), where the flesh would be devoured by wild animals (a way to avoid polluting earth with the corpse). While these have largely gone out of fashion in modern times, many of the other practices of this ancient religion have been kept remarkably alive, despite considerable hardships, by the small and constantly dwindling community of Zoroastrians in Iran.

NOTES

1. Koran, 24:35.
2. Koran, 24:55.
3. Koran, 33:33.
4. Paraphrased from the translation of a Shi'ite prayer in Dwight M. Donaldson, *The Shi'ite Religion: A History of Islam in Persia and Irak* (London: Luzac & Co., 1933), 356.

5. Michael Fischer, *Iran: From Religious Dispute to Revolution* (Cambridge, MA, and London: Harvard University Press, 1980), 61–63.

6. One such site, operating as of 2006, is http://movaghat.blogsky.com/. For a detailed study of the institution of *mot'a* marriage, see Shahla Haeri, *Law of Desire: Temporary Marriage in Shi'i Islam* (Syracuse, NY: Syracuse University Press, 1989).

7. It is impossible in the space available here to do justice to this great array of religious notions; interested readers may make reference to the many examples of popular religious ideas and practices cataloged in Henri Massé, *Persian Beliefs and Customs* (New Haven, CT: Human Relations Area Files, 1954).

8. Reinhold Loeffler, *Islam in Practice: Religious Beliefs in a Persian Village* (Albany: State University of New York Press, 1988), 246.

9. It has been suggested, for example, that the shrine of Bibi Shahrbânu in Rayy, now a suburb of Tehran, took the place of what had been a site for the worship of Anahita, the Zoroastrian goddess of the waters; see Mary Boyce "Bibi Sahrbanu and the Lady of Pars," *Bulletin of the School of Oriental and African Studies* 30(1967):30–44.

10. Shaikh 'Abbas Qomi, quoted by Hamid Algar in "Emâmzâda," *Encyclopaedia Iranica* (London; Costa Mesa, CA; New York: Routledge, Mazda, Bibliotheca Persica, 1985–in progress), 8:395. This important article contains a detailed survey of sites and practices related to these institutions.

11. Quoted in Henri Massé, *Persian Beliefs and Customs* (New Haven, CT: Human Relations Area Files, 1954), 403.

3

Literature

A discussion of the role of literature in Iranian culture should begin with several caveats. First of all, the discussion in this chapter is limited to Persian literature. There are, of course, other languages in Iran that have a literary tradition, but it is not possible to try to deal with them here. This is not to demean or neglect their importance in any way, but it can perhaps be justified not only by necessity but on the grounds that Persian literature, unlike those other literatures, is the common heritage of all Iranians: Not many Persian speakers would be at all familiar with, say, Azeri Turkish literature, but it is a safe bet that an educated Azeri would be very knowledgeable about Persian literature and take as much pride in it as his Persian compatriot.

At the same time, it has to be remembered that Persian literature is international in character and not confined to the nation-state of Iran. Some of the great masters of Persian literature had no real connection with Iran at all, but rather lived in Anatolia, India, or central Asia. For example, the great mystic poet Jalâl-od-Din Rumi (1207–73) was born in Balkh (now part of Afghanistan) and spent most of his life in Konya (in modern Turkey and then ruled by Saljuq Turks). Historically speaking, Rumi is arguably of greater importance for Saljuq and Ottoman Turkish culture than for Iran. Most of his poetry, however, was written in Persian, and the greatest of his works, the long didactic poem known as the *Masnavi-e Ma'navi* ("Profound Couplets"), is often held to be the equivalent of "the Koran in Persian," were such a thing possible. Certainly, no comprehensive survey of Persian literature could ignore such an author, any more than one of English language literature could exclude Robert Burns or Ernest Hemingway. As a practical matter, however, such an approach would vastly expand the scope of this chapter, which will have to concentrate on authors with closer connections to Iran proper.

Finally, it should be kept in mind that mass literacy in Iran is a very recent phenomenon. For most of its history, literature was produced by and for a small elite, and this has affected its character in many ways. Yet some of this literature definitely had a mass impact, especially poetry, which was particularly susceptible to being memorized and recited at public and private gatherings. At the same time, the country has produced a vast amount of folk literature, perhaps the best guide to key features of authentic Iranian culture. In more recent years, increased literacy rates and contact with non-Iranian literatures have dramatically altered both the genres and the nature of Persian literature.

THE PERSIAN LANGUAGE

New (or Modern) Persian is one member of a great family of Iranian languages that have been spoken across Asia in both ancient and modern times. Its linguistic ancestry is as diverse and complex as that of English, and this has made it just as richly expressive as a means of communication. The core of the language has been inherited from the language of pre-Islamic Sasanid Iran, itself a descendant of the Old Persian of the Achaemenids. Over the centuries, it has been enriched by many borrowings from other languages it has encountered, notably Arabic and, to a lesser extent, Turkish and Mongolian (and more recently European languages).

In the period immediately before the Arab conquests, the most important languages in Iran were Middle Persian and Parthian (the latter used in the eastern parts of the Iranian world). Except among some diehard Zoroastrians, who compiled in the ninth century A.D. a number of sacred texts in what is called "Pahlavi" (a form of Middle Persian written in a script derived from Aramaic), little effort was made to keep these alive as written languages. For over two centuries, when people of Iranian origin produced literature they did so mostly in Arabic—in fact, Iranians played a prominent role in shaping both classical Arabic literature and the scholarly study of Arabic grammar and philology. For certain types of writing, such as works of science, philosophy, and especially religion, Arabic never really disappeared in Iran and was often the language of choice. As a spoken language among ordinary Iranians, however, Arabic did not take root as it did in other areas conquered by the Arabs; the Middle Persian/Parthian dialects survived in numerous forms and were in common use among the people. In fact, even many of the Arabs who settled in the conquered Iranian territories began to use the local vernacular language for ordinary discourse. By the ninth century A.D., poetry, probably just in oral form, was being composed in this language as well. As rulers of Iranian ethnic heritage began to appear, some encouraged this trend: Perhaps the best-known example is the Saffarid commander Ya'qub Lays (861–879), who supposedly rejected panegyrists who attempted to praise him in Arabic, a language he scornfully boasted he did not understand.

In ways and for reasons that are still imperfectly understood by historians, a method for writing the New Persian language in the Arabic script was perfected and efforts to promote it as a literary language began. As a literary language, New Persian developed over the course of the ninth and tenth centuries in the eastern Iranian lands ruled by the Samanid dynasty, where it was known as *dari* ("court" Persian, as the language is still called in Afghanistan) or *pârsi* (Fârsi, as the main dialect spoken in Iran today is called). This was apparently first encouraged by bureaucrats in the Samanid chancery who wanted to make it the official language for state documents and records. One Samanid ruler in particular, Mansur I (961–976), gave official sanction and impetus to this movement by ordering the translation from Arabic into Persian of two renowned works on history and exegesis. From that time onwards, Persian was established as a viable literary language.

The Persian language itself is deceptively simple yet capable of the most eloquent and subtle expression. It has no distinction of gender for verbs, nouns, or pronouns: the pronoun *u,* for example, can mean he, she, or it. There is also no definite article. (Not surprisingly, Persian-speakers trying to learn English thus typically have a great deal of trouble trying to master the use of gender and especially the use of the word *the.*) There are no complicated case endings, inflections, or declensions to worry about, apart from the use of the affix *râ* as a marker of a direct object. With a couple of exceptions, all verbs are regular and conjugate predictably from the infinitive to every tense and in every person. Syntax is flexible, but usually in the order subject-object-verb. If the language has a difficulty, at least for a non-native speaker trying to learn it, this probably lies in its tendency for words to have multiple meanings and its vast array of highly idiomatic expressions. Take, for example, the remarkably pliable word *dastgâh,* literally "hand-place": It can mean anything from factory to a modal scale in music; it is used to refer to the operating mechanism of numerous different devices from looms to telephone dials; and it has a number of figurative meanings such as wealth and wisdom too. Conversation in Persian is regularly peppered with a stock of colorful polite words and phrases— referring to oneself as *bandeh* ("slave"), or responding to a routine greeting with *qorbân-e shomâ* ("may I be your sacrifice," roughly meaning "you're welcome" or "sincerely yours"). Social status plays an important part in the choice of such phrases, and the context or a slight change in nuance could easily change what would normally be polite flattery into mockery. This linguistic combination of studied ambiguity and rhetorical extravagance can be seen as hallmarks not just of Persian language but of Persian culture itself, which tends to put a high value on wit, cleverness, ingenuity in concealing motives and objectives, projection of social status, and cultivation of social ties. These qualities come fully into play in Persian literature as well.

One other aspect of the language that should perhaps be discussed here pertains to the script. The writers who developed New Persian as a literary language did not attempt to use an older script for that purpose, nor to devise a new one. Instead, they adapted Arabic script for that purpose. The shortcomings of using Arabic script for Persian have been discussed earlier and need not be repeated here. It is worth noting, however, that Persian shares with Arabic a great fondness for the art of calligraphy, and certain styles of writing the Arabic script have become closely associated with this art in Iran. The most elegant and popular is undoubtedly the style known as *nasta'liq* (derived from *naskh*) a particularly clear and legible style, and *ta'liq,* a florid decorative style often used in formal chancery documents. Literary manuscripts, personal correspondence, and calligraphies used for decoration are often done in this style. Calligraphic designs, with both religious and nonreligious motifs, are found not only on papers but also on ceramics, pottery, floral drawings, decorative scrolls, and ceilings and walls of mosques, palaces, and even luxury houses. Iranian Muslims have always been fond of inscribing the precious words of their holy book, the Koran, in intricate calligraphic designs.

Recently, after the Islamic Revolution, the use of calligraphic writings, as a form of native art work versus Western or modern art, has again become very popular and many artists, of all kinds, utilize it as an enhancing element in their work. Traditional calligraphy used images to transform poetry into visual art, words into design, and writing into mystery. Modern calligraphy has developed new forms, even incorporating calligraphy elements into three-dimension art as in sculptures by the contemporary artist Parviz Tanâvoli. Such calligraphic forms metamorphose words into new meanings and meanings into new experiences. The meanings are no longer embedded in fixed words but in they way they look and feel as the viewer experiences a calligraphic piece. Words lose their fixed meanings and enter a fluid world of senses and intellect beyond the reach of language and dictionary. The art is no longer a fixed reality but a medium of dialogue between senses and intellect, producer and viewer, seller and buyer, and the work and objects surrounding it.

CLASSICAL PERSIAN LITERATURE

A vast amount of Persian prose literature, in fields ranging from history to philosophy, was produced during the pre-modern period. This prose literature certainly has its value, and much of it is in print and read by Iranians today. However, it is fair to say that it is mostly of interest to specialists and academics of one sort or another rather than to any general audience, and there is no particular need to discuss it here. The greatest achievement by far of classical Persian literature was rather in the field of poetry, and it is this poetry which still resonates most vibrantly and extensively with contemporary Iranian audiences. No survey of Persian culture and customs which ignored the role of poetry would be adequate.

An appreciation of classical Persian poetry requires taking into account three major factors that have influenced it. First, this poetry developed against the background of the Arabic poetic tradition, which was based on a very complex and rather rigid theory of prosody and on very specific genres, the *qasideh* or panegyric ode being the most important. So far as can be determined, pre-Islamic Persian poetry was a popular, oral art which had neither a formal system of prosody nor sharply defined genres. The Persian poetry of the Islamic period, however, tried as far as possible to adapt the theory, technical vocabulary, and practice of the Arabic model to its own needs. This applied in the first instance to the rhythm of the poem: The metrical units were not based on stress, as in English poetry, but on the alternation of long and short vowels (or their metrical equivalents as determined by a rather complicated system of prosody), as in Arabic. Specific patterns of vowels, for example short-long-short-long-long, constituted the foot and meter of the poem. These were assembled into the key building block of the poem, the *bayt* or verse, itself composed of two units of equal length (the *mesra'* or hemistich). Each *bayt* needed to express a complete thought and could stand independent of the *bayt*s which preceded and followed it. The convention in Arabic was for the final words of each hemistich of the first verse to rhyme with each other, and the last word of each subsequent verse to match that rhyme throughout the entire poem, which could be quite long. Monorhyme was also the case for certain genres in Persian, especially the *qasideh* and the shorter *ghazal,* or lyrical ode. However, Persian poetry also readily accepted poems with multiple rhyme schemes, most famously the *masnavi* or "couplet," where the rhyme only had to be kept between the hemistichs of each verse, as well as genres such as the *robâ'i* or "quatrain" (actually two verses where three or all four hemistichs rhyme). In any case, systematic meter and rhyme became essential qualities of Persian poetry.

A second factor of great importance was the role of court patronage in the production of Persian poetry, or rather one very specific type of Persian poetry. The symbiotic relationship between certain rulers and poets was very clear. A bevy of poets was a normal accoutrement of any court worth the name. The poet produced a poem of praise, the *qasideh,* which celebrated the noble qualities and great accomplishments of the ruler and served to spread his fame far and wide. The ruler reciprocated by lavishing gifts and coin on the poet. If he did not, he would likely find himself the object of scorn, not praise, in a satirical *qasideh* penned by the poet from the safety of a rival court. The panegyric had to conform to a strict format, both in terms of prosody as discussed above and in content: The poem was expected to begin with an appeal to emotion (the *nasib,* usually an amorous lyric, and *tashbib,* an effort to win the sympathy of the listener) and then proceed to a section of praise (*madh*) which would eulogize the patron and encourage him to be generous. Given these constraints, one *qasideh* tended to distinguish itself over another through the use of the most refined and extravagant rhetorical devices, obscure words and allusions, and so forth. As a result, the Persian *qasideh*s, like the Arabic ones, can be very tedious poems, although some did transcend the genre to make statements of great import and beauty. They are also often of considerable historical interest since they were composed to commemorate important events such as military campaigns or court ceremonies and festivals.

Finally, classical Persian poetry in its maturity became so deeply steeped in the tradition of mystical Islam, Sufism, that the two are almost inseparable. The origins of Sufism are obscure, its manifestations are variegated, and its doctrines are difficult to describe—which may well be why poetry is a prime vehicle for its expression. Essentially, Sufism, like all forms of mysticism, holds that God is the supreme truth or reality of the universe, and everything that is good and beautiful comes from Him. All extant beings are His creations and part of His reality; temporally separated from Him and trapped in physical form, they long to know Him, to escape the bonds of matter, and to be reunited with His Unity (*vahdat*), annihilating the self in His oneness. The Sufi was thus above all one who loved God and whom God loved. Through his efforts at devotion, which could take many forms or "paths" (*tariqât*), a Sufi might attain that desperately desired goal of an actual spiritual contact with God, a knowledge of Him directly without the intermediaries of prophet or scripture. For many Sufis, such a desperate seeker of God need not be bound by ordinary religious practices, and one who gained communion with God might be liberated entirely from their constraints. As a result, the behavior of many Sufis was, to say the least, nonconformist, which got some of them in serious trouble with the authorities. Their sentiments could, however, easily be expressed in veiled form through poetry, with its themes of the lover and the beloved, its celebration of beauty, its metaphors about wine and intoxication or music and dancing, and its mockery of staid religious conventions. By the twelfth century, this was established as a main current in Persian poetry, and its influence has extended far beyond Iran itself due to the popularity among non-Persian audiences of poets like 'Omar Khayyâm and Rumi.

Virtually all the major poets of the early era, during the Samanid, Ghaznavid, and Saljuq periods, worked within the court tradition. They included such masters as Rudaki (d. 940?), Daqiqi (d. ca. 976); 'Onsori (d. 1050?); Farrokhi (d. 1038?), and Manuchehri (d. 1041?). In their hands, the *qasideh* was not at all the tiresome and overly refined vehicle of flattery it later became. Their language was fresh, clear, and direct, and their mastery of the techniques of metaphor and simile superb. Although they maintained the traditional elements and framework of the Arabic *qasideh,* they made it Persian in spirit as well as language. This is perhaps most obvious in the opening part of the poem, where they typically celebrated the beauty of nature as found in Iran rather than the conventional descriptions of deserts and caravans typical of the Arabic equivalents. These lyrical sections or fragments of the *qasideh* could often stand on their own as independent poems, much like a *ghazal.* As an example, one might cite a few lines from a famous *qasideh* by Farrokhi on an occasion in the spring when the ruler's horses were being rounded up and branded:

> Gardens all chameleon-coated, branches with chameleon whorls,
> Pearly-lustrous pools around us, clouds above us raining pearls!
> On the gleaming plain this coat of many colours doth appear
> Like a robe of honour granted in the Court of our Amir.
> For our Prince's Camp of Branding stirreth in these joyful days,
> So that all this age of ours in joyful wonder stands a-gaze.
> Green within the green you see, like stars within the firmament;
> Like a fort within a fortress spreads the army, tent on tent.
> Every tent contains a lover resting in his sweetheart's arms,
> Every patch of grass revealeth to a friend a favourite's charms.
> Harps are sounding midst the verdure, minstrels sing their lays divine,
> Tents resound with clink of glasses as the pages pour the wine.[1]

The greatest poem of this era, however, was written by a poet who broke almost all the norms of Persian poetry as we have just described them. Abo'l-Qâsem Ferdowsi (d. 1019 or 1025) did write some *qasideh*s and short poems, and he did try to seek out the patronage of the famous ruler Mahmud of Ghazna, but he devoted his life and work above all to writing a great epic poem which would preserve the stirring legends of pre-Islamic Iran (completing a task which had been begun by Daqiqi). This masterpiece, the *Shâh-nâmeh* or "Book of Kings," took over 30 years to finish and ran to some sixty thousand verses, written in *masnavi* form (rhymes between the hemistichs of each verse) and the popular *motaqâreb* meter (scanned in each hemistich as short-long-long/short-long-long/short-long-long/short-long). The basic outline of the "Iranian national history" on which the *Shâh-nâmeh* is based has been described earlier and need not be repeated here. The diversity of the stories which make it up prevent the *Shâh-nâmeh* from being the kind of intense, concentrated epic one finds in the *Iliad* or even a sprawling epic story of a single hero like the *Odyssey* (although the cycle of stories about the great Iranian champion Rostam resembles that genre in some ways). The unity of the *Shâh-nâmeh* rather derives from its sweeping moral vision of a continuing struggle of good against evil and order against chaos, coupled with its fervent devotion to the land of Iran.

Ferdowsi came from the social class of the *dehqân*s, the proprietors of small landed estates who had traditionally been responsible for the defense and fiscal administration of Iran at the village level. They had played a role of inestimable importance in keeping alive the culture and customs of pre-Islamic Iran, and the *Shâh-nâmeh* clearly represents their outlook on the world. The tales of the *Shâh-nâmeh* are the stories of their heroes, who face their dilemmas and challenges. The social mores reflected in the poem, especially those pertaining to the business of "fighting and feasting," are theirs. The fundamental sadness of the poem, shown in its frequent allusions to an Iran that has finally been beaten down by its enemies and that has lost its past grandeur, no doubt is rooted in the despondency of this warrior class as it realized it was gradually fading away. The art of the poem, however, transcends these social norms; few poets have ever excelled to such a degree as Ferdowsi in the ability to describe the clamor of battle and the tragic turmoil of human existence.

Unlike other types of poetry, there was no Arabic prototype for a work such as the *Shâh-nâmeh;* the many stories it contained were Iranian in origin, and Ferdowsi wanted it to be pure Persian even in language, using as few words of Arabic origin as possible (some say none at all). This patriotic aspect of the poem is perhaps its most enduring and endearing feature, and Iranians often quote from it to express their love of country: One of its most popular lines is the declaration *na-bâshad be-Irân tan-e man ma-bâd,* "were it not for Iran, I myself could not exist." During the intensely nationalistic period of Pahlavi rule in twentieth-century Iran, not surprisingly, this aspect of the poem and its place in Persian literature was both exalted and exploited, not least in how it was misrepresented as an apology for monarchy and blind obedience to foolish kings. This produced something of a reaction against the poem following the Islamic revolution, but that has largely passed. Indeed, such a line may resonate even more for many secularized Iranians, both inside and outside of the country, who have become frustrated with the theocratic government in Iran. To combat the Islamic rule, which ultra-nationalists view it as an extension of Arab rule and culture, such Iranians still tend to exalt the *Shâh-nâmeh* as a book representing their national identity. As a grand epic, though, the *Shâh-nâmeh* ultimately transcends politics and validates the author's own assessment of his legacy. Those final lines of the poem may be cited here as a sample of the poet's craft:

az ân pas namiram keh man zendeh-am
keh tokhm-e sokhan man paragandeh-am
har ân kas keh dârad hosh o ray o din
pas az marg bar man konad âfarin

Henceforth, I shall not pass away, I will live on;
For I have sown the seeds of my speech.
Anyone who has intellect, insight, and faith,
Will, after I die, say blessings for me.

The recitation in collective settings of verses from the *Shâh-nâmeh* or stories based on it (*Shâh-nâmeh-kh*ʾâni* or *naqqâlî*) became an important part of entertainment in traditional Iranian society. Such recitations might take place either in private homes or in public settings. For example, parts of the *Shâh-nâmeh* would be read out in the traditional sports facilities known as the *zur-khâneh* ("house of strength"). In teahouses, the recitation was often done dramatically by an individual (known as a *naqqâl*) who might utilize a drum, hand clapping, singing, and pictures on curtains hung on the wall to enhance the story. It was not unusual for these *naqqâls* to embellish the original stories for dramatic effect. They were narrator, actor, and director at the same time, recreating and animating scenes while engaging the spectators. Although the art of *naqqâli* has been declining in Iran, its elements have been revived in modern theatrical performances and still can be seen in some traditional settings. Recently, a type of restaurant based on traditional forms of dining has emerged in Iran, known as a *sofreh-khâneh*, in some of which *naqqâli* is offered as a form of entertainment to the customers.

Two other masters of classical Persian poetry, beloved in Iran and famous around the world, are Mosharref-od-Din Saʿdi and Shams-od-Din Hâfez. Both lived in the fabled city of Shiraz, the heartland of Persian culture; Saʿdi (ca. 1213–92) at the beginning of the Mongol period, and Hâfez (ca. 1325–1389) toward the end of that era.

Shaykh Saʿdi, as he is known, wrote many fine poems, including a highly-regarded collection of lyrical odes (*ghazals*). His greatest accomplishment, however, lay in two rather unusual long poems, the *Bustân* ("Herb-Garden") and the *Golestân* ("Flower-Garden," which mixes prose and poetry). The titles of these works are most appropriate as indicators of their organization and content. Like a bouquet of useful herbs or beautiful flowers from a garden, the poems are anthologies of what is often referred to by the cliché of "wisdom of the East." Moreover, Sa'di lived in a very troubled time, when the Muslim lands were being ravaged by the Mongols, but he was fortunate enough to find safe haven in Shiraz—much the way a garden is for Iranians a tranquil refuge from the anxieties encountered beyond its walls. His poems are collections of ethical advice on how, figuratively speaking, to make that spiritual garden one needs in order to cope with living in such a turbulent world; they are often drawn, or so he claims, from the experiences of his own life and travels. They are thus best described as didactic or moralizing poetry, using short ver-sified anecdotes and stories to make a philosophical point, yet thanks to Sa'di's poetic touch they are largely free of the tiresome tone such a rubric implies.

The poems are definitely Sufi in spirit, especially the *Bustân*. In its opening lines, it emphasizes both the majesty and the compassion of God:

The heads of kings, neckexalting,
Are at His court, on the ground of supplication.
He does not instantly seize the froward;
He does not drive away with violence those excuse bringing.
And though He becomes angry at bad conduct,
When thou didst return He canceled the past circumstance in the book of sins.
The two worlds (this and the next) are like a drop in the sea of His knowledge;
He sees a crime, but in mercy covers it with a screen…
He places the ruby and the turquoise in the backbone of the rock;
The red rose, on the branch of green color.
From the cloud He casts a drop toward the ocean;
From the backbone of the father He brings the seed into the womb.
From that drop He makes an incomparable pearl;
And from this He makes a form of man like the lofty cypress.
The knowledge of a single atom is not hidden from Him,
To whom the evident and the hidden are one.
He prepares the daily food of the snake and the ant;
Although they are without hands and feet, and strength.
By His order He portrayed existence from nonexistence;
Who, except He, knows how to make the existing from the nonexisting?[2]

Sa'di's Sufism, however, has a light and decidedly pragmatic touch, teach-ing, for example, that telling a lie that does good is better than telling a truth that does harm. Indeed, the stories often skewer the false piety of the hypocritical or misguided 'âbeds (ostentatious worshippers) and *darvish*es (mendicant Sufis). Sa'di's view of the proper Sufi attitude is suggested in this anecdote from the *Golestân*:

A gang of dissolute vagabonds broke in upon a darwesh, used opprobrious lan-guage, and beat and ill-used him. In his helplessness he carried his complaint before his ghostly father, and said, Thus it has befallen me. He replied: O my son! the patched cloak of darweshes is the garment of resignation; whosoever wears this garb, and cannot bear with disappointment is a hypocrite, and to him our cloth is forbidden.

> A vast and deep river is not rendered turbid by throwing into it a stone.
> That religious man who can be vexed at an injury is as yet a shallow brook.
> If thou art subjected to trouble, bear with it;
> For by forgiveness thou art purified from sin.
> Seeing, O brother! that we are ultimately to become dust,
> Be humble as the dust, before thou moulderest into dust.[3]

Significantly, both the *Bustân* and the *Golestân* open with chapters on kingship and good government. They were clearly intended as admonitions to rulers to act in a spirit of justice grounded in Sufi values. A good example comes from the *Golestân:*

A king ordered an innocent person to be put to death. The man said, Seek not your own hurt by venting any anger you may entertain against me. The king asked, How? He replied, The pain of this punishment will continue with me for a moment, but the sin of it will endure with you for ever.

> The period of this life passes by like the wind of the desert.
> Joy and sorrow, beauty and deformity, equally pass away.
> The tyrant vainly thought that he did me an injury,
> But round his neck it clung and passed over me.
> The king profited by this advice, spared his life, and asked his forgiveness.[4]

Finally, one of the delights of reading Sa'di's stories is finding that they can also be playful or humorous in nature, and the verses which adorn them like proverbs—even though some contemporary Iranians, using modern standards, view these as sexist and old-fashioned. For example, there is an anecdote in the *Golestân* of a man whose beloved wife died young but who was required by the terms of his marriage contract to continue to take care of the unpleasant mother-in-law. Thus he complained to his friends:

> They plucked the rose and left me the thorn;
> They plundered the treasure, and let the snake remain.
> To have our eye pierced with a spear were more tolerable than to see the face of
>   an enemy.
> It were better to break with a thousand friends than to put up with one rival.[5]

Hâfez, a pen name meaning "one who has memorized the Koran," is the supreme master of the *ghazal* genre of poetry. Virtually all literary critics, Iranian and non-Iranian, express their admiration of the exquisite, gemlike quality of his verses, and there is really no doubt that his lyrical odes are unsurpassed in both their technical perfection and the depth and subtlety of their expression. Even though Hâfez often uses some of the most hackneyed metaphors in Persian literature—the garden, the rose and the nightingale, the beauty of the city of Shiraz, the wine cup, the tresses of the beloved—they always seem fresh and appropriate in his poems. Hâfez's ability to employ color and striking images can make a poem seem like a miniature painting. An exquisite example is the *ghazal* beginning with the line *raftam be-bâgh sobhdam-i tâ chenam gol-i/âmad be-gush nâgahan âvâz-e bolbol-i,* ably translated into English by Arthur J. Arberry:

> I walked within a garden fair
> At dawn, to gather roses there;
> When suddenly sounded in the dale
> The singing of a nightingale.
> Alas, he loved a rose, like me,
> And he, too, loved in agony;
> Tumbling upon the mead he sent
> The cataract of his lament.
> With sad and meditative pace
> I wandered in that flowery place,
> And thought upon the tragic tale
> Of love, and rose, and nightingale.
> The rose was lovely, as I tell;
> The nightingale he loved her well;
> He with no other love could live,
> And she no kindly word would give.
> It moved me strangely, as I heard
> The singing of that passionate bird;
> So much it moved me, I could not
> Endure the burden of his throat.
> Full many a fair and fragrant rose
> Within the garden freshly blows,
> Yet not a bloom was ever torn
> Without the wounding of the thorn.
> Think not O Hafez, any cheer
> To gain of Fortune's wheeling sphere;
> Fate has a thousand turns of ill,
> And never a tremor of good will.[6]

Hâfez's themes are among the most profound in literature, complex and inexhaustible in the ways they can be interpreted: the anguish of unrequited love, the capriciousness of fate, the transience of life, disillusionment with the world, the mystery of existence. In such poetry, the inherent peculiarities and ambiguities of the Persian language become great assets. For an example, one need look no further than the opening lines of what is probably Hâfez's most famous and often discussed *ghazal: agar ân tork-e shirâzi be-dast ârad del-e mârâ/be-khâl-e henduyesh bakhsham samarqand o bokhârârâ.* This was first translated into English by Sir William Jones as a conventional love poem:

> Sweet maid, if thou would'st charm my sight
> And bid these arms thy neck infold;
> That rosy cheek, that lily hand,
> Would give thy poem more delight
> Than all Bocara's vaunted gold,
> Than all the gems of Samarcand.

But of course Persian has no gender, and it is not all that clear who is being addressed or why. Literally, the verse says "If that Shirazi Turk would take our heart in his/her hand, for the mole on his/her face I would give Bokhara and Samarqand." Thus some critics might read this as an actual love poem addressed to a young lass (or lad), while others would take it as a Sufi allegory or even a political appeal to the Turko-Mongol ruler of Shiraz. This kind of quandary runs throughout his poems: When Hâfez speaks of taverns and wine drinking, are these just Sufi metaphors for the world and the intoxication that comes from the love of God, or do they reflect a real celebration of libertinism? When he mocks pious zealotry, is he following the conventional Sufi disdain for formal religion or was he a genuine agnostic? Guessing at what lies so elusively behind Hâfez's incomparable artistry is a major component of his appeal. That is why Hâfez's poems can be used equally by religious leaders to support their religious views, by Sufis to support their love of God, by secularists to denounce clerical hypocrisy, by musicians as lyrics for both mystical and romantic music, and, recently, by Iranian homosexuals as historical evidence for the existence of homosexuality in Iranian culture.

Quite apart from the literary significance of his work, the importance of Hâfez in Iranian culture, even at the popular level, cannot be emphasized too much. For example, his *divân,* or collection of poems, is one of the books, along with the Koran, most often used for the purpose of taking an omen (*fâl*), letting it fall open and taking advice from a randomly selected verse. Many secular Iranians use a copy of the *Divân,* instead of the Koran, on the special table they prepare in celebration of the Iranian New Year (see the chapter on holidays and festivals). Beyond that, the affection and respect which Iranians have for Hâfez is shown quite well in a personal anecdote related by Manuchehr Farmanfarmaian, formerly an official with the National Iranian Oil Company and Iranian ambassador to Venezuela. On returning in 1954 via Pakistan from a trip to the United States, he found himself being harassed a bit by a border guard at Zâhedân, who started rummaging through his baggage:

Suddenly he gave a start as he saw a little volume of poetry by Hafez that I always traveled with. "You have a Hafez?" he asked. I nodded dumbly. I had become addicted to Hafez and could not sleep at night without reading a passage or two. I was not alone in this appreciation. The guard took the book reverently in his hands and, opening it, read a page silently to himself. His eyes shone as he looked back at me. "You may close your bags now, sir," he said with respect, handing the book to me on the flat of his rough, cracked palms. For a moment we stood looking at each other, such vastly different men who nonetheless were brothers through the love of poetry.[7]

Apart from these great masters, Iran produced a vast number of other poets in the classical period. The *tazkereh*s, or biographical dictionaries compiled by various literary authorities, record the names of literally thousands of these poets, but most are now largely forgotten or known for just a memorable line or two. Others are quite important, though not on a level with Hâfez or Sa'di. The most famous outside Iran is undoubtedly Omar Khayyâm, thanks to the superb adaptation of his poetry into English by Robert Fitzgerald. Prior to that, Khayyâm was more highly regarded by Iranians as a mathematician than as a poet. He was, of course, a competent poet, being quite skilled at the genre known as the *robâ'i* or *do bayti* (a kind of quatrain). Anvari (d. 1191?) and Khâqâni (d. 1199) excelled at the writing of *qasideh*s. Nezâmi (b. 1141?) wrote very fine long narrative poems that blended the epic tradition of Ferdowsi with the mystic outlook of a Sufi *masnavi;* five of these were combined in his work known as the *Khamseh:* a mystical and philosophical introductory poem (*Makhzan al-asrâr*); the story of the romance of Khosrow and Shirin; the love story of Majnun and Layli; the stories told to King Bahrâm Gur by seven princesses (*Haft paykar*); and an Alexander romance. Farid-od-Din 'Attâr (d. 1230?) was a mystic poet almost on a par with Rumi. These were all very serious poets, but it should not be overlooked that Persian poetry, like Persian culture, also had a comic side that reveled in the display of wit, humor, invective, and ribaldry. The undisputed master of this style of poetry was the inimitable 'Obayd-e Zâkâni (d. 1371). It is a delicious irony that he, probably Iran's most brilliant and impertinent humorist, lived in the era of one of its most dour and humorless rulers, the ruthless Timur (Tamerlane). The last truly great poem of the classical period was Nur-od-Din Jâmi (d. 1492), who wrote in many of the established genres but is best known for a collection of seven *masnavi* poems known as the *Haft awrang*.

Poetry continued to be produced in Iran after the Mongol period and right down to contemporary times but in generally diminishing quality if not quantity. There are many possible reasons for this decline. For example, in the Safavid period—otherwise such a brilliant chapter in Persian history and culture—it is fairly clear that patronage for poets had dried up in favor of the writing of religious literature, so that many of the best Persian poets decided to pursue their careers at the far more lucrative courts of the Moguls in India. Beyond that, it seems that the traditional genres and topics of Persian poetry had been pretty well exhausted by the previous masters, and it would be particularly difficult for anyone else to breathe something fresh and lively into them. In that sense, it was not until the concept of poetry itself began to change that prominent new poets could appear. That process began in the nineteenth century under the Qâjâr rulers. Some poets of that time looked back to the earliest generation of Persian poets as models of clear and simple language that should be emulated, as opposed to the ornate and highly polished language of the later classical period. Others, such as Qâ'âni (d. 1854), probably the greatest of the Qâjâr poets, began to bridge the gap that had developed between the literary language and the language of the people by writing in ways that used Persian as it was actually spoken. Still others began to be influenced by non-Persian, specifically European, poetry, which was reflected in the unconventional topics and expressions they used. Ultimately, this led in the twentieth century to the development of wholly new modes and genres of poetry in Persian.

Against the background of the Constitutional Revolution at the beginning of the twentieth century (1905–1911), Iranian poets also began experimenting with new ideas. Poets like Malek-osh-Sho'arâ Bahâr, Iraj Mirzâ, 'Âref, Mirzâdeh 'Eshqi, Abo'l-Qâsem Lâhuti, Taqi Raf'at, and 'Ali-Akbar Dehkhodâ all tried to advance the quality of the poetry by transposing rhymes, creating new expressions, and introducing new themes. The most dramatic changes in Persian poetry emerged along dramatic changes in the Iranian society after the World War II when poets unhappy with the rigid structure of traditional style dispensed with the rhyme and consistent meter and adopted a free verse language. Works of this group are known as *she'r-e now* ("new poetry"). The father of this new genre was 'Ali Esfandiâri (1895–1959), who used the pen-name Nimâ Yushij. Born in Yush, a village near the Caspian Sea, Nimâ first received traditional schooling and then went to a Roman Catholic school in Tehran where he received instruction from a lyric poet, Nezâm Vafâ (1883–1960). Nimâ's early attempts at imitating classical poets like Jâmi, Rumi, and Khayyâm were unsatisfactory. As time passed and he became more familiar with new poetic devices and the culture of urban life, he found old devices too self-limiting for the free flow of his ideas. While working with rhythm and rhyme, he soon stopped bothering with the conventional Arabic meters and the limitation they put on the length of his lines. He found it useless to break the continuity and integrity of a thought, or idea, by the fixed pattern of rhymes in a *bayt*. Thus, he wrote poems centered on an idea, rather than form, with lines of varied length. For him, the length of a line was to be determined by the depth of the expressed idea. In 1937, adapting the *vers libre* of French symbolists, he wrote his first free verse, *Qoqnus* ("The Phoenix"). These innovations did not go well with traditionalists and Nimâ found himself isolated, ridiculed, and unnoticed. But time was on his side. As the country was going through rapid modernization under the rule of Rezâ Shah, young poets were becoming tired and unhappy with classical devices. Nimâ's innovations in form and style, coming as they did at the same time as the innovations in prose by the master Iranian novelist at the time, Sâdeq Hedâyat, attracted young poets of his time and brought him respect and recognition. What became particularly attractive to these young poets was Nimâ's symbolism, allowing them to use ordinary words as symbols representing deeper and hidden meanings. Experiencing the oppressive policies of a young shah, words like "night" and "dawn" became respectively symbols of tyranny and enlightenment. Soon, young poets were experimenting with a form of poetry full of political symbolism—a tradition which has continued until today. Nimâ's most important works include *Afsâneh-ye Nimâ* ("Nima's Fable"), *Shahr-e shab, shar-e sobh* ("City of Night, City of Morning"), *Nâqus* ("Bell"), *Mâkh Ulâ*, and *Mâneli*.

An important poet who appeared in twentieth century Iran, one who was recently declared a "national poet" by the government, was Sayyid Mohammad-Hosayn Behjat-Tabrizi (1906–1988). He used two pen names, Haydar Bâbâ in Turkish (from the name of a hill near poet's native village, Khoshknâb, in Tabriz) and Shahriâr in Persian. An Azeri Turk, Shahriâr composed poems in both the Persian and Turkish languages and followed the traditional poetic forms. Having composed the first and most famous Turkish poetry collection ever written by an Iranian, Shahriâr is regarded by Azeris as one of the first contemporary poets exposing the potentialities of Azerbaijani poetry and its importance in shaping Azeri identity. The simplicity of his words and frequent use of slang and colloquial Persian make his poems both accessible and memorable among ordinary people. Though he mostly wrote lyrical poetry, he also composed quatrains, couplets, odes, and elegies in both Persian and Turkish.

A contemporary poet whose works resembled those of Shahriâr and received widespread attention among the public was Fereydun Moshiri (1927–2000). Moshiri composed poems in both classical and modern forms and bridged the gap between traditional *bayt*s, with equal strength and length, and the modern poetry's emphasis on thematic integrity. A humanist in perspective and modern in outlook, he avoided sensationalism, worked on difficult themes, and yet kept his poem accessible to broader audiences.

Several important poets followed Nimâ Yushij's thematic and expressive style and became influential and important in their own turn: Nâder Nâderpur, Fereydun Tavallali, Esmâ'il Khoi, Yâdollâh Royâ'i, Nosrat Rahmâni,

Ebrâhim Golestân, Ahmad-Rezâ Ahmadi, Mohammad-Rezâ Shafi'i Kadkani, Siâvash Kasrâi, Mas'ud Farzâd, Manuchehr Âtashi, Yâdollâh Maftun Amini, Hushang Ebtehâj, Manuchehr Nistâni, Mohammad-'Ali Sepanlu, Sa'id Soltânpur, M. F. Farzâneh, 'Ali Bâbâchâhi, and Mahmud Kiânush. Called "New Wave" poets, they wrote prose poems and experimented with Dadaism, automatism, formalism, futurism, surrealism and other trends. Mahdi Akhavân-Sâles (1928–1990) is one of those poets who started with classical poetry and became an important heir to Nimâ. Like Ferdowsi, Akhavân-Sâles' forte was epic and his poetry contained a complex set of metaphors, symbols, and far-fetched similes. He was one of the contemporaries whose poems are widely interpreted as political. A disciple of Akhavân-Sâles is Esmâ'il Khoi, who divides his verses into very long hemistiches. Khoi is one of the best-known political and philosophical Persian poets living in exile today. A poet of this same generation who has tried to create a synthesis of various styles in modern poetry is Mohammad-Rezâ Shafi'i Kadkani. Influenced by classical poets such as Hâfez and Rumi, and modernists such as Nimâ and Akhavân Sâles, Kadkani composes lyrical poems, but they also often reflect the social and political environment.

The most popular, and for that same reason controversial, contemporary Iranian modernist poets are Ahmad Shâmlu and Forugh Farrokhzâd. Shâmlu (1926–2000) started his career as a journalist and began writing sentimental, lyrical, and patriotic prose poems. Having experimented with a variety of styles, Shâmlu soon abandoned the traditional forms of rhythm and rhyme and wrote poems with the natural music of the Persian language. Deeply influenced by Paul Eluard, Garcia Lorca, Luis Aragon, and the great Turkish poet, Nazim Hekmat, he found his own style by using soft and harmonious words in manner different from ordinary prose. A playwright, translator, broadcaster, and literary historian, Shâmlu's career exposed him to much larger audiences than other contempory poets and made his views and poems, especially those with political overtones, very controversial. He was seen a threat by both the government and the traditionalist poets who resented his rise to fame among the educated youth.

Forugh Farrokhzâd (1935–67) is arguably one of the most original and influential of modern Persian poets. One of her earliest volumes of poetry, published in 1957, was entitled 'Esyân (Rebelliousness), a quality well represented in both the unconventionality of her life and the originality of her art. She quit school early, married at 16 against her parent's wishes, got divorced three years later, briefly entered a psychiatric hospital, once attempted suicide, and engaged in a series of what were by Iranian standards of the time scandalous romantic affairs. Not only was she equally unusual in being a woman who gained recognition in a field that had been so thoroughly dominated by men, everything about her poetry was iconoclastic. First of all, she followed Nimâ Yushij by breaking completely with the Persian classical tradition to write in a style comparable to that of free verse in modern Western poetry. Beyond that, she wrote about subjects and themes, often clearly drawn from her own personal life experience as a woman, that were virtually taboo in polite Persian discourse. The rebelliousness drew from her awareness of the pains of existence. Much of her poetry thus spoke of her frustration with the place assigned to women in Persian society, her own search for love, and her disappointment and bitterness at men who were incapable of moving beyond physical passion. Moreover, no amount of rebellion could dispel the feeling that she was, in fact, trapped, as suggested by the titles of her other early volumes of poetry, *Asir* (The Captive) and *Divâr* (The Wall). True liberation, the subject of one of her last collections of poetry (*Tavallod-e digar,* "Rebirth"), came only through realization of one's individuality and the solace of art. Yet even this was tempered by a sense of the fragility and brevity of life, expressed in her poetry by references to "the sucking mouth of the grave," a "cold season," a "young pair of hands buried beneath the falling snow." These now seem almost like premonitions of her own tragic and untimely death in an automobile accident in 1967. As a female rebel challenging conservative social norms, Farrokhzad's poetry was banned for more than a decade after the Islamic Revolution. Eventually, the government could not resist her popularity anymore and allowed her works to be openly circulated again, albeit only with modest pictures of her. Today, an industry has developed in Iran around collections of her poetry, books and movies about her life and art, recordings of her voice, and a short documentary film she made on leprosy called *Khâneh siyâh ast* ("The House Is Black").

After her death, Forough became an influential role model for a generation of young female poets: Shâdâb Vajdi, Maymanat Mir-Sâdeqi (Âzâdeh), Zhâleh Mosâ'ed, Minâ Asadi, and Simin Behbahâni. Behbahâni (b. 1928) has established herself as one of the most distinguished contemporary female poets. She has written poetry in both modern and traditional forms and has produced her own style of lyrical ode (*ghazal*). What distinguishes her poetry from those of past poets is her ability to incorporate theatrical subjects as well as contemporary issues into her poems. She is a political activist, was nominated for the Nobel Prize in Literature in 1997, and was awarded the Carl von Ossietzky Medal in 1999 for her struggle for freedom of expression in Iran.

Finally, mention should be made of Sohrâb Sepehri—an important contemporary modernist poet whose popularity inside Iran has increased after his death. Sepehri (1928–1980) had a very close relationship with nature and maintained a solitary life. He was painter as well and his poetry is often in dialogue with his painting. His verses are full of images, symbols, and the music of nature. They represent conversations with nature in a style blending Islamic mysticism, Zen-Buddhism, and even pre-Islamic Zoroastrianism. Some of his poems, along with those of Nimâ, Akhavân-Sâles, and Shâmlu have been used in musical productions and are listened to by many contemporary Iranians.

MODERN PERSIAN PROSE LITERATURE

Although poetry still holds an important place in the creative literature of contemporary Iran, it has in recent years come to be rivaled in popularity and importance by prose fiction—the novel, the novella, and especially the short story. The rise of these genres represents a considerable innovation in the nature of Persian literature; it reflects and is directly related to broader changes in Iranian society and culture. Story-telling was certainly important in earlier periods but typically only in the context of formal verse or in orally-transmitted folktales (a very important mirror of traditional culture). Prose literature was produced mostly by and for a small educated elite and tended to be almost exclusively in the form of nonfiction and scholarly writing such as history, prosopography, geography, or philosophy. This began to change towards the end of the Qâjâr period as writers began to experiment with new genres of prose literature and to try to address broader, popular audiences. In the vanguard of this effort were writers such as Mirzâ Malkom Khân, Zayn-ol-ʿÂbedin Marâghehi, and ʿAli-Akbar Dehkhodâ. These trends intensified during the Constitutional Era, as prose writing increasingly imitated Western genres, made use of a journalistic style, sought to write in a clear and accessible manner, avoided the use of words of Arabic origin but incorporated new Western words for which there were no equivalents readily available in Persian (e.g., polemic, class, parliament, cabinet, etc.). This touched off a lively debate between the modernists and the defenders of the traditional style of writing, especially during the period 1921–41. Taqi Rafʿat, Mohammad-Taqi Bahâr (1886–1951), Nimâ Yushij, Mohammad-Ali Jamâlzâdeh (b. ca. 1895; d. 1997) Sâdeq Hedâyat (1903–51), Saʿid Nafisi (1895–1976), Mohammad Hejâzi (1900–1973), Rashid Yâsami, and Yahyâ Reyhân were some of the authors involved in this debate. Two other developments during that period are noteworthy: the emergence of modern romantic writings and satire. The most noted author of the first genre was H. M. Hamidi, pen-named Hosaynqoli Mostʿân. The second genre is credited to two works, *Charand Parand* ("Nonsense") by Dehkhodâ and *Yaki bud yaki na-bud* ("Once Upon a Time") by Jamâlzâdeh.

One of the most important consequences of these trends was the emergence of prose fiction as a major form of Persian literature. This was partly the result of Iranian writers becoming familiar with and influenced by the types of literature popular in Europe—initially spurred, appropriately enough, by a Persian translation of the famous picaresque novel by James Morier entitled *The Adventures of Hajji Baba of Isfahan* (first published in 1824). At the same time, some Iranian intellectuals were attracted to fiction as they realized it could be a relatively safe outlet for veiled or not-so-veiled sociopolitical commentary that might lead to censorship or repression if expressed in other forms of writing. The two writers who were the most influential in establishing prose fiction as a legitimate literary genre and shaping the course of its development were Jamâlzâdeh and Hedâyat.

Jamâlzâdeh's father was one of the most popular preachers and orators in Iran during the Constitutional Era and was eventually imprisoned and murdered for his outspoken pro-Constitutionalist views. Jamâlzâdeh himself had been sent to study at a Catholic school in Beirut in 1908 and, except for occasional visits back to his homeland, spent the rest of his long life outside Iran. Despite, or perhaps because, of his physical separation from Iran, Jamâlzâdeh developed an intense interest in Persian language and culture and came to express his affection for them through fiction. In 1921, he published a collection of short stories under the title of *Yaki bud yaki na-bud* ("Once Upon a Time"); probably no other work has done so much both to revolutionize the character of Persian literature and to make prose fiction one of its key genres. The most important of its stories is undoubtedly "Fârsi shekar ast" ("Persian is Sugar"), a very humorous account of the enforced encounter in jail of a religious cleric, a Europeanized modernist, and an ordinary Iranian from the countryside. The comedy derives from the situation, from the satirical presentation of the characters, and above all from the bewilderment caused by the different types of language used by the protagonists—as opposed to the simple and clear Persian of the bumpkin, the cleric's speech is peppered with Arabisms and the modernist's with borrowings from French. In theory, they are all compatriots speaking the same language, and yet they border on mutual unintelligibility to the point of seeming to come from different worlds. Behind the farce, however, there is the serious issue of what actually constitutes an authentic Iranian or Persian identity in modern times. In that sense, the story also symbolized, in ways Jamalzâdeh may not have fully anticipated, the central dilemma of contemporary Iranian history as the nation's people have been pulled between the attractions of two periods of their past (pre-Islamic and Islamic) and two styles of culture (the glamour of the West and the comfort of the traditional). In any case, Jamâlzâdeh's plea for the use of a Persian style in closer conformity to actual speech, his satirical technique, and his biting political commentary all resonated with many subsequent writers.

Hedâyat also came from a distinguished family, in his case one that had produced a considerable number of writers and bureaucrats during the Qâjâr period. In a sense, he carried on the intellectual tradition of the family, but in the style of the eccentric bohemian artist for which he had apparently cultivated a taste during his student days in Paris—a habitue of cafes with a misanthropic disdain for "the happy and the stupid," a fanatic vegetarian and champion of animal rights, a vehement nationalist critic of Arabic and Islamic elements in Iranian culture who admired India and Buddhism. He also had a morbid and enduring fascination with death and the occult that resulted in at least two attempts at suicide, one unsuccessfully when he jumped from a bridge into the Marne River (around 1928) and one successfully, again in France in 1951, when he opened the gas tap to his kitchen stove. His writings span the range from polemical essays to vitriolic satires to historical drama and short stories, but looming over them all is his novella *Buf-e kur* ("The Blind Owl"). This enigmatic, controversial, and highly influential work really cannot be described in brief; the plot, setting, and characters are all as ambiguous as they are detailed. Essentially it has two parts, both written as first person narrative. The first part seems to be the tale of a tortured recluse, an artist who decorates pen-cases by drawing the same picture (of a beautiful woman offering flowers to an old man) on them over and over. He glimpses this "ethereal woman" through a hole in his wall and searches for her but cannot find her; when she mysteriously appears in his bed, he murders and dismembers her. In the grave dug for her, he finds a jug bearing her image, the prototype for his own obsessive drawings. He is somewhat comforted by the thought that in the past there was someone just like him. He smokes opium, falls into a coma, and emerges as the narrator of the second part, a man who is also completely alienated from the rest of mankind (the *rajjâleh-hâ,* who are described as "the imbeciles" who lead normal lives) and lives in fear of arrest by "drunken policemen." He had a wife with whom he is infatuated and yet impotent (she is supposed to look just like his mother); he encouraged her to be promiscuous, only to murder her "accidentally" after he succeeded in making love to her in the disguise of "a grotesque old hunchback" who was the most significant of her paramours. He returns home and, looking in the mirror, realizes that he *is* the old hunchback; the shock of this awakens him. This is not so much storytelling as it is the capturing of a dream or drug-induced hallucination in which the countless parallels and highly symbolic images make it is impossible to say what is real and what is illusion. It has also given rise to many divergent interpretations of how it should be read. Just as Jamâlzâdeh's work contributed to new conceptions of how the

Persian language could be used, Hedâyat's work in *Buf-e kur* demonstrated the possibilities of what could be done in Persian fiction, and few subsequent novelists of any significance escaped its influence. In particular, its emphasis on the alienated intellectual, its exploration of psychological character, and its surrealistic atmosphere would be repeated in many other works. Finally, it should be mentioned that Hedâyat was a politically conscious writer concerned about his country's domestic and international status. He was critical of the cultural and religious environment in which he lived and was a harsh critic of both the political and clerical establishment. *Hâji Âqâ*, a novel published in 1945, was a direct attack on religious superstition and despotic rule. To Hedâyat, the underdevelopment of Iranian society was due to the dominance of Islamic culture. For Iran to move forward, it had to eradicate the legacies of the Arab domination and go back to its pre-Islamic roots. Hedâyat joined a group of intellectuals who worked for cleansing the Persian language of Arabic words.

A third period in the history of Persian prose fiction began in the early 1940s and continues to the present time. Features of the fiction of this period include: the use of more scenery and images, avoidance of foreign words either Arabic or European, representation of rural sub-culture, and resistance against political oppression. It has given rise to many different types of novels: realist versus surrealist, purely artistic versus committed art, nihilistic, romanticist, and even crime fiction.

Although the models of style, humor, satire, and surrealism set by Jamâl-zâdeh and Hedâyat continued to be emulated by many Persian writers, as the Pahlavi regime became more politically repressive, and as the influence of socialist ideas increased among the intelligentsia, social criticism became the dominant theme of prose literature. This might be from the point of view of the alienated intellectual or the oppressed masses, especially those of rural society and the urban poor; the critique was sometimes open but often veiled in order to avoid censorship or political persecution. The most important writers of this type were probably Gholâm Hosayn Sâ'edi (1935–1985) and Jalâl Âl-e Ahmad (1923–69). Sâ'edi is best-known for his plays and short stories. Âl-e Ahmad became popular for a nonfiction work, *Gharbzadegi* ("Afflicted by the West"), which fiercely denounced Western cultural influences in Iran, and his novel *Modir-e madraseh* ("School Principal"), a devastating critique of the educational system in Iran (something he knew first-hand having worked as a teacher himself). Among the many other authors who mixed politics and social criticism with fiction were writers like Sa'id Nafisi (d. 1966), Mosh-feq Kâzemi, Mohammad Mas'ud (1861–1947), Bozorg 'Alavi (1907–97), Mahmud E'temâdzâdeh (pen-named Behâzin), Samad Behrangi (1939–68), Sâdeq Chubak (1916–95), and Taqi Modarresi (1932–97). One result of this emphasis on social criticism was the reaction of government in the form of censorship and harsh treatment of writers. Since the establishment of a ministry in charge of cultural issues in Iran, there have always been officials assigned to screen fiction and nonfiction works prior to their publications. This has resulted in suppression of many artistic works, which often found their way into an underground market with greater public interest in them. For instance, Bozorg Alavi's book, *Chashm-hâyash* ("Her Eyes") was banned in Iran, and if it was found in anyone's library, it would result in the incarceration of its owner. The same was true of one of Samad Behrangi's books, *Mâhi siâh-e kuchulu* ("The Little Black Fish").

Prose writing during the Pahlavi era produced important novels, each appearing at different times and capturing the imagination of the public. 'Alavi's works attracted broad audiences in the 1950s. In the 1960s, 'Ali-Mohammad Afghâni's voluminous novel, *Showhar-e Ahu Khânom* ("Mrs. Ahu's Husband"), became popular and increased public interest in reading novels. In the 1970s, Dowlatâbâdi's *Kelidar* and novels by other writers like Simin Dâneshvar (1921–), Bahrâm Sâdeghi (1936–1986), Jamâl Mir Sâdeghi (1933–), Iraj Pezeshkzâd (1927–), and Ahmad Mahmoud (1931–2002) continued to enrich Iranian literature. Simin Dâneshvar's masterpiece novel, *Savushun* ("Mourning"), published in 1969, was the first novel written by an Iranian woman and from a woman's perspective. *Savushun* is set in Shiraz under British occupation during World War II and examines issues arising from both foreign domination and a patriarchal society. It has been reprinted more than 16 times and continues to be read by the young Iranian generation. In 1964, *Dâ'i jân Nâpoli'un* (Uncle Napoleon) by Iraj Pezeshkzâd captured public attention and became the basis for one of the most successful serials in the history of Iranian television. This comic novel focuses on the paranoia Iranians have developed over what they think is British control of all affairs in their society. Another author of significance in this period was Hushang Golshiri (d. 2000), whose novel *Shâzdeh Ehtejâb* ("Prince Ehtejab") greatly influenced the direction of Iranian literature. Golshiri's influence on modern Iranian literature was two-fold: the impact of his own novels and his legacy of producing writers in his workshop for novelists. Golshiri is known for his use of complex structure, vivid language, and subtle manipulations of narrative time in his novels. If Hedâyat provided Iranian writers with a model for surrealism and Âl-e Ahmad, 'Alavi, and Dowlatâbâdi with a model of realism influenced by socialist ideas, Hushang Golshiri, Bahrâm Sâdeqi, and Ebrâhim Golestân, Bahman Forsi, and Rezâ Barâhani are novelists who set an independent approach to the novel: structuralism. For these writers, a novel has to have its own structure, congruent with its language, theme, and internal dynamic. The efforts by these writers reflected not only the socio-cultural concerns of the Pahlavi era, they also dealt with issues of Iranian identity as it experienced modernity and Westernization.

The Islamic Revolution of 1979–80 produced new challenges and new opportunities for the development of Persian literature. Authors using secular images insensitive to religious norms found it difficult to produce works. The new Ministry of Culture and Guidance issued instructions banning protagonists' names containing the word *shâh*, such as Jahânshâh, Shâhvali, and so forth. Anything giving credence to signs and symbols of the Pahlavi era in particular and monarchy in general was banned. Not knowing what the exact rules were and how far they could push the boundaries, many authors either left the country or simply put their pens down for a while. Those who dared to produce and publish their works underground were subject to arrest and imprisonment. Several authors were killed during the 1980s for their political and cultural defiance of government policies.

As the dust of the revolution settled and the rules became clearer, old and new writers began to publish their works, albeit within new limits. The rules insisted on the moral function of the artistic work and warned against glorification of norms antithetical to Islamic values. New novels were to promote native cultural values, emphasize the glory of homeland, depict the negative aspects of Western culture and society, and promote moral values based on Islam. The Iran-Iraq War during the 1980s contributed to the emergence of a new genre of works variously called "martyrdom literature" (*adabiyât-e shehâdat*), "revolutionary literature" (*adabiyât-e enqelâb*), and "war literature" (*adabiyât-e jang*). These works were moralistic fictions promoting heroism, nationalism, Islamic ideology, and religious devotion. Later in the decade, secular writers began to work again. Their silence was broken with the publication of *Samfoni-ye mordegân* ("Symphony of the Dead") by 'Abbâs Ma'rufi in 1988. Ma'rufi portrayed the life of a family with four children in provincial Ardabil. His sophisticated narration of the conflict between two brothers and his frequent symphonic-like changes of voices, views, places, and levels of discourse represented a fresh style in an environment dominated by repetitive styles. Ma'rufi was the publisher of a literary magazine called *Gardun*. In 1996, his critical commentaries caused his journal to be shut down and resulted in a sentence of six months in jail and twenty lashes with a whip. His works were banned in Iran, and Ma'rufi escaped the country and now lives in Berlin.

With the Iran-Iraq War behind it, the Islamic Republic began the 1990s with a determination to open up to the world, normalize its relations with its neighbors and European countries, reconstruct the war-torn country, and liberalize the cultural atmosphere in the country. Cultural activities picked up pace, new magazines and newspapers appeared on the scene, and authors began to push limits further. Increase in literacy and population size laid the ground for the emergence of young novelists, poets, and play writers. Translation of Persian literature into Western languages brought further attention to modern Iranian writers, encouraging further developments at home. It is still early to try to assess fiction writing during this contemporary period, but perhaps the most striking change has been in the willingness of writers (and filmmakers as well) to explore the ethnic and linguistic diversity of Iran and experiment with what Iranian authors call "multivoices" (*chand sedâi*). Linguistic diversity was strongly discouraged during the Pahlavi period in the interest of promoting a Persian-based Iranian nationalism (some of the best writers, for example, were actually Azeri Turks who were effectively blocked from writing and publishing in their native language and had to write instead in Persian). Recent fiction, however, often emphasizes provincial settings, regional dialects, and the interaction of Persians and non-Persians in an Islamic Iran. This is quite noticeable in the work of Mohsen Makhmalbâf, a novelist as well as a film director, who pays much attention to ethnic minorities; Moniru Ravânipur, one of Iran's best women writers, who uses language and settings drawn from the southern coastal area; or Mahmud Dowlatâbâdi whose epic, 10-volume novel *Kelidar* about life and society in the northeastern province of Khorâsân may be one of the greatest works in all of modern Persian fiction. A multi-voice novel, in the tradition of Russian author Leo Tolstoy, it focuses on more than one protagonist and develops multiple characters with diverse voices and views. The same applies to situations, themes, and forms. Ahmad Mahmud's works are also good examples of this style.

After the revolution, works of a new generation of authors, especially female novelists, have received attention from both critics and the public. These writers include Fattâneh Hâjj Sayyed Javâdi, 'Ali-Ashraf Darvishiân, Amir Hasan Cheheltan, Farkhondeh Âqâi, 'Adnân Gharifi, Goli Taraqqi, Javâd Mojâbi, Ebrâhim Yunesi, Shams Langarudi, Nâder Ebrâhimi, Banafsheh Hejâzi, Nâtâshâ Amiri, Mortezâ Kâkhi, Mohammad Bahârlu, Mohammad Qâ'ed, Esmâ'il Fasih, Bijan Najdi, Shahriâr Mandanipur, Amin Faqiri, Sayyed-'Ali Sâlehi, and 'Emrân Sâlehi.

Another interesting recent development in the literary culture has been the influence of a new genre of works produced by Iranian writers living abroad. Though officially banned from distribution within the country by the government, their works are still read widely in Iran. These authors and poets include Esmâ'il Khoi, 'Abbâs Ma'rufi, Rezâ Barâhani, Nasim Khâksâr, Mirzâ Âqâ 'Asgari, Shahrnush Parsipur, Ebrâhim Nabavi, Hâdi Khorsandi, 'Abbâs Safari, and Majid Nafisi.

THE MEDIA

The writing of prose fiction was not the only cultural innovation in Iran that can be attributed to a combination of Western influence, social consciousness, an increasing rate of literacy among the general population, and the development of the means for mass production and distribution of printed material. Just as striking, and perhaps even more important, has been the growing national appetite for other forms of reading material, information, and entertainment, notably in the form of newspapers, magazines, radio, television, and cinema. Precisely because these are such highly popular and potentially subversive means of communication, they have all had to struggle with problems of censorship and state control, yet they have nonetheless managed to flourish and produce at times spectacular results.

The first newspapers to appear in Iran were official government gazettes intended primarily to keep courtiers and bureaucrats informed about events in Iran and abroad. The earliest was a lithographed publication issued weekly and entitled *Ruz-nâmeh-e vaqâye'-e ettefâqiyeh* ("Diary of Current Events") that appeared in February 1851. After the office of the government press was taken over by Abo'l-Qâsem Khan Sani'-ol-Molk (latter known as E'temâd-os-Saltaneh) in 1860, it was renamed *Ruz-nâmeh-ye dowlat-e 'aliyeh-e Irân* and began to include engravings, some of which were remarkably well done, to illustrate the text. It continued to be published, with some interruptions and changes in title, down to at least 1911. These newspapers are of considerable historical interest, but they did not have the cultural impact of the privately printed and circulated newspapers that soon followed. Even though these papers had limited circulation numbers—usually only a few thousand and even the most popular about ten thousand—they were important because they were read by members of the elite. In some cases, they could also reach even larger audiences among the still mostly illiterate general population by being read out in teahouses and at public gatherings. The earliest and most influential Persian language papers, all printed outside of Iran and thus able to avoid censorship, were *Akhtar* ("The Star"), published at Istanbul; *Habl-ol-Matin* ("The Firm Rope"), published at Calcutta; and *Qânun* ("The Law"), published (and mostly written) by Malkom Khân in London. All played an important rule in introducing concepts of political reform to Iran. With the coming of the Constitutional Revolution, the number of such papers—and the political interests they represented—proliferated dramatically. Well over three hundred newspapers are known from that period, though most were short-lived. Probably the most popular and highly regarded was *Sur-e Esrâfil* ("Esrafel's Trumpet"). It was unabashedly secularist, anti-clerical, and constitutionalist in outlook and, with articles by 'Ali-Akbar Dehkhodâ (see above), had some of the very best satirical writing in Persian. Indeed, the paper was so effective that it became a main target of the reactionaries after the anti-Constitutionalist coup of 1908 that initiated the period of the "Lesser Despotism"; Mohammad-'Ali Shah ordered the owner and editor of the paper, Mirzâ Jahângir Khân Shirâzi, to be strangled to death.

The general restriction of freedom of expression during the Pahlavi period also affected the press. Essentially, any paper that flourished during that time was at least suspected of collusion with either the government or a foreign power. Still, some papers did aspire to the norms and standards of professional journalism as best they could. Foremost among them was *Ettelâ'ât* ("The News") founded in 1926 as the organ of the Iranian News Agency. It tried to incorporate features of a popular, mass-circulation daily newspaper and was not always uncritical of the government; however, the editor, 'Abbas Mas'udi, was close to Rezâ Shah, and it eventually acquired the aura of a semiofficial paper. It was also for a while the most widely-read paper in Iran. Its chief competitor was *Kayhân,* which appeared in May 1941. By the 1970s, *Kayhân* had a circulation almost twice as large as that of *Ettelâ'ât* and was probably even more widely regarded as the official voice of the government. It was a vicious article in that paper attacking the reputation of Âyatollâh Khomeini that sparked the Islamic Revolution. After the Revolution, both *Ettelâ'ât* and *Kayhân* along with their subsidiary publications, were taken over by the Foundation for the Oppressed (Bonyâd-e Mostaz'afân).

It could hardly be said that the Revolution brought a genuine freedom of the press to Iran. Through control of licensing procedures and the supply of critical materials such as newsprint, the government still had considerable influence over the press. Nonetheless, the environment for newspapers was in many ways reminiscent of that of the Constitutional Era. The stranglehold of the big papers was broken, and there were numerous political factions that sought to push their ideas and agendas through affiliated newspapers, which began to appear in profusion. Papers that went too far in their views might be banned, only to reappear immediately under a different title. Especially after the electoral victory of the Khatami as president, the political disputes between conservatives and reformers were reflected—and sometimes fought out—in the press. Numerous newspapers and magazines emerged, reflecting the diversity of ideas, politics, and factional affiliations: *Abrâr, Âftâb-e Yazd, 'Asr-e âzâdegân, Entekhâb, Ebtekâr, E'temâd, Hambastegi, Ham-Mihan, Hamshahri, Hayât-e Now, Irân, Jâma', Jâm-e Jam, Jomhuri-e eslâmi, Jomhuriyat, Khorâsân, Khordâd, Mehr, Mellat, Neshât, Qods, Resâlat, Tus, Vaqâye'-e Ettefâqiyeh* and *Yâs-e Now.*

As the tug of war between the conservatives and reformists continued, over 40 newspapers, including several of the ones mentioned here, were banned, especially after a crackdown in April 2000. Investigative reports about some officials generated harsh reactions. Probably the most daring example of independent investigative journalism was the work of Akbar Ganji, a reporter for several reformist newspapers, who exposed government involvement in the murder of several dissident intellectuals in 1998. He was arrested in 2000 and sentenced to 10 years in jail—a sentence reduced to 5 later. Among the better known contemporary newspapers, *Jomhuri-e eslâmi, Resâlat,* and *Keyhân* are regarded as proconservative, while *Sharq* and *E'temâd* have been proreformist. A few, such as *Ettelâ'ât* and *Irân,* try to follow a moderate or centrist line. *Hamshahri,* one of the most widely read newspapers in Iran, used to be a reformist paper, but with the appointment of Mahmud Ahmadinejâd in 2003 as the mayor of Tehran, and his election in 2005 as the president, it has shifted to a proconservative position.

NOTES

1. Given here in the translation by E. G. Browne, *A Literary History of Persia,* (Cambridge: Cambridge University Press, 1928), 2:126–27.

2. Translated in Charles F. Horne (ed.), *The Sacred Books and Early Literatures of the East,* vol. 8: *Medieval Persia* (New York: Parke, Austin, and Libscomb, 1917).

3. As translated by James Ross, *Gulistan, or, Flower Garden* (London: W. Scott, 1890), 160. Bestowal of the cloak or mantle was a sign of acceptance into a Sufi order; "ghostly father" here is better understood as spiritual guide (i.e., the head of the order).

4. Slightly modified from the translation by Ross, *Gulistan,* 117.

5. Following here the translation by Ross, *Gulistan,* 221.

6. In A. J. Arberry, *Fifty Poems of Hafiz* (Cambridge: Cambridge University Press,, 1953), poem no. 44. By convention, the poet would mention his own pen name in the last line of the poem.

7. Manucher Farmanfarmaian and Roxane Farmanfarmaian, *Blood and Oil: Memoirs of a Persian Prince* (New York: Random House, 1997), 312.

4

Drama and Cinema

Drama and cinema in contemporary Iran can be said to have some roots in older, more traditional forms of similar cultural activities. The first type of dramatic expression, for example, was probably connected to the veneration by ancient Iranians of the sun-god Mithra, when worshipers constructed a public stage and wore masks to perform certain religious rituals. We also know that after Alexander's invasion of Iran, performances of Greek plays were held there well into Parthian times. As discussed in an earlier chapter, dramatized presentations of the epic stories and legends of ancient Iran were performed by bards (*gosân*s) and storytellers (*naqqâl*s) in Parthian, Sasanid, and early Islamic times, and later on the Shiʿite passion-play (*taʿziyeh*) became a well-established form of dramatic presentation. The Turks and Mongols also brought some customs of popular drama and public performances such as shadow-puppet plays to Iran. Iranian rulers often patronized jesters, entertainers, and other performers for the amusement of the court elites. For ordinary people, the bazaars and public squares were places where jugglers, magicians, comedians, storytellers, and entertainers offered their dramatic performances to the public.

In addition to *taʿziyeh* and *naqqâli*, traditional forms of dramatic performance include those known as *ruhowzi* or *siâh-bâzi*, *pardeh-dâri*, and *khaymeh-shab-bâzi*. *Ruhowzi* is a comic type of folk drama similar to *commedia dell'arte* but with rapid verbal rather than physical humor. It is often performed at weddings and at teahouses. It is called *ruhowzi* or "over the pool" because it is typically performed on a board placed over the pool commonly found in the yard of a Persian home. *Ruhowzi* usually involves several players engaging in comic dance, music, and song. The dialogue is colloquial and filled with satirical impersonations of local people and events. The play often involves participation by, or exchanges with, the spectators. *Pardeh-dâri* is performed by a single narrator who chants a narrative, using a screen with pictures as a prop to illustrate the story he is telling. This is somewhat similar to *naqqâli* except that the subjects of the story are usually of a religious nature. *Khaymeh-shab-bâzi* is basically puppet theater, performed with glove dolls or marionettes.

EARLY DEVELOPMENT OF CINEMA

Cinema in Iran has its origins in the foibles of court entertainment in the late nineteenth and early twentieth century. In 1900, the Qâjâr king, Mozaffar-od-Din Shah, went to France for a state visit. While there, he became fascinated with the camera and what it could do. He ordered his photographer, Mirzâ Ebrâhim 'Akkâsbâshi, to buy a cinematograph. Later, using the newly acquired equipment, Mirzâ Ebrâhim documented the presence of Mozaffar-od-Din Shah at a ceremony in Belgium. This documentary is the first film made by an Iranian. Mirzâ Ebrâhim brought his camera equipment back to Iran, and the king set up a demonstration for the court. The king also had a movie made of court eunuchs playing with each other in the palace courtyard. Film had become a part of court entertainment, and the various films made by Mirzâ Ebrâhim probably represent the first ethnographic footage taken in the history of Iranian film.

Films made during the Qâjâr period may be divided into three categories: documentation of court ceremonies, social-cultural scenes around the capital, and scripted action films. Royal and religious ceremonies were often filmed, and the films would later be shown at weddings of members of the elite, at family gatherings, or at court parties. Also, a number of documentaries were produced in this period.

In 1905, Mirzâ Ebrâhim Khan Sahhâfbâshi, an antique dealer, was the first private entrepreneur to import a film projector to Iran. He converted the backyard of his shop into an open-air theater and began public screening of films in Tehran. He showed a mostly upper class audience silent movies imported to Iran via Russia. The fate of this courageous venture was thrown into controversy when rumors circulated claiming that the films shown there included unveiled female characters. This led to condemnation by the religious leader Âyatollâh Fazlollah Nuri, who demanded the closure of the theater. This, along with other political problems, resulted in the closure of Sahhâfbâshi's theater, confiscation of his financial assets, and his exile to India in 1907.

Under the patronage of Mohammad-'Ali Shah, a Russian-born court photographer, Mahdi Rusi Khân, became a cinema manager and replaced Sahhâfbâshi as a presenter of films for elite viewers in Tehran. In 1909, Rusi Khân made a film of the Moharram mourning processions, but it was only shown in Russia. With the restoration of the Constitution and the exile of Mohammad-'Ali Shah, Rusi Khân fell out of favor and his films were confiscated. Though the new theater he had opened on the second floor of a printing shop in Lâlehzâr Avenue remained open for a while, he decided to leave Iran for Paris in 1911.

By 1912, a number of movie theaters had been built, mostly by foreign-born Iranians, especially from Russia. The only person who was able to keep his theater open for more than a decade was an Armenian businessman by the name of Ardashir Khân Bâtmângariân. His theater, known as Sinemâ Jadid ("New Cinema"), opened in 1913 in collaboration with a French company.

A unique contributor to the evolution of cinema in Iran was an elderly French woman by the name of Mme Bernadotte. She owned a bookstore in Tehran and sometimes showed newsreels and war documentaries in a small projection room to her predominantly French-speaking customers. It is reported that some of these films contributed to the spirit of nationalism at the time and generated a stir amongst the Iranian public. Some people, however, accused her of witchcraft, claiming that she called forth Satan on the screen—accusations which resulted in the closure of her "little cinema." Another contribution to the development of film culture was the Iranian-British Cultural Center, which in the 1920s screened documentaries to a select group of Iranians.

In the 1920s and 1930s, more movie houses were established. In 1925, 'Ali Vakili was able to build the largest movie theater at the time in the Grand Hotel on Lâlehzâr Avenue and later published the first magazine on show business in Iran. At the beginning of Rezâ Shah's rule, there were 8 theaters in Tehran. By the early 1930s, there were 15 theaters in Tehran and 11 in other provinces. The existence of such an infrastructure encouraged people to attend movie theaters.

Movies made during this period included some documentaries by Khân Bâbâ Khân Mo'tazedi, who had previously worked with a film studio in France. The first Iranian-made feature films also began to appear. The main pioneer in this effort was an Armenian immigrant, Hovhannes Ohanian (Âvânes Uhâniân), who established an acting school in Iran in 1930. With actors from this school and Mo'tazedi as his cameraman, he made a popular slapstick comedy, *Âbi o Râbi* ("Abi and Rabi") that same year. This was followed in 1932 by *Hâji Âqâ âktor-e sinemâ* ("Haji Aqa, Movie Actor")—the story of a woman and her fiancé who wanted to become film actors but had to defuse the opposition of her religiously-minded father to their plan. The script was written by one of the most prominent Iranian authors of the time, Sa'id Nafisi, and the film employed an Armenian woman, Asia Ghostantin, as the actress. The film was meant to demonstrate the desirability of the new media through the use of humor. This blend of comedy and melodrama would remain a popular genre of Iranian film into the 1970s. One of Ohanian's students, Ebrâhim Morâdi, established his own studio and released a film in 1934 called *Bu'l-hawas* ("The Lustful Man"). This film contrasted the simple and natural life in rural areas with the unexpected and often uncomfortable aspects of city life—another durable theme in Iranian cinema. This was also the last Iranian feature production done within Iran's borders until the end of the World War II. Morâdi's efforts were very important for the new industry in Iran. He also employed the first two Iranian Muslim women to work as actresses, namely Qodsi Partovi and Âsieh.

The first Persian-language movie with sound, *Dokhtar-e Lor* ("The Lor Girl"), was made in Bombay in 1933 by 'Abd-ol-Hosayn Sepantâ, a Zoroastrian poet and writer from Isfahan. Sepantâ wrote the script for the film and also played the role of the character Ja'far in this movie. "The Lor Girl" was such a success that it landed Sepantâ an offer from the Iranian government to produce films about the glory of the country's past and the desirability of a modern lifestyle, but this did not work out exactly as intended. In 1935 the Ministry of Education commissioned Sepantâ to make a film about the life of the poet Abo'l-Qâsem Ferdowsi, but parts of his film *Ferdowsi* were rejected and had to be redone because the shah did not like the film's negative portrayal of Sultan Mahmud. Sepantâ continued to produce movies inspired by classical Persian literature and Iranian history, but mostly outside the country and without government support. Sepantâ's last film *Layli o Majnun,* based on the classical love story of Layli and Majnun, appeared in 1937. With their use of Persian dialog accompanied by songs, music, and dance, Sepantâ's films were quite popular, but a combination of political, financial, and bureaucratic difficulties forced him to leave the movie industry.

SOCIOLOGICAL CHALLENGES OF INTRODUCING FILM TO A TRADITIONAL SOCIETY

The introduction of modern film to a traditional Iran was not without its sociological problems. As mentioned earlier, cinema started as a court entertainment and remained available only to the cultural and political elite for over a decade. When the government began to encourage this industry, it still had to confront the opposition of the *'olamâ* and a public unprepared and unwilling to do away with traditional modes of entertainment. Theaters were declared by the 'olamâ to be centers for all kinds of vices. They were labeled "houses of Satan" and subjected to mob attack or forced closure. The public perception marked people attending theaters as "immoral people engaged in sinful activity." In light of these criticisms, theater owners and others involved in this industry, along with government officials, took great pains to promote the theater as a respectable place that the police prevented "loose women, depraved youngsters and hecklers" from entering. On one occasion during Rezâ Shah's reign, the opposition to the establishment of the first theater in the southern part of Tehran, which was and still is very traditional, was so strong that police had to force people to go to this theater.

At a more practical level, in the early years the government had to make special efforts to keep the cost of attending movie theaters low enough to attract nonelite segments of the society. This was a problem for theater owners as well. As the number of movie theaters increased, theater owners had to compete for viewers. They tried to attract viewers by offering free tickets, ice creams, nuts, and other food items. Some owners even hired musicians to play music, interpreters to walk around the hall and explain the scenes in a loud voice, and Armenian female employees with heavy makeup in order to attract viewers.

A second problem had to do with the translation and presentation of foreign films. Since films shown in the early days were in their original language, there had to be brief pauses for live translation. Every 10 minutes or so, the film would be interrupted by a Persian caption explaining previous or forthcoming events. Some theaters hired story tellers to convey what was involved in the films so they did not have to stop the show intermittently. It also took a while for the Iranian viewers, unaccustomed to the new technology, to know how to adjust their feelings and behaviors to the realities of this new phenomenon. Some cinemas had to hire policemen to control the viewers' behavior during the show. On one occasion, when a lion jumped in a scene of a Tarzan film, a policeman attending the theater shot at the screen in an attempt to subdue the lion!

The third problem confronting the development of a film culture was the presence of women both in the film and in the theater. By 1920, Iranian film viewers were used to seeing unveiled women in foreign movies. However, showing Iranian women in film was a new challenge for filmmakers and theater owners. Since the first Iranian films involved Armenian women of Iranian origin, there was not much public objection. However, when films with sound were produced, the participation of Muslim women in filmmaking became a major controversial issue. The first actresses were subjected to ridicule, harassment, and social isolation. These were courageous women whose passion for the art and profession surpassed their need for income or a costly fame. The perseverance of these actresses and their film producers paved the way for breaking a social taboo and easing modern media into Iranian society.

A related problem was how to allow women to visit the theater because it was not possible to allow men and women to attend the theater at the same time. Theaters experimented with having dedicated hours for each sex. This did not work well. Later, they tried to designate some theaters as exclusively for women. Mo'tazedi founded two such theaters for women in 1925, and three years later, Vakili created a female-only theater in a Zoroastrian school hall. This did not work well for attracting women to the theater either. Also, it was financially inefficient. Then, they tried to allow both sexes in the same theater, but with women seated in the balcony. This did not last long either. Finally, they tried having women and men sit in separate parts of the theater. This worked until 1936, when women were freed from wearing the veil by the order of Rezâ Shah and wives could sit next to their husbands in the theater.

A final problem had to do with the spread of cinema beyond the capital, especially in areas with a heavy concentration of ethnic population. Since not all ethnic groups spoke or even understood the Persian language, showing films to non-Persian speaking audiences posed a serious challenge. For instance, Sinemâ Khorshid in the city of Abâdân, then heavily populated by Arabs, could not stay open more than three nights a week because of the lack of an audience, even with free admission.

CINEMA DURING THE REIGN OF REZÂ SHAH

With the establishment of the Pahlavi dynasty, the secularized state became a social and cultural force to encourage the spread of new ideas through new modes of communication. Rezâ Shah was a strong leader determined to push modernization of Iran against any opposition, even from the religious quarters. He supported the film industry as long as the filmmakers produced newsreels documenting the rapid development of the country's infrastructure. His attitude paved the way for the growth of contemporary art forms, particularly cinema in Iran. While the industry was in its infancy and in need of support, Rezâ Shah's rule was also new and in need of means to demonstrate its power. Rezâ Shah saw cameras as tools to show the country as he wanted it to be seen. No one could even own a camera without authorization from a court. He hired Khân Bâbâ Mo'tazedi to film various ceremonies at the palace, the parliament, and the opening ceremonies of the trans-Iranian railway system, the National Bank of Iran, and the Pahlavi communication center. These newsreels were shown at court, in army barracks, and at some theaters.

After viewing an impressive documentary about the Anglo-Persian Oil Company in Khuzestân, Rezâ Shah ordered the construction of new movie theaters in Tehran. Lâlehzâr, a street in what was then the north of Tehran, but is now in the middle of the city, was where the theaters were built, along with European-style hotels. Lâlehzâr became an attractive location in Tehran for movie houses and was viewed as a venue for lovers, pleasure seekers, and those seeking amusement. Rezâ Shah's program thus found a receptive audience among the country's elite and the relatively small middle class. Since all the movie theaters were located in the northern part of Tehran, the government provided aid to build a theater in the southern part of Tehran in a poor neighborhood. Sinemâ Tamaddon ("Civilization Cinema") was built there as a symbol of the shah's determination to educate the Iranian population to modern ways of life.

Once attendance by the so-called lower classes increased, a new hierarchy emerged among theater halls: elite and popular theaters. The former showed high-quality films of the time and were attended by educated people who were familiar with the Western literature from which those films were adopted. The latter showed foreign, comic, and action and adventure films and were attended by the less sophisticated public. Interestingly, the music played in these theaters was also geared to this hierarchy: whereas the elite theaters played Western music, the popular theaters played popular Persian music.

Unfortunately, most films shown during Rezâ Shah's reign were imported films from Europe, the United States, and Russia. His cultural policies fostered a favorable environment for the influx of Western films. During 1928–1930, over 1,000 foreign films were imported into Iran, nearly half of them from the U.S. and the rest from France, Germany, Russia, and other countries. As Rezâ Shah's sympathy to Germany increased, so did the number of German films shown in Iran. This was also helped by the absence of security prerequisites on foreign exchange to purchase German films.

Not surprisingly, Rezâ Shah's cultural policies fostered an environment openly conducive to the influx of Western films. American films flooded Iranian market during the 1920s, and German films gained a significant market share towards the turn of the decade and well into the 1930s. The success of the later was not unrelated to Germany's increased cultural and technical presence in Iran following World War I. While this flood of American and German films into the country enabled the expansion of a foreign film market in Iran, it inhibited the development of the local film industry. With Rezâ Shah's departure in 1941, German films rapidly disappeared from the landscape of Iranian cinema, as was the case with most French productions as well. The result was an increase in American films, rising from 60 percent in 1940 to 70–80 percent by 1943. In the 1930s, significantly more theatre halls opened. The young Iranian film industry also demonstrated its capacity for local production, no matter how limited.

DOMINANCE OF FOREIGN FILMS AND THE GROWTH OF THE DUBBING INDUSTRY

From 1937 till 1947, foreign films continued their dominance, and Iran did not produce any films locally. During the 1940s, numerous restrictions were imposed on Iranian cinema resulting in the stagnation of local production. World War II also caused serious political and economic difficulties for the country and brought the fragile Iranian motion picture industry to a virtual standstill. Yet, as mentioned before, foreign movies poured into the Iranian market and a sizable portion of the growing Iranian working class and the emerging middle class was attracted to film as a form of legitimate entertainment. This was not lost on investors in the motion picture industry. To satisfy the newly-developed appetite, more movie theaters were built, and the industry found dubbing of foreign films into Persian as both an improvement in the quality of services provided to viewers and a profitable venture. A number of producers began dubbing foreign movies outside of Iran and then importing them to Iran for competition with Hollywood movies. One of these was a young Iranian, Esmâ'il Kushân, who dubbed two foreign films in Turkey and imported them to Tehran for show in 1946 with spectacular success. Soon, local dubbing studios were set up, creating competition for foreign operations.

As early as 1943, the first dubbing studio, called Iran-Now Film, was established in Tehran. By 1961, dubbing foreign films into Persian in Europe ended, and almost all foreign films were dubbed in Iran. Utilizing the availability of improved technical facilities as well as comparatively more cost-effective local dubbers and actors, the local studios were able to create products superior in quality to films dubbed in Italy. Some of these studios later engaged in film production as well. Dubbing was challenging, but the industry was able to overcome most of its early difficulties. Interestingly, dubbing provided Iranians with both an opportunity for creativity and censorship. In the case of creativity, Iranian dubbers adjusted dialogues, and even music, to Iranian taste by utilizing Persian idioms close to the foreign expression used in the original dialogue. For instance, a song by Jerry Lewis in the movie *Patsy* was replaced with an Indian song in order to fit the Iranian taste, which was much closer to Indian culture than to American. In terms of censorship, "morally unacceptable words" were replaced by sanitized Persian equivalents. In turn, dubbed movies came to stifle Iranian originality by getting Iranian viewers so much used to their plots and dialogues that Iranian producers began to dub local production and actors emulated their foreign counterparts' use of inflection and tone. For instance, Mohammad-'Ali Fardin's voice in *Gedâyân-e Tehrân* ("The Beggars of Tehran") was a direct imitation of Peter Falk's voice in *A Pocketful of Miracles*. Also, the majority of films were shot on location without sound—sound was introduced later into the film through dubbing in studios. Except for those actors who had the benefit of stage experience, most actors in the film industry lacked appropriate vocal abilities—their voices would be replaced by dubbers who accentuated aural effects and otherwise compensated for these actors' shortcomings.

A number of business organizations, jointly financed by both Americans and Iranians, were set up exclusively to produce films. These centers facilitated the transfer of technical know-how and related information to Iranians, particularly in the art of producing newsreels and documentary films. The American presence in Iran during World War II also contributed to this expansion. The United States Information Service (USIS) in Iran began to distribute documentary and news films, dubbed into Persian, throughout the country. The Iranian government used 40 mobile cinema units to show these films to villagers and town people. In 1951, 60 films and 38 strips "on technical and instructional themes" were produced and distributed. Between 1951 and 1953, a number of magazines dealing specifically with acting and cinema appeared: *'Âlam-e Honar, Sinemâ va Teâtr, Setâreh-e Sinemâ,* and *Payk-e Sinemâ.* After the overthrow of Mosaddeq's government in 1953, the shah's new cultural policy of favoring Western products, especially American films, contributed to an increase in screening of foreign films in local cinemas. The number of foreign films shown in Iran increased from 100 in 1953 to close to 400 in 1961. This was due to a general lack of support for domestic films by the government, an increase in taxation on local films, and a reduction in duty on imports of foreign films.

THE EMERGENCE AND DOMINANCE OF *FILM FÂRSI*

Following World War II, a breakthrough for Iranian cinema came when Esmâ'il Kushân channeled his profits from dubbing foreign films into the production of films with sound in Iran. In 1947, he established a film studio, Mitrâ Film, followed by the production of Iran's first feature-length sound film in 1948, *Tufân-e zendegi* ("The Tempest of Life"), directed by Mohammad-'Ali Daryâbaygi. Despite the magnitude of its achievement, the movie did generate any enthusiasm and resulted in a financial loss, thus forcing some of Kushân's colleagues to abandon him. Despite serious difficulties, Kushan opened Pârs Film studio, under which his first venture was *Zendâni-e amir* ("The Prince's Prisoner," 1948), followed by his independently produced

musical comedy the next year, called *Vâryeteh-ye bahâr* ("The Spring Festival").
Hushang Kâvosi, producer of *Yusuf o Zolaykhâ* ("Joseph and Zolaykha"), was
one of the first directors working at Pârs Film. Kushân's efforts were followed
by Farrokh Ghaffâri's introduction of Iranians to alternative and artistic
foreign films. Ghaffâri founded the National Iranian Film Society at the Irân
Bâstân Museum in 1947, and directed his first successful film, *Janub-e shahr*
("Downtown").

Though Kushân's earlier films received somewhat lukewarm reactions, the
release of his new film, *Sharmsâr* ("Disgraced"), was significant due to his
employment of a heavy dose of songs and music—an imitation of Indian
movies that remained very popular in post–World War II Iran. An Iranian
ballet group that had successfully performed in Europe was in this movie
about a rural girl who is seduced by an urban boy and then become a successful
performer in a cabaret in the city. The impact of "Disgraced" extended into
promoting the career of the female singer, Delkash, who sang eight songs for
the film. Delkesh became the first popular singer involved with the cinema.

The success of "Disgraced" laid the foundation for commercial filmmaking in Iran, encouraging investors, producers, and directors to view film
production as a potentially lucrative venture. Kushan's success opened up
a different avenue for filmgoers who were no longer interested in subtitled
films—Persian-language films featuring renowned Iranian singers and dancers
became a real and attractive alternative. Furthermore, "Disgraced" also added
another layer to the popular themes which were to dominate Iranian cinema
for decades: simplicity of rural life versus corrupted city life, innocence of
rural girls versus deceptive city men, and rich versus poor lovers whose parents
opposed their union—themes that came to define what scholars later called
Film Fârsi. These were dreamlike melodramas imitating Indian movies. The
happy endings offered an optimistic view of the society and changed viewers' taste for movies. Much of their content were copied from stage productions—stories which, in turn, were drawn from classical Persian literature.

A period of urban expansion and rural-urban migration in the 1950s and
1960s saw the expansion of a cinematic culture in the country, an increase in
commercial film production, and growth in the number of cinemas all over
the country. Most films produced in this period were adaptations of novels,
plays, and Western films. While high in quantity (over 1,000), the quality
of these films was not very good because production companies focused
mainly on profit and pandered to the common tastes of the public for love
stories, sex, violence, and horror. Sâmuel Khâchikiân was a major director
involved in production of such films. Others included Majid Mohseni (*Lât-e
javânmard,* "The Gentleman Vagabond," based on Sâdeq Hedâyat's short
story, "Dâsh Âkol"); *Bolbol-e mazra'eh,* "The Nightingale of the Farm,"

1957; and *Parastu-hâ be-lâneh barmigardan*, "Swallows Come Back to the Nest," 1963); 'Atâollah Zâhed (*Chashm be-râh*, "In Waiting," 1958), and Farrokh Ghaffâri, whose "Downtown" (1958) was banned by authorities after five days of showing. Mohseni's "The Gentleman Vagabond" was the first film in Iranian cinema to focus on the prototype of the *jâhel* (a kind of good-hearted hooligan), thus setting the tone for over 200 similar productions during the 1960s. Films in this period, filled with music and dance and focused on melodramatic themes of traditional hooliganism (*jâheli*), love, and simple contrasts of rural purity and innocence versus urban corruption and decadence or good guys (lower class and poor) versus bad guys (emerging upper middle class and rich), were to be characterized in the 1970s with the negative label of *Film Fârsi*.

The number of films produced in this decade ushered Iranian cinema into what many would consider a phase of professional development during which an overwhelming majority of productions were grounded in *Film Fârsi*. Several important actors associated with this genre of films were Taqi Zohuri, Esmâ'il Arhâm Sadr, Nosratollâh Vahdat, Mohammad-'Ali Fardin, and Nâser Malakmoti'i. Some actresses in this category included Puribanâi, Foruzân, and Jamileh. In 1965, a "poor boy meets rich girl" tale used by Siâmak Yâsami's *Ganj-e Qârun* ("Qârun's Treasure") became a box office hit. This was a combination of love and family melodrama with a heavy dose of comedy and musical. As such, it was a sequenced imitation of fantasized Hollywood productions whose revenue surpassed any film ever produced in Iran up to that time. It also became a model for many films to be produced in the coming decade. This film, and the others subsequently made in imitation of it, generated enough support for Iranian domestic production to withstand the onslaught of foreign films.

NEW WAVE CINEMA

In the late 1950s and early 1960s, young critics and new filmmakers, who had studied film in Western universities, returned home. They were familiar with modern techniques and sensitive towards artistic quality and technical standards in the film. Their views refreshed the movie scene with new ideas different from common tradition. They viewed Iranian films produced in the 1950s and 60s as "inferior," both technically and artistically. They certainly had a cultural bias as well: those films glorified the working class, peasants, and artisans as well as their culture.

Towards the late 1950s and into the early 1960s, while commercial films gradually gained a foothold in Iranian cinema, the new filmmakers challenged the *Film Fârsi* establishment not only by criticism but also by making their own films. Some of these films included Forugh Farrokhzâd's documentary about people afflicted with leprosy, *Khâneh siâh ast* ("The House is Black") in 1962, Ebrâhim Golestân's *Kesht o âyeneh* ("Mudbrick and Mirror") in 1965, and Shâhrokh Ghaffâri's *Shab-e quzi* ("The Night of the Hunchback") in 1964. These films were works meant to be categorized as "art films" or "intellectual" or "progressive." *Siâvosh dar Takht-e Jamshid* ("Siâvosh at Persepolis") was produced by the poet, Fereydun Rahnemâ, in 1967. In the same year, Dâvud Mo'lâpur produced *Showhar-e Âhu Khânom* ("Mrs. Ahu's Husband") based on a popular novel of the same name by 'Ali-Mohammad Afghâni. Based on a script by Gholâm-Hosayn Sa'edi, Daryush Mehrjui made the celebrated film *Gâv* ("The Cow") in 1968. Other films included: *Moghol-hâ* ("The Mongols") by Parviz Kimiâvi in 1973; *Cheshmeh* ("The Spring") by Ârbi Âvânesiân in 1970; an adaptation of Sâdeq Chubak's novel *Tangsir* by Amir Nâderi in 1973;, *Yek ettefâq-e sâdeh* ("A Simple Incident") by Sohrâb Shahid-Sâles in 1973, *Qeysar* in 1967 and *Khâk* ("The Earth") in 1973 by Mas'ud Kimiâi; *Toqi* by 'Ali Hâtami in 1969; and *Gharibeh va meh* ("The Stranger and the Fog") by Bahrâm Bayzâi in 1974.

These new films questioned the old cinematic tradition in content, form, and even technique and offered Iranian viewers an alternative cinema. They came to be known as the "New Wave" (*mowj-e now*). The New Wave represented "committed art" which demanded reflection and social responsibility, rather than escapist entertainment where the viewer remains passive and receptive. As was to be expected, their thematic content attracted substantial disfavor from the Iranian censors. What proved controversial was the stark realities they portrayed, often highlighting issues which until that point had been hidden from the public eye. Mo'lâpur's "Mrs. Ahu's Husband," for instance, concerned itself with the issue and implications of polygamy in Iranian society. Some other films which sparked controversy, particularly with the censorship authorities, were Ghaffâri's "The Night of the Hunchback" and Farrokhzâd's "The House is Black." Films categorized in this genre were much less optimistic about the direction of society and often symbolically criticized prevailing cultural norms and policies. They were also considered subversive to the dominant political system and viewed as antiestablishment for challenging, either overtly or covertly, the status quo.

Another feature of some of the New Wave films was their focus on universal issues surpassing national considerations. These films strived to deal with basic human questions and conditions that transcended the Iranian context. That is why some of these films traveled outside of the country, won international awards, and gained international fame for Iranian cinema. Two such films were Mehrjui's "The Cow" and Shahid-Sales' *Tabi'at-e bi-jân* ("Still Life"), made in 1974. Both won prestigious international prizes and became the symbols of New Wave Iranian cinema.

In general, the New Wave movies were regarded as elitist and some had difficulty attracting average Iranians as viewers. Some of these films showed only one or two nights in Tehran, never making it to provincial towns. They attracted many intellectuals and provided fodder for critical commentaries in newspapers but remained financially unsustainable and too culturally sophisticated for the general public. The disparity between the intellectual and lower classes in Iran denied these young filmmakers commercial success and pitted them against critics who viewed them as elitists. Yet, some of them did receive considerable attention in foreign countries. Rahnemâ's "Siâvosh at Persepolis" was one such film. The financial failure of these films discouraged their producers, in turn putting pressure on filmmakers to make films which were more viable financially. In fact, a number of films made in this period combined elements of both artistic and commercial considerations such as *Yârân* ("Comrades") in 1974 and *Mâhi-hâ dar khâk mimirand* ("Fish Die on Ground") in 1976, both by Farzân Delju. By and large, these films were successful in shifting public interests from violence and sex to a more refined and constructive taste. Starting in 1968, public interest in *Film Fârsi* began to decline and some of the new intellectual films began to attract public attention. For instance, Mas'ud Kimiâi's *Qeysar* made a dynamic breakthrough into the domestic film industry by winning both critics' and viewer's attention. Other films which caught the interest of both critics and the public were *Âqâ-ye Hâlu* ("Mr.Simpleton," 1970) *Dâsh Âkol* (1971), and *Gavazn-hâ* ("The Deer," 1974).

The cultural policy adopted by the Pahlavi regime with the onset of the White Revolution in 1963 assumed somewhat of a greater intensity in the late sixties and early seventies. The policy attempted to enforce a homogenization of diverse Iranian ethnic cultures, to depict the monarchy as the best form of government, and to give a positive picture of modern Iran to the international community. Aware of the widespread accessibility to and influence of the many forms of Iranian media, the government encouraged the expansion of cultural centers. By 1965, Tehran had 72 movie theaters, while other provinces had 192. The government also exerted more control over older establishments like the Ministry of Information and the Ministry of Culture and Arts. National Iranian Television (NIT) was transformed to National Iranian Radio and Television (NIRT), expanding its influence into other cultural domains. A large budget was allocated to feature-filmmaking, predominantly in the public sector, with full government control. The NIRT established the College of Television along with a powerful production company named *Telefilm*. The latter was responsible for training young Iranians in the art of filmmaking and finding common ground between the stage theater and film. Tehran University housed the Faculty of Dramatic Arts and the Faculty of Fine Arts.

Expansion of outlets for developing interest and professional expertise in the cinematic arts continued with government initiatives like The Free Cinema of Iran, various festivals featuring films like the annual Shiraz Art Festival, the Educational Festival (1967 onwards), the International Festival of Films for Children and Young Adults (1967), the Free Cinema Film Festival (1970), the National Film Festival (1970), the Tehran International Film Festival (1972) and the Asian Young Film Festival (1974). In 1969, the Center for the Intellectual Development of Children and Young Adults, along with UNESCO, helped with making films for children. A significantly large number of young filmmakers branched away from the established film industry to form an independent collective, called "the New Film Group," while the government actively censored and/or prohibited several Telefilm-NFG productions.

These developments, along with increased activities of New Wave filmmakers led to a historical revival of the country's domestic filmmaking industry—encouraging film critics to speak variously of *sinemâ-ye now* (New Cinema), *sinemâ-ye javân* (Young Cinema), *mowj-e-now* (New Wave), or even *sinemâ-ye demokrâtik* (Democratic Cinema). The foundation of what would emerge later in the postrevolutionary period was put down in this period.

IRANIAN CINEMA AFTER THE REVOLUTION

On August 10, 1978, three men set fire to the Rex Theater in the city of Abâdân, killing 300 people who were trapped inside. At the time, this was widely blamed on agents of the shah's secret police (SAVAK). However, as the country went through the revolutionary turmoil, theater-burning became a common act by Islamic activists for protesting the shah's regime. These incidents set the mood for the national attitude toward cinema in the years following the revolution. During the revolutionary period, close to 200 cinema houses were burned, demolished, or shut down by the revolutionaries who viewed them as "centers of corruption." Immediately after the revolution, the entire film industry virtually came to a complete halt and cinematic development in the country was once again disturbed. The Islamic Revolution aimed to change dramatically the direction of Iranian culture as it had evolved during the Pahlavi period. The impact of a new theocratic government was highly visible on the film industry—an industry so closely tied to Western and modern cultural products. This put the whole industry in jeopardy.

From when the Islamic republic was first established in 1979 until 1982, funds were cut off to the film industry and the government imposed a ban on the screening of new or existing films in the country. During 1980–1983, very few new films were produced in the country because filmmakers were unable to work in an environment of hostility, arbitrary rules, and no financial support. Filmmakers and entertainers were associated with the influences of western culture and corruption of society marked by the shah's government. Many were threatened with legal charges, others were imprisoned, some even executed. With almost no production of new films in the country, the government began to encourage the screening of older films with more traditional values and imported foreign films with morally and politically acceptable themes, namely the struggle of oppressed peoples against colonialism and imperialism. Religious leaders' initial reaction to cinema and theater was, and continues to remain as of this date, ambiguous: some wished to forbid them entirely, some to allow them with tight supervision, and some to use them to the advantage of the new state. Apparently the government saw the potential usefulness of cinema as a tool and, rather than banning the art form altogether, decided to use it as a means of promoting good Islamic values and helping usher in an Islamic culture. Thus, the Islamic Republic set about its mission of creating a strictly ideological cinema. Films, as the new religious leaders viewed them, were a good tool for educating people, especially about moral values. The government encouraged local production by discouraging and reducing the number of films imported. The reduction of municipal taxes on local films was also accompanied by generous long-term bank loans to producers and availability of foreign exchange funds for importing equipment and supplies.

In 1982, the Ministry of Culture and Islamic Guidance was in charge of supervising the film industry. It issued a set of new regulations which would dictate the distribution of exhibition permits needed by films before they could be screened legally. The review involved examination of script, issuance of production and final exhibition permits, and the final assessment of the completed production. New guidelines disallowed portrayal of women without the *hejâb* (veil). They were to be portrayed as modest and chaste women, good mothers, and God-fearing Muslims. Films were to be devoid of sexual scenes, violence, any negative portrayal of Islam or the Islamic government, and any dialogue or interaction deemed "immoral." A film could be refused a permit if it contained any of the following violations: insult to Islam or other recognized religions; insult to the Islamic Republic; encouragement of prostitution, drug addiction or other bad behavior; negation of equality whether based on color, language, or belief; and the depiction of violence or torture.

In the early 1980s, films were made for propagandistic purposes, and nearly no Iranian citizen was interested in seeing them. Yet, as time passed, new rules took effect, and early purges of Iranian actors and actresses ended, the industry searched for a new identity and figured out how to transcend the new restrictions. Directors learned to illustrate controversial subjects by using safer and more symbolic methods. For instance, in one film, a man plays playing with a ring on his finger to hint at an intimate encounter. Therefore, despite a comparatively large number of restrictions put upon cinema, the end result of efforts by Iranian directors and producers was surprisingly positive. Since the focus of film producers was no longer profit-making, Iran's filmmaking improved considerably, gaining popular support and international acclaim. Despite efforts to completely "Islamize" cinema, the revolution sparked, in filmmakers, an innovative spirit which would begin to appear in the next few years as regulations and bans were slightly loosened and resources became available to the industry. Much of this innovation emerged out of the existing confusion and constraint. Because of this continued struggle, however, most films made during the early 1980s failed to reflect the political and ideological climate of Iran. Due to general and ambiguous guidelines, filmmakers often censored themselves almost as much as the government did in an attempt to avoid entanglement.

As the speed of movie production picked up after the revolution, two different kinds of cinema emerged alongside one another: The "Islamic cinema" advancing moral values and the "artist cinema" offering symbolic critique of social conditions under the Islamic government. The Iran-Iraq war (1980–1988) became a major theme of Iranian cinema and spurred an entire film genre referred to as "Sacred Defense" cinema, which would be a prevalent theme for the next eight years. Fiction films produced during the war dealt with fighting and military operations or the war's social and psychological effects. They reflected the problems created by the war, and many featured stories of brave soldiers and martyrs. Unfortunately these early war-era films amounted to little more than propaganda and held little artistic or social value, failing to give a realistic representation of the issues of war. Sacred Defense cinema was as much a spiritual cinema as it was war cinema, meant to build national and ideological support for the government.

Immediately after the revolution, women became the source of most tensions in film-making. In an attempt to move away from the moral corruption of *Film Fârsi* and to create a completely ideological cinema, women all but disappeared from the screen due to the numerous regulations placed on them. Women were treated either as "bad" or "good" based upon their chasteness, but for the most part they were ignored altogether. This initial tendency to ignore women as anything other than complacent housewives also resulted in ignoring many other social problems like domestic violence, prostitution, drug addiction, and infidelity. Many filmmakers avoided stories involving women; female characters were placed in the background as quiet, obedient housewives. They were mostly shown seated to avoid attention on their bodies which were deemed "provocative distractions." In war movies, women were rarely depicted, unless as the mothers or wives of soldiers, and the chief messages were directed at portraying more of a feeling of virtuousness in the face of adversity.

Furthermore, this policy toward women in the film made it very difficult for cinema to be a realistic representation of Iranian society in regards to women and issues surrounding love relationships. Government regulations forbade filmmakers to portray any physical contact between a man and a woman, and women were expected to dress according to the full Islamic dress code at all times, which meant covering nearly every part of her body including hair. This, in particular, took away many realistic aspects of female life in cinema because even during scenes where a woman would normally be unveiled, such as when in bed, she had to remain covered in front of the camera. This insistence on veiling kept female actors from being completely natural in their roles and injected feelings of artificiality into the films. In films involving relationships between men and women, where a situation would normally call for physical interaction, for the purpose of comforting or aiding someone who is hurt, there could be none. Indeed, the regulations went so far as to advise that direct eye contact between a man and a woman should be avoided, as it might be construed as a look of desire.

While most "Sacred Defense" films went unnoticed, several films in the artistic category dealing with the war received wide attention. The first was *Bashu: gharibeh-ye kuchek* ("Bashu: The Little Stranger"), directed by Bahrâm Bayzâi (1988) and produced by the Center for the Intellectual Development of Children and Young Adults. This film not only examined the tensions created by war but also offered a sharp critique of a society in which a young boy loses both his family and his own "self." The second was *'Arusi-ye khubân* ("Marriage of the Blessed"), written and directed by Mohsen Makhmalbâf and produced by the Institute for the Cinematographic Affairs and Jânbâzân Foundation in 1988. This film also depicted the agonies of a war veteran who sees his "revolutionary society" deviating from the Islamic ideals for which he fought. Finally, in the unreleased *Josteju* ("The Search," 1981) Amir Nâderi focused on the authorities' attitude toward soldiers missing-in-action at the beginning of the war.

The end of the war with Iraq and the death of Âyatollâh Khomeini marked the end of Iran's revolutionary period and a new phase of "reconstruction" began. The new government, headed by President 'Ali-Akbar Rafsanjâni, felt that ideological values had been adequately infused and wanted to boost morale by allowing more room for cultural discussion. It relaxed restrictions on cultural products and allowed the screening of some previously banned films. Also, the Ministry of Culture and Islamic Guidance introduced a new rating system which increased the revenue received by producers by allowing them to screen highly rated films in more upscale theaters. As a result, the quality and quantity of films produced in Iran due to measures taken by the government increased. But these policies were opposed by conservative clerics and their followers. The press, cinema, and music industry became arenas where the conservative, liberal, and radical political factions flexed their muscles. Conservatives were able to force the relatively liberal cleric Mohammad Khâtami to resign from his position as the Minister of Culture and Islamic Guidance in 1992. The new minister appointed was an ultra-conservative. The Islamic codes were again strictly reinforced, and many films which would have been allowed previously were banned.

Protesting the new restrictions, 134 Iranian writers wrote a letter demanding that the government relax censorship of the press and cultural products—a letter which brought severe hardships to its signatories. A month later, two hundred film directors and actors published another public letter in which they requested an end to government control of the Iranian motion picture industry. The response from conservatives was entirely negative. The clergy, the Parliament, the judiciary, and the Council of Guardians escalated the cultural offensive. From late 1994 through mid-1997, Iran witnessed the most repressive campaign since the 1979 revolutionary upheaval. For instance, in 1996, virtually none of the 1500 fiction manuscripts and screenplays under review in the Ministry of Culture and Islamic Guidance received approval. Instead, new rules were enforced, including no use of makeup, no women running, and no antagonists with the name of a sacred Islamic figure—such as Mohammad, 'Ali, Hasan, or Hosayn. Violations of these rules resulted not only in censorship, but also in outrage and attack by religious vigilantes. For example, Hezbollâhi militants attacked two movie theaters in Tehran because they were showing *Tohfeh-ye Hend* ("Present from India"), a popular comedy in which an Iranian merchant married an Indian woman. What sparked the violence were the joyous wedding scenes, including a four-minute segment showing little girls dancing. The attack ignited a panic—and then a stampede in which several moviegoers were trampled underfoot and a pregnant woman was pushed down the stairs. The protest amounted to a warning, the local press reported, about the government's "negligence" in issuing permits for the movie to be made and then screened. The Ministry of Culture and Islamic Guidance resolved the issue by censoring that four-minute segment of the movie and forcing the director to re-cut the film.

All that changed with the election of Khâtami as president in May 1997. Immediately, Khâtami declared his intention to allow a freer cultural environment by removing many of the past restrictions. He appointed 'Atâollâh Mohâjerâni to reform the Ministry of Culture and Islamic Guidance. Upon his appointment, Mohâjerâni openly declared his intention to strengthen national movie industry without putting restrictions on the import of foreign movies. He lifted the ban on previously banned movies, signaling that the past restrictive measures were not going to be exercised anymore.

The film that benefited the most from this measure was *Âdam barfi* ("The Snowman") which had been deemed "un-Islamic" because of one segment in which the male protagonist pretends to be a woman in order to marry an American man in hopes of obtaining a visa to America. In 1995, the Ministry of Culture and Islamic Guidance had banned the movie indefinitely. When it was able to be screened in Iran, "The Snowman" made far more money than any other movie that year, and the main actor, Akbar 'Abdi, was nominated for the best actor in an Iranian version of the Oscar. However, conservatives again created problems because they did not approve of the film being shown. On the day it was to premiere in Isfahan, militant Hezbollâhis attacked the local theater, destroyed posters, and threatened people lined up for the show. The theater shut down as a result. Nevertheless, promoters of the film persevered, and it was shown in November 1997 in 22 other cities in Iran.

Social criticism began to rise to the surface, posing questions regarding the hold of the Islamic regime over society. Intellectual debate was spurred over religion, modernity, and development. The overall liberalization policies that began in the late 1980s, and ebbed and flowed over the next decade and a half, led to a shift of themes in cinema and an increase in production of the films. Furthermore, despite its indirect attempts to encourage domestic film production, the government found itself directly involved in film production to keep the industry afloat. In 1987, over a third of films produced were funded by the government supported agencies. The government-run Fârâbi Cinema Foundation became a major financial supporter, distributor, and promoter of Iranian movies.

After the war with Iraq, the themes used in Iranian films began to change: from war, revolution, and morality to love, adventure, children, poverty, freedom, and gender discrimination. Women's voices began to be heard, especially those who had suffered economic distress during the war. After losing the men in their family, many women were forced to become the sole source of income for their family. So, as women's role in society began to change, the need for accurate portrayal became more apparent. To combat this misrepresentation, women began seeking creative control behind the camera, trying to prove that it is possible to portray women in a realistic light and still be in line with morality codes. Several female Iranian filmmakers began to make themselves known in the late eighties and early nineties. As a result, women's issues have become a major theme in recent Iranian cinema, and interest in them has even spread to male directors who have been persuaded to reevaluate their own portrayals of women. Once female filmmakers became known, films with better and more diverse representations of women began to appear. The nineties saw the emergence of more dynamic female roles from the screen. Films such as Rakhshân Bani-E'temâd's *Banu-ye Ordibehesht* ("The May Lady," 1998) and Tahmineh Milâni's *Do zan* ("Two Women," 1999) challenge the society's standards for women by presenting women as dominant characters, faced with difficult situations involving relationships.

When explicit critique of the human condition remained out of reach, and so determined was the will of the government to keep cinema keenly focused on ideological values that adults could not be portrayed in any manner which could be equated to real life, Iranian filmmakers began to use children as the main characters. This allowed filmmakers to evade the censors and go places where adults could not. Drawing on a popular saying that "truth can be heard from children," they cast children to explore facets of everyday life. Several internationally celebrated examples of such films include: 'Abbâs Kiârostami's *Khaneh-ye dust kojast?* ("Where Is the Friend's House?," 1987) and *Mashq-e shab* ("Homework," 1988); Bayzâi's "Bashu, the Little Stranger"; Samira Makhmalbâf's *Sib* ("The Apple," 1988); 'Ali-Rezâ Dâvudnezhâd's *Niyâz* ("The Need," 1992); Ja'far Panâhi's *Bâdkonak-e safid* ("The White Balloon," 1995) and *Âyeneh* ("The Mirror," 1997); and Majid Majidi's *Bahcheh-hâ-ye âsman* ("Children of Heaven," 1997) and *Rang-e Khodâ* ("The Color of Paradise," 1999).

The relationship between children and adults in these films is used to represent Iranians themselves. Many filmmakers may use the idea of power wielded over children by strong adult figures to portray the constraints placed on Iranian society. In this way, children bear a lot of the weight of societal issues which cannot be expressed through adults, and in many films they are portrayed as wiser and very mature. The use of children to portray Iranian society brought about a different kind of realism in Iranian cinema. This kind of cinema tends to focus on reality rather than fantasy, and to that end, many directors use untrained children to give their films a natural quality. Children see and take in the world differently than adults. They are viewed as completely innocent, sexless, and void of the cynicism and corruption seen in adults. In this way, children are capable of portraying platonic love. Their presence in front of the camera is more real and more natural.

In the 1990s, Iranian cinema moved in two directions: back to *Film Fârsi* and a resurgent New Wave. Ironically, the two are closely related and move in the opposite direction of each other. The New Wave films produced in Iran by filmmakers like Kiârostami, Makhmalbâf, and Panâhi do very well abroad but very poorly in the local market. As opposed to this trend, there is a resurgence of *Film Fârsi* after the revolution too. These are action films replete with violence and adventure. What differentiates post-revolutionary *Film Fârsi* from the prerevolutionary one is the replacement of sex with an overabundance of violence. These films generally do much better in local markets, especially in provincial cities.

Nevertheless, the Iranian cinema has been under the international spotlight in the past decade, gaining the attention and praise of film festivals and critics—a movement which gained momentum with Kiârostami's success at the Cannes Film Festival, as he won the "Palme d'Or" for *Ta'm-e gilâs* ("The Taste of Cherry") in 1997. Kiârostami, in fact, has had an enabling role in the current New Wave because several of the new awardees are either his students, or have worked on his scripts, or have been inspired by his style. Since 1995, Iranian films have garnered hundreds of international awards at Cannes and other festivals around the world. They have won in many fields: best picture, best foreign film, best director, best script, best actor, best documentary, and best short film. Since then, Iranian cinematographers have become a regular feature of jury in international festivals. Critics rank Iran as the world's most important artistic national cinema, producing works comparable to Italian neo-realism.

Although Iranian cinema has, by now, become a global phenomenon, Iranian filmmakers still battle with government censorship. Their success had come through negotiation and innovation in the midst of ambiguity and conflict. Surrounded by all these confusing regulations and societal taboos, filmmakers have had to find new and creative ways of getting their messages across, of saying what they want to say without angering the censors. The experience has proved to be a learning process for both the artists and the Islamic government about how to allow freedom of expression to flourish within a theocracy. That makes Iranian cinema what it is: a cinema of subtlety and suggestion, giving rise to multiple interpretations and wide imagination; a cinema now grounded in the aesthetics of simplicity, modesty, social contradictions, and humanistic language.

MODERN DRAMA

The development of drama in Iran, like cinema, is intertwined with and influenced by the political and economic developments in the country. Since cultural and political policies often applied to both of these arts, and had similar consequences for both, the following is a brief presentation of the history and nature of drama in Iran.

Modern drama in Iran began in the late 19th century when Iranians educated in the Western countries came back home, translated Western plays into Persian, and promoted modern arts. A series of plays, written by Iranian intellectuals at the time, came to set the tone for thematic of modern drama. For instance, plays written by Mirzâ Fath-'Ali Âkhundzâdeh in Turkish and published in the Caucasus stimulated Mirzâ Âqâ Tabrizi to write several plays in the 1870s. As was the case at the time, most intellectuals were concerned with the backwardness of Iranian society and the despotic rule of the Qâjârs. These themes filled the plays written at the time and strengthened the "critical" aspect of traditional Iranian dramatic expressions. Drama became a medium of social criticism and satire. The most distinguished playwrights of the time included Mortazâqoli Khân Fekri Ershâd Moayyad-ol-Mamâlek, Ahmad Mahmudi Kamâl-ol-Wozarâ, Mirzâdeh 'Eshqi, and Abo'l-Hasan Forughi.

As discussed in the case of cinema, Rezâ Shah's ascendance to power was accompanied by his desire to modernize the country; thus his support for modern theater. However, his support was conditioned by his intolerance of any criticism of the regime. Plays glorifying pre-Islamic culture, supporting the shah's modernization plans, promoting nationalism, and critical of traditional superstitious aspects of the culture received support and encouragement from the government. Several examples of this genre include: Sa'id Nafisi's *Âkherin yâdgâr-e Nâder Shâh* ("The Last Memento of Nâder Shah," 1926) about the glorious memories of victory by an old Iranian soldier who had been in Nâder Shah's army during the war with Russia; Hasan Moqaddam's popular comic *Ja'far Khân az Farang âmadeh* ("Ja'far Khân Returns from Europe," 1922) dealing with confusions arising from encounters between Iranian and European cultures; Zabih Behruz's *Jijak 'Alishâh* (1923); and Sâdeq Hedayat's *Parvin, dokhtar-e Sâsân* ("Parvin, Daughter of Sâsân," 1930).

The "Spring of Freedom," as the period after Rezâ Shah's abdication in 1941 was called, saw a revival of drama in Iran. Various political parties and groups used this medium as an instrument for furthering their cause. The most successful effort in this regard was that of 'Abd-ol-Hosayn Nushin, who had graduated from the Conservatoire de Toulouse and was an active member of the communist Tudeh Party. In 1947, Nushin brought a number of professional actors together to stage modern dramas in Ferdowsi Theater in Tehran. In 1948, Nushin was arrested for his political activities and the Tudeh Party was outlawed. However, his colleagues opened Sa'di Theater in 1951 and continued to stage Western plays translated into Persian. The 1953 coup d'etat against Mosaddeq resulted in the burning of the Sa'di Theater and the imprisonment of some of its actors. But none of this could stop political-protest drama in Iran. Over the next decade, when Iranian authorities censored any serious drama with political overtones, the bulk of works translated, adapted, and staged from Western playwrights consisted of critical drama. The role of the Tudeh Party in the 1940s and Iranian leftist intellectuals in the 1950s and

1960s cannot be overstated. The German Communist playwright Bertolt Brecht was one of the strongest Western influences on Iranian dramatists prior to the revolution.

The return of Mohammad-Rezâ Shah to Iran in 1953 resulted in stricter censorship, thus forcing Iranian dramatists to focus more on techniques than content. By the end of the decade, a number of theaters opened and numerous efforts were made for promoting drama. Yet, two major factors slowed those efforts: censorship and the emergence of *Film Fârsi*. As urbanization grew and people became more familiar with the modern communication medium, cinema was a much cheaper and more accessible venue for entertainment than theater.

In the 1960s, Iranian drama had an experience similar to Iranian cinema: the arrival of a young generation of Iranian graduates from America and Europe with training in new cinema and theater. Under the influence of these young playwrights, Iranian drama developed a character of its own. Dramatists staged both foreign and native works. Works of major foreign playwrights, both modern and classical, were translated to Persian and staged. Given the political sensitivities of the authorities to plays with social themes, both classic and modern Western works were easier to stage and in fact many of them were staged by some of the most able Iranian directors. Numerous theater halls opened up in Tehran and other major cities. Even smaller towns lacking theater halls began staging drama in facilities adaptable to occasional performances. Aside from academic departments established for teaching drama in major universities, some high schools encouraged students to develop "drama clubs" for writing, performing, and staging. The decade of the 1970s was one of the most productive periods of drama during the Pahlavi period. Some of the most able and enduring names in Iranian drama performance and directorship started their career in this period. Many are still performing in Iran, even though some have retired and some others have passed away.

It is important to note that as the artistic and political dramas increased, the older popular dramas receded to Lâlehzâr, the street in the middle of Tehran where both cinemas and theaters existed. Viewers and audiences at Lâlehzâr were mostly working class and peasant migrants who choose theater purely as an entertainment. Dramas produced in these theaters were often farcical comedies which contained a subtle social criticism or moral tone. Two of the most popular actors in the history of Iranian comedy, who started and continued their careers in this type of drama, were Nosratollâh Vahdat and Esmâ'il Arhâm Sadr—both later drawn to cinema as well. Tapes of their comedies are still played in private homes, despite the government's negative view of their works. "Lâlehzâri Drama" was a negative label used by New

Wave critics and audiences to refer to these farcical dramas produced for pure entertainment.

A major force in the development of drama in this period was the government. The Ministry of Culture and Arts, the Faculty of Fine Arts at Tehran University, and the Iranian National Television all established special school, workshop, or festival for drama. Beginning in 1967 the government also sponsored an Arts Festival in the city of Shiraz in order to promote Iranian drama to world community. As the Festival gained more popularity, it attracted avant-garde artists and dramatists. Many Iranian dramatists also renewed traditional forms in newer styles. Nevertheless, all these developments were overshadowed by the continutation of censorship by government authorities and by the harsh treatment of politically motivated artists. Works of several playwrights were banned, and plays that were staged were closed if they generated unexpected stirs in society.

Confronted with this ambivalent attitude, just as in cinema, Iranian dramatists developed a shared language, symbolism, and metaphors for themselves. As the language of these dramas become more symbolic and sophisticated, the Iranian theater lost its appeal to commoners and soon became an exclusive domain attended by an educated, and often politically motivated, elite. Exceptions to this were a few plays whose success encouraged their directors to seek a broader audience in cinema. Still, there were dramatists who followed the realist tradition and blended their new ideas and techniques with traditional forms and themes. For instance, 'Ali Nasiriân's *Bongâh-e te'âtrâl* ("The Theatrical Agency," 1978) was an adaptation of traditional *ruhowzi*. Bijan Mofid's *Shahr-e qesseh* ("City of Tales," 1969), was a satirical portrait of a hypocritical religious cleric presented in a musical form. This was one of the most popular Iranian plays of all times, running for seven years in Tehran before the revolution, and for a while afterward it was broadcast by its admirers from the rooftops of their homes in Tehran in protest against religious leaders. In general, the decade of the 1970s was one of the most productive in the history of Iranian drama.

Toward the end of the Pahlavi era, there was a short period of openness which preceded the revolution and lasted about a year afterward until the establishment of the Islamic Republic. During this period, dramatists became responsive to the mood of the time and staged a number of politically motivated plays with much more direct language. Two such dramas were Mahmud Rahbar's *Qânun* ("The Law," 1977) about the abusive and corrupt policies of the government and Farâmarz Tâlebi's *Pâdegân dar shâmgâh* ("The Barracks in the Evening," 1977) which questioned the government's recruitment of young villagers for confronting political demonstrators. A more interesting and daring project was Sa'id Soltânpur's *'Abbâs Âqâ, kârgar-e Irân Nâsiyonâl*

("Abbâs Âqâ, a Worker for the National Iranian [Oil Company]), which was staged in the streets.

This period was short lived. Before long, restrictions imposed by the new Islamic government led to a period of decline in drama, accompanied by imprisonment of some political dramatists, forceful retirement or exile of some others. Sa'id Soltânpur was executed for his political activism, Gholâm-Hosayn Sâ'edi, Parviz Sayyâd, Parviz Kardân, Bijan and Bahman Mofid, as well as most actors and actresses, had to flee the country to avoid persecution for their allegedly "corrupt" past writings and performances. With the start of the war with Iraq, the country went into a mood of depression and established dramatists had to either quit or continue their work in an "Islamic" manner—something they had to learn.

Ironically, the Islamic Republic found performing arts to be an important tool for propaganda. The Ministry of Culture and Islamic Guidance provided various forms of support for dramatists who were willing to work within the confines of new rules. Young and inexperienced dramatists with Islamic credentials took the stage, while the older and more experienced dramatists waited for a better working environment. As the decade proceeded and rules became clear, the older dramatists began producing works, albeit commensurate to new rules. The 1980s became a transitional period during which dramatists became more cautious, conventional storytelling techniques became more popular, and the experimentations of the previous decade came to an end. *Ta'ziyeh,* which had been losing popularity, became important again as a useful means of promoting religious, moral, and national values. The tropes of the *ta'ziyeh* were now employed in a variety of dramas and even cinema. This was not done just by Islamic-minded dramatists and filmmakers. The secular filmmaker and dramatist Bahram Bayzâi utilized this type of drama in his *Cherikeh-ye Târâ* ("Guerilla from Târâ," 1978) and *Mosâferân* ("Travelers," 1992). Recently 'Abbâs Kiârostami staged a newly-styled *ta'ziyeh* presentation in Europe as well.

As was the case with cinema, the liberalization policies of the 1990s helped artists find creative ways to express themselves while abiding by the rules. Works produced in the past 15 years can be classified into two types, Islamic and secular. Works produced by Islamic dramatists use drama as a means of promoting religious and moral causes. For instance, Hamid-Rezâ A'zam's *Shegerd-e âkhar* ("The Last Technique," 1989) utilizes the traditional *naqqâli* technique to recount the bravery of the youth who fought in the war against Iraq. The secular works are those whose concerns remain social criticism and have a veiled antiestablishment tone. These works are produced either by older dramatists who are still living in the country or the new generation of secular artists trained after the revolution. Some of these still follow the course of development established prior to the revolution. Bayzâi and Akbar Râdi are two of the earlier dramatists who are active and produce new works. Some of the older actors and actresses, like Mahin Oskui, 'Ezzatollâh Entezâmi, 'Ali Nasiriân, Pari Sâberi, and Jamshid Mashâyekhi, are still working and have adjusted themselves to the new restrictions.

Iranian drama has thus become more varied in its styles of expression. Some dramatists continue to follow the traditional style, and others have remained loyal to the New Wave traditions of the 1960s and 1970s. Alongside urban modern drama, traditional folk drama continues to be performed in rural towns, village fairs, and various national holidays. Recently, the younger graduates of Iranian universities are experimenting with a variety of contemporary theatrical theories and forms. Many have tried using a less text-oriented genre and rely on a combination of performing arts such as dance, music, and storytelling. Women now have been incorporated into new plays, albeit fully but creatively covered.

Today, as in the past, the major force behind the established theater in Iran remains the government. The Ministry of Culture and Islamic Guidance has commissioned the Dramatic Arts Center to represent the performing arts on the national and international levels by organizing annual festivals and tours for performances, developing guidelines for state financial and technical assistance to theater, supporting drama schools and groups in the country. The annual Fajr Festival, widely attended by both national and international artists, has become a major vehicle for promotion of drama in the country. Although government grants remain significant for major productions, the majority of over 140 drama groups listed on the main webpage for Iranian theater (www.theater.ir) are nonprofit, and their members support themselves with jobs other than drama. To support dramatists, a new "House of Theatre" was established recently. There are now numerous journals, newsletters, and Web pages dedicated to information about Iranian drama and dramatists.

5

Architecture

Iran has a rich and varied architectural history going back over 3,000 years, and the remains of Iranian architectural monuments can be found from Syria to India and China. Iranian architecture make uses of a great variety of techniques such as stone carving, stucco and plasterwork, tile and brickwork, mirror and glasswork, and other ornamental elements. As in any architecture, geographical, religious, political, technological, and natural factors determine the quality and quantity of architecture. Many of the diverse architectural designs and structures in Iranian lands resulted from the availability of suitable natural resources and consideration of factors such as climate. The landscape itself is a source of both constraint and freedom. The Iranian *kavir* (desert) imposed enormous limitations on the structural designs and the kind of buildings Iranian architects could produce. However, the challenge of working with the vast tracts of desert land has offered Iranian architects the chance to be creative with both their designs and responses to societal needs. Another important variable shaping architectural characteristics is the technological knowledge and skills available in the region. Some good examples of responses to these technological and environmental challengse are the Iranian *bâdgirs* (wind-catcher towers), *qanâts* (underground water channels), and *âb-anbârs* (water reservoirs).

Since much of Iran is desert, Iranian cities and towns were confronted with the challenge of dealing with water shortages, high levels of heat, and at times strong winds. Given the limited resources available to builders in these towns, building materials consisted mainly of mud and its derivatives. Mud and mortar excavated from construction sites are often used for buildings, thus creating a modicum of self-sufficiency. Baked or unbaked bricks and mud effectively resist the incessant rays of the sun in the hot summer months. During the cold season, little heat is used for warming the interiors because hardened, unbaked brick walls act as good insulation. Buildings are often constructed with tall walls, arched roofs, water reservoirs with arched domes, and air traps or wind catchers. Residential structures often are positioned at a specific angle to collect maximum heat and allow for winds to bring cooler air into the structure.

The *bâdgir* ("wind-catcher tower") was an architectural innovation to capture cool air in a desert environment. These towers were set at a specific height on the roof of a building to capture a breeze and transfer it underground within the structure in order to bring cool air into large rooms and halls in the hot days of the season. *Bâdgirs* served as ventilators using wind energy to operate. They were placed on a part of the structure where they could collect maximum air flow. Ducts were located at the four corners to capture the wind from any direction. When capturing wind from one direction, ducts in the other three directions would be closed. Some *bâdgirs* had an arched roof that absorbed heat from the strong sunshine during the day and radiated it back more quickly at night. In this way, *bâdgirs* worked as simple air conditioners in arid and dry regions. In some houses, a water reservoir was built underground, and the air from the *bâdgir* was routed to it to cool the water in the reservoir. The impact from the airflow would also stir the water and prevent stagnation.

Another necessity of desert living was controlling water distribution in very high temperatures. Iranians were among the first to construct underground water systems. They also constructed dams, canals, bridges, and means for adequately distributing the water to both residential and agricultural areas. A number of these dams, bridges, and water canals from earlier times are still found in Iran. The city of Isfahan has the most magnificent bridges built over the Zâyandeh Rud, a river dividing the city into south and north, with 12 bridges from the Sasanid through Safavid periods crossing it. The oldest of these bridges is the Shahrestân from the Sasanid period. The Allâhverdi Khân bridge is a 1181-foot long, 46-foot wide bridge with 33 spans built in A.D. 1602 The Khâju Bridge, in two stories and with a 438-foot length and 40-foot width, is a dual-function structure built during the reign of Shah 'Abbâs II (1642–1666) in order to serve as both a bridge and a dam. Wide and thick timbers were used to change its function from one to the other. The second floor of the bridge included fantastic pavilions decorated with stucco carvings and inscriptions. The main parlor was often used for royal receptions and national festivals.

Underground water reservoirs, called *âb-anbârs*, were used (occasionally in conjunction with a *bâdgir)* to help cool water. These reservoirs were built deep underground and often covered by a domelike roof with a few ducts. Water was transferred from *qanâts* and used for various purposes in the house. The city of Yazd, located in the middle of the Iranian desert, is known to have hundreds of these *âb-anbârs*. Another structure used in conjunction with water reservoirs was the traditional icehouse (*yakhchâl*). The icehouse took advantage of cold temperatures at night temperature or in winter to transform water into ice. The icehouse was typically a big pit about 35–50 feet deep along with several shallow rectangular water lagoons. Walls of different heights were built around the lagoons to allow for freezing and to keep out the sunlight. Once the ice was formed, it was cut into manageable pieces and transferred to the underground storage place.

Aside from environmental and technological factors influencing the relationships between people, environmental resources, and various forms of constructions, sociological variables affected Iranian architecture. Many distinctive features of Iranian architecture are determined by cultural variables, including a desire for security, religious considerations, and attitudes towards private and public life. The distinct qualities of Iranian architecture separate it from arts produced by culturally different people in the same territorial environment. Certain design elements have persisted throughout the history of Iranian architecture: extensive decorations, the high-arched portal set within a recess, columns with bracket capitals, columned porches (*tâlârs*), domes on arches, networked courts, interior courts with a pool, and tall towers.

Three elements defined the archetypal traditional Iranian house: energy, space, and boundary. Energy determined the utilization of various units of space (a room or special hall) at different times for generating flow and interaction. The space in these houses was flexibly defined and could be redefined to suit new needs. The boundary established the relationships between people inside the house and protected them against the outside world. The space connected different units of the interior. Given the numerous attacks on Iran in the course of history, and the existence of nomadic populations moving around all the time, even cities felt insecure to leave themselves exposed. Many cities had a large surrounding wall, thus turning these cities into fortified communities. The best example is the city walls of Yazd, which historically has served as a shelter for Persian imperial dynasties holding out against the Arab, Saljuq, Mongol, Timurid, Safavid, and Afghan invasions of Iran.

Religious life also has been a main inspiration behind much of Iranian architecture throughout its history. The Zoroastrian emphasis on light as a source of beauty and clarity continued to exert influence even in the Islamic period. The Arab invasion in the seventh century and Islamic culture influenced Iranian architecture and gradually affected the native structures. Islam limits interactions between men and women who are not related to each other and demands much more privacy from women than other religions. This restriction has had an impact on Iranian architectural design, city planning, and housing plans. Since families had to keep female members out of public view, Iranian houses are all walled and not easily accessible to passersby. The internal dispositions of houses convey a sense of being more inward looking. From an architectural perspective, most buildings in the more traditional cities like Yazd and Natanz represent a form of contained and closed space. What separates a house from the outside is a wooden, or today metal, door lacking any glass or see-through material. The door secures the inside from the outside. This inward-looking attitude has also affected the exterior of housing, especially prior to modern housing in the twentieth century. The exterior architectural design does not reflect the sophistication and crafts-manship applied to the interior. The quality of artwork on the door and its entrance were the only visible markers of social class observable from the outside. Much of the artwork and design are visible in the interior and the courtyard (*hayât*).

The *hayât* is an important buffer zone separating the interior space from the outside world and also providing resources not deemed appropriate in the interior. These resources included water and washing facilities, which traditionally were often kept on the opposite side of rooms in the yard. At the center of *hayât*, there was always a small pool called *howz*, surrounded with flowers, grape vines, and trees, especially pomegranates and figs. The *hayât* also served as a transitional stage for entering or departing the house. Rooms never opened directly onto the street or public arena—a phenom-enon rarely observed in current apartment buildings. Houses had a small enclosed transitional space called *hashti*, which itself directed into a hallway (*dâlân vorudi*). The internal space was set up to accommodate different daily and nightly activities, gender relationships, various religious and cultural ritu-als, and functional situations. Balance, symmetry, harmony, symbolism, and rhymes were important elements of interior design in the housing structures. Rooms were designed in such a way that they would angle toward Mecca, the direction Muslims face when praying. The interior of houses were also subject to cultural variables such as status hierarchy and a collectivist culture, which did not allow for much privacy. Traditional homes of the affluent con-tained rooms that often opened to each other and did not allow for the kind of privacy found in modern Western housing. The influence of this collectiv-ist attitude is also found in the act of building itself. Construction of housing in rural areas has been a communal effort that enhances the community's solidarity.

Two other factors have played a decisive role in the development of archi-tecture in different periods of Iranian history. Depending on their social, political, religious, and financial status, patrons made special demands reflecting their priorities. Religious patrons demanded religious motifs; the political elite were more interested in motifs of grandeur; some female patrons showed interest in reflecting women's concerns in both the decorative arts and structural designs. Religious endowments and charities led to the construction of mosques, mausoleums, cemeteries, religious halls (*takiyeh*), cisterns (*âb-anbâr*), and other public facilities. By their nature and support, these resources contributed to the cohesive structure of communities (*mahaleh*) within the city. Another factor contributing to the cohesiveness of these communities was their functional separation. Traditional Iranian cities separated residential quarters from commercial centers (bazaar and caravansaries) and public squares (*maydân*s). Religious and often ethnic minorities each lived in their own quarters. These quarters were named accordingly (such as *mahaleh-e tork-hâ*, meaning "Turkish neighborhood" or *mahaleh-e arâmaneh*, meaning "Armenian neighborhood"). All cities contained a bazaar, a grand mosque (*masjed-e jâme'*), and a citadel (*arg*). Traditional cities did not divide along class lines. Rich and poor were mixed in traditional neighborhoods. The separation of affluent neighborhoods from slums in the city, the north-south divide, and other economic divisions are all products of modernization and the introduction of Western economic relationships.

The bazaar, as the center of commercial and civic life, was a key feature of urban life in Iran and the Islamic world in general. Bazaars were built in the heart of the city and housed many public facilities such as mosques, baths, and caravanserais for both city dwellers as well as tourists. Major cities like Tehran, Isfahan, Shiraz, Tabriz, Yazd, and Mashhad have well-known and frequently visited bazaars. Smaller towns also have bazaars as the center of economic activities. The architectural design of these bazaars was no simple matter as most were domed and covered large expanses of shops and other public facilities.

Finally, it should be noted that aside from the recent Western influence on Iranian architecture (to be discussed later in this chapter), even traditional architecture has been influenced by foreign styles, either those of neighboring countries or of those of peoples that invaded and dominated Iranian society. Iranian builders and designers, though maintaining their cultural and national identity, often looked outside of their borders to enhance the horizon, scope, and richness of their work. However, Iranian architecture often absorbed those foreign elements while remaining true to its originality and beauty. Though influenced by Arab, Mongol, Turkish, Chinese, and central Asian cultures, the unique architectural style developed in Iranian society is the result of thousands of years of work by master artists and architects who were inspired by faith, national pride, and original creativity.

To have a better understanding of the diversity and richness of Iranian architecture, it is appropriate to describe its evolution during distinct historical periods. For the purpose of this chapter, we will present Iranian architecture in three periods: pre-Islamic (to the seventh century A.D.), Islamic (to the end of the nineteenth century), and contemporary (twentieth century). What follows is not a comprehensive survey of building and construction styles but a brief description of architectural developments across the wide region historically known as Iran. It should be mentioned that much of what is being described concerns settled life, not that of the nomads who were also a part of this stretch of land and found among ethnically diverse groups and lifestyles. Nomadic abodes were varied and often depended on the ecological system in which nomads lived. Available resources for nomadic constructions were often few, and the nomadic life style did not allow for accumulation of many goods and permanent settlement. Materials produced for constructing their tents were easy to pack, yet delicate and full of decorative elements, demonstrating a creative and self-generative culture.

IRANIAN ARCHITECTURE IN THE PRE-ISLAMIC PERIOD

Examples of prehistoric and pre-Islamic architecture are found in ancient huts, remnants of old towns and villages, fortresses, temples and fire temples, mausoleums and palaces, dams and bridges, bazaars, highways and roads, towers and outposts, garden pavilions, and monuments. The earliest forms of architecture known in Iran include peasant huts and farming hamlets. These structures were made of mud bricks and mortar and featured painted walls. From the fifth millennium B.C., handmade bricks instead of wood were used to make huts.

One of the earliest examples of prehistoric architecture can be found at Zâgheh Tepe, a building complex from the late seventh and early sixth millennium B.C., in the environs of what is now Qazvin. The Zâgheh Tepe, consisting of a fireplace, two storerooms, and a living room with decorated and red painted walls, was probably used for social and religious gatherings. Another prehistoric remnant of this period is Tepe Sialk, built in the late sixth or early fifth millennium B.C., near what is now the city of Kâshân. It is believed that the oval-shaped houses built from handmade sun-dried mud brick in this settlement represent the first rudimentary housing techniques used by humans at the time. Several other significant excavated sites of this period are Tepe Hasan near Dâmghân, Tell-e Iblis near Kermân, and Tepe Hasanlu in western Azerbaijan. The last of these preserves the earliest structure in which wood was used as a supporting column.

Between the thirteenth and eighth centuries B.C., many wooden towers featuring entrance gates, paved courtyards, rooms, and nooks were constructed. Cone mosaics and colored and glazed bricks were used in huge ziggurats such as the marvelous five-storied Chogâ Zanbil temple, constructed by the order of an Elamite king, on the bank of the Karkheh river ca. 1250 B.C. This monument had such an imposing dimension and superior quality of construction that its reconstructed remnants reflect a magnificent historical monument. A novelty in this structure is the construction of a portable water system used for both worshipers and the people of the city. Architecture during the time of the Medes, the first Iranian kingdom, established in the eighth century B.C., was extremely well planned and constructed. Ecbatana, the capital of the Medes, was one of the earliest towns in Iran built based on planning and what can be considered at the time as urban principles. Another structure of importance in this period is the two-story royal palace of the Median kings at Ecbatana, surrounded by fortifications and towers. Stone-carving art found in later Achaemenid architecture seem to have its roots in this Median period.

The Achaemenid period (ca. 550–330 B.C.) offered the first great era and the richest collection of architectural works to the pre-Islamic Iranian history. Stretching from the Indus River in India to the Nile River in Egypt, from the Danube in Europe to central Asia, this vast empire produced huge gray and slender stone palaces, mausoleums, and fire-temples, some of which have survived and are among the most attractive tourist sites in Iran and the neighboring countries. Persepolis, an impressive complex of palaces, was planned by Darius, not only as the seat of his government but also to showcase imperial receptions and festivals. Columns, reliefs, terraces, stone towers and pedestals, and pediments typified the architecture in this period. Glazed bricks in blue, white, yellow, and green with animals and floral ornaments in palaces with large halls represented a somewhat new development in Iranian architecture and are indicative of a high-level of skill. The Achaemenids made full use of known technologies and the materials available in their environment. By using long Lebanese cedar beams instead of stone lintels, they achieved greater height with the fewer and thinner stone columns.

The Pasargadae palace in Shiraz—built during the reign of Cyrus the Great (ca. 550–530 B.C.)—and majestic Persepolis, also near Shiraz and begun during the reign of Darius I (522–486 B.C.), have come to represent the identity of pre-Islamic Persian architecture and even non-Islamic Iranian national identity. Persepolis is so vast and so rich that it took some 100 years to be completed. The Palace of Xerxes, the Palace of Darius I, the Treasury, the Hall of a Hundred Columns, the Apadana Palace (with a large terrace of 37 columns, each 72 feet high), and the Throne Hall of Xerxes are among the most majestic structures at Persepolis. The "Gate of All Nations" was the venue through which the representatives of different Iranian nations passed in order to reach the audience hall. The latter was completely destroyed by Alexander in 330 B.C. The magnificent Persepolis complex served successive Achaemenid kings a venue where vassal states would come for their annual tribute to the king during the celebration of the spring equinox. The tomb of Cyrus the Great, located in the south of Pasargadae, is a respected national shrine for many Iranians. It is a stepped platform surmounted by a peak-roofed structure. The building used whitish limestone and was built by artists from Media, Egypt, and Lydia.

Following the victory of Alexander the Great over the Persian army in 331 B.C. and the death of Darius III, the Iranian Empire came under Alexander's control. In 330 B.C., Alexander looted Persepolis and carried away many of its treasures. The Seleucids, who succeeded Alexander the Great, were very much under the influence of Hellenistic designs, and they mixed these designs with Iranian forms. Greek geometric designs were used in the construction of some cities and monuments. The Parthians (ca. 238 B.C.–A.D.224) succeeded the Seleucids and gradually began to move away from Greek designs. Parthian architecture had several unique features, including prominent use of a form known as ogee to Europeans, the emergence of the element of *ayvân* (an audience hall leading to a domed chamber), extensive use of cut stones and stucco for making walls and ceilings, and the common use of the vaulting technique with mud and fired bricks. Parthian reliefs still exist at Bisotun and Susa. Also, the oldest known Iranian tower, Mil-e Ajdahâ, was constructed at what is now Nurâbâd in the Mamasani district of Fârs province during the Parthian period. At the time, this tower served as a guidepost for caravans traveling through the territories. Later, such towers became common as guideposts for cities, towns, caravanserais, and lighthouses in coastal areas.

The Sasanids, who followed the Parthians, remained faithful to their Iranian predecessors and revived the earlier Achaemenid architectural glory. Unique features of the architecture of this era were the size of constructions in the form of large monuments and huge towns like Bishâpur, built by Shâpur I in Fârs; the advancement of stucco art used for palace decoration; the widest high-rising baked-brick vaults known at the time, such as the splendid Tâq-e Kesrâ palace at Ctesiphon in what is now Iraq; and the use of stone and gypsum as construction materials. Wall painting thrived during this period, and the artists not only decorated palaces and rock carvings but also arched dams. The Sasanids built elaborately decorated bridges and dams like the Shushtar dam on the Kârun River in Khuzestân. They also build numerous fortresses.

In Sasanid arcitecture, domes, gates, floors, and walls were decorated with colorful mosaics. Master sculptors created beautiful stone-carved reliefs like

Naqsh-e Rostam at Dârâbgerd (Fârs province) during the reign of Shâpur I. This monument depicts the victory of Shâpur I over the Roman emperor Valerian (A.D. 260). Sasanid architectural influences persisted into the Islamic era and traveled far beyond the borders of Iran to India, China, Syria, Asia Minor, the Balkans, Egypt, and Spain.

THE ISLAMIC PERIOD

The invasion of Iran by the Arabs and the introduction of Islam to Iran substantially altered the appearance of classical Iranian architecture. First and foremost, in the new Islamic Iran, the construction of mosques replaced the construction of fire temples. New mosques were built throughout the land, and in some cases former Sasanid temples were incorporated into mosques, as in the one at Yazd-e Khâst between Isfahan and Yazd. In the early period, mosques were fairly simple in design and functionality. As time went by, Iranian architectural know-how and taste influenced the construction and aesthetics of the mosques. Palace designs also began to acquire Islamic character.

Although not many structures remain from the first two centuries of Islamic rule, there was rapid construction and expansion of Islamic buildings after the third century. The most distinctive architectural features of the Islamic period are the extremely elegant calligraphy, stucco, tile, mirror, and mosaic work used for decoration; the construction of tall towers; and the use of domes for mosques. Examples of the towers exist at Gonbad-e Qâbus (the tomb of Qâbus b. Vashmgir, built in A.D.1006 with a height of 167 feet above and 35 feet below ground), at Shahr-e Rayy (the Gonbad-e Toghrel, built by the Saljuq ruler in A.D.1139), and the Kâshâneh funerary tower at Bastâm (built ca. A.D. 1308). Mud brick towers from earlier periods have not survived, but those made from high quality brick and mortar still stand and are in good condition. The fact that many of these towers still remain is miraculous for a country prone to many devastating earthquakes.

A spectacular feature of traditional Islamic architecture in Iran was the use of *moqarnas*. *Moqarnas* is an Arabic term to describe: a kind of stalactite decoration consisting of small nichelike components combined with each other in successive layers to enclose a space and generate surfaces rich in three-dimensional geometric shapes. This technique is thought to have originated in eastern Iran and then to have spread throughout the whole of the Islamic world. Another impressive feature of ornamentation in Islamic architecture in Iran is its extensive use of calligraphy and floral designs in tiles and on doors. Calligraphic designs on tiles of deep azure blue, using phrases from the Koran or hadiths, have been used in almost all religious buildings. Walls, minarets, domes, and doors of religious shrines use these calligraphic designs not only for decoration and artistic quality, but also for producing a holy ambiance in the environment in which they are used. Most Islamic structures combine tile work, stucco and stone carving, illumination and *moqarnas*, joinery, gilding, embossing, latticework, inlay, raised work, and painting. The shrines of the Eighth Imam, Rezâ, in Mashhad; of Fâtemeh the Immaculate (Hazrat-e Ma'sumeh) in Qom; of Shâh 'Abd-ol-'Azim in Rayy; and of Shâh Cherâgh in Shiraz are some of the most famous religious complexes in Iran, combining many forms of art in architecture and religious expression. The vast Imam Rezâ shrine (Âstân-e Qods) consists of 33 buildings with halls, porticos, *ayvâns,* and minarets all decorated with tile work, inlay, mirror work, stucco and stone carving, painting, illuminations, and *moqarnas*.

Tiles are a major component of Islamic art and architecture, and the tile makers of Isfahan, Kâshân, and Rayy were known for their masterful work. As mentioned earlier, glazed brick had been an important element in the Iranian architecture and decorative arts since ancient times. Most of these glazed bricks were different from the kind of tiles used today. Brick and stucco were widely used for decorating buildings up to the tenth and eleventh centuries A.D. The acceptance of Islam increased the interest in the use of all kinds of designs, especially floral and calligraphic, in glazed bricks and tiles. Almost all mosques built in the Islamic period are decorated with these. The mosques at Nâ'in and Nayriz are the best examples of extensive use of geometric patterns in decorative bricks from the Buyid period. The mausoleum of Pir-e 'Alamadâr and the tomb-tower of Mihmândust are other examples from the eleventh century A.D. Other cities have mosques with marvelous architectural work from this period, notably the congregational mosques (*masjed-e jâme'*'s) of Golpâyegân, Zavâreh, Qazvin, and Ardestân, all built during the twelfth century.

The Il-Khanids in the thirteenth century A.D. used tiles not only for the exterior but also for the interior surfaces of the walls and domes. In fact, in this period, the use of tiles reached perfection in the form of mosaic-style design known as *moraqqa'*. Based on this technique, a panel is filled with previously cut and carved small pieces of tiles and then glazed. These glazed tile panels are more durable and weather resistant. The best early examples of these panels can be seen seen in the Timurid monuments of Herât, Samarqand, and Bukhârâ. Later monuments decorated with this technique include Gowharshâd Mosque in Mashhad, the Jâme' mosques of Yazd and Varâmin, and the Madraseh-ye Khân in Shiraz.

Luster tile panel is another design consisting of square, rectangular, hexagonal, octagonal, and polygonal forms with human, floral, and geometrical motives. Most of these panels contained poetry, proverbs, and hadiths from religious or historical personalities. Sites at Takht-e Solaymân (especially from the palace of Abâqâ Khan in the Il-khanid period); Gorgân; Kâshân; and Khorâsân offer many examples of these panels. The calligraphic script known as *ta'liq* became popular on tiles in the eleventh through fourteenth centuries A.D. Used in luster and under-glaze decoration, these tiles were inscribed with poems from Ferdowsi, Hâfez, Rumi, Sa'di, and other famous Persian poets. During the Safavid period, *naskh* and *soluth* scripts also became popular.

During the Saljuq period, the dome chamber type of mosque became the dominant model. The first double-shell domes were constructed. A defining feature of Saljuq architecture was stone and stucco carvings. The *mehrâbs* of the Jâme' mosques of Qazvin and Ardestân represent two examples of stucco-carving in this period. The Mongol invasion slowed artistic and architectural production until the thirteenth century A.D. when the Il-Khanids accepted Islam and became interested in promoting the arts. A new form of stucco art, found in the Haydariyeh Madraseh at Qazvin, was introduced during the Mongol period. A different kind of vaulting technique that required precise calculation of size and dimension in the construction of domes was also introduced under the Timurids. Designs of these domes are indicative of some Chinese influences. The Vaqt o Sâ'at complex in Yazd is another example of the sophistication of structures in this period. Commissioned by Sayyed Rokn-od-Din and completed around 1326, it originally included a mosque, library, seminary, and observatory. Part of the complex, usually called the Masjed-e Vaqt o Sâ'at, a domed building decorated with *naskh* and *kufi* calligraphic inscriptions, still stands today.

The Safavids were great supporters of the arts, and one of the most productive artistic periods in Iranian history developed under their patronage. The city of Isfahan in particular was turned into a virtual museum of exquisite architectural monuments, adding to the city's already rich cultural heritage. The infrastructure of the city was greatly improved, and attention was given to not only the construction of palaces and mosques, but also to utilitarian structures such as caravansaries, bridges, bazaars, bathhouses, water reservoirs, dams, and pigeon cots. Magnificent gardens and palaces were built. The garden plays a symbolic role in Persian imagination and is the landscape on which the Iranian sense of beauty grows, but the palace is the ultimate desire of Iranian ruling elites. A fine example of a Safavid palace and garden in Isfahan is the Chehel Sotun, a palace built in the middle of the Jahân-namâ Garden. Its ceilings are supported on tall wooden columns on stone plinths decorated with fine wooden frames of different geometrical designs; the walls have latticed windows, mirror-work, and paintings of Safavid rulers, battles, and ceremonies. The large pool in front of the palace creates a natural mirror for the reflection of the palace. The heart of Safavid

Isfahan was the Maydân-e Naqsh-e Jahân, a huge square at the center of the city flanked by the Masjed-e-Shah (now called Masjed-e Emâm), Masjed-e Shaykh Lotfollâh, and the 'Âli-qâpu Palace (a government structure built at the time with six stories). The tiles in the mosques on the Naqsh-e Jahân are decorated with beautiful inscriptions of verses from the Koran in deep azure blue. The northern part of the Naqsh-e Jahân square leads to the great bazaar of Isfahan—one of the most attractive and frequented bazaars in Iran. In general, the Safavids concentrated on the exterior grandeur of their buildings, which they emphasized by building recessed structures like niches and entrances that gave a sense of depth. Tile work was also implemented on a larger scale and covered vast surfaces. These buildings have been subject of numerous books by art historians and architectural experts. The Safavids also built a number of magnificent bridges. In Isfahan, the Khâju bridge served as both a bridge and a dam, It is one of the most elaborate combined bridge-dams in the world. The second floor of the bridge contains beautiful pavilions decorated with stucco carvings and inscriptions. Finally, it should be mentioned that the policies of Shah 'Abbâs encouraged the transfer of a large number of religious minorities to Isfahan. This resulted in construction of some beautiful Armenian churches in Jolfa on the southern side of the Zâyandeh Rud river as well as in Shiraz.

During the Afsharid and Zand periods, there were few new developments, except the application of different colors in glazed tiles. The Kâkh-e Khorshid palace and the observation tower in the city of Kalât were built during the reign of Nâder Shah. Karim Khân Zand, who made Shiraz his seat of government, built a citadel, a bazaar, and several bathhouses, all named after him. A distinctive pink tile, known as Zand tile, was developed during this period.

Overall, Iranian architecture experienced a decline in the Qâjâr period as many old monuments remained in disrepair. Though many new structures were built, none could reproduce the grandeur and the glory of the previous era, especially the Safavid period. Several city gates, with monumental decorative ceramic works, and many mosques, with numerous *ayvâns,* networks of cupolas, and more windows for lighting were built. Buildings erected in this period had deeper courtyards and ceilings and walls decorated with mirrors. Military architecture received new attention as Iran began to learn about new European military developments. Members of the elite enthusiastically built palaces, mansions, pavilions, and hunting and summer resorts. The Masjed-e Shâh and Masjed-e Sepahsâlâr are two of the important mosques built in Tehran during this period.

The arrival of Europeans resulted in the construction of a number of new churches, adding to the number built in Iran in earlier periods. During the reign of Fath-'Ali Shah, the crown prince and governor of Azerbaijan, 'Abbâs Mirzâ, ordered new structures to be added to the Saint Tâtâvus monastery, known as the Qara Kelissâ. The Saint Tâtâvus Church, located in one of the oldest districts of Tehran, was also built during Fath-'Ali Shah's reign. A church built in this period in Bushehr represents one of the best examples of the application of Iranian architecture to a Christian building. The artwork and windows were all based on old Iranian designs.

TWENTIETH CENTURY

During the late Qâjâr period (i.e., at the beginning of the twentieth century), the continuity of Iranian architectural forms and urban structure was broken. Exposure to and arrival of European styles changed the demands as well as the requirements of housing construction and urban designs. Early imitations of European designs are reflected in the appearance of structures built in this period, especially government buildings and public facilities. In the early period of Pahlavi rule, this trend penetrated first into the interior of public buildings and then into private homes as well. The European influence emerged in two forms. The first was the adaptation of French academic architectural style as taught at the Ecole des Beaux-Art in Paris. Known as neoclassical style, this European tradition was a modern rendering of ancient Roman and Greek architectural designs. Dominant during fascism in Italy, Stalinism in the Soviet Union, and Hitler's Germany, neoclassicism represented the glory and grandeur of the state, and promoted nationalism and loyalty to tradition. As Rezâ Shah's modernization of Iranian society and industrialization necessitated the fast importation of foreign models of development, centralization of power became the basis for the development of state buildings. Thus, new structures were built based on their functionality without any consideration of native architectural designs. Many factories built in the early twentieth century followed this European structural model: large spacious cubic styles with heavy use of cement and steel. During the period 1930–40, many European architects (some of whom were also archaeologists and art historians), especially from France, Italy, and Germany, worked for the Iranian government, helping in the construction of modern government offices. They included Nikolai Marcoff, Ernst Herzfeld, Erich Shmidt, Arthur Upham Pope, Andre Godard, and Maxime Siroux. The first college of architecture built in Iran followed the Beauxian model. The Marmar and Sa'dâbâd palaces were also built mostly along European design, with some Persian touches. As time went on and nationalism became an integral part of Rezâ Shah's modernization, architects were encouraged to employ elements of Achaemenid and Sasanid architectural designs for the appearance of some of these state buildings. The new form, called the national style (*sabk-e mellî*), combined Western frames, technological foundations, elements of calligraphic design drawn from the Achaemenid period, and ceramic works from the Islamic period. In Tehran, buildings for the first Iranian railroad station, the Ministry of Justice, and even the University of Tehran were constructed in this manner. The appearance of buildings constructed for the Sherkat-e Farsh-e Irân (The Iranian Rug Company) and the Central Police Station in Tehran both had large Roman style poles with crowns designed after pre-Islamic forms. Soon, as George Nathaniel Curzon put it in 1892, Tehran began to "clothe itself at a West End tailor's."[1]

In Tehran, the government began urban planning by building wide roads in new areas, encouraging stores to use glass doors rather than old wooden doors, and ordering city dwellers to avoid building walls taller than 3 meters for one-story houses and 8.5 meters for two-story houses. Additionally, monuments and statues in public squares (*maydâns*) were constructed, replacing the old tradition of mosques and public buildings around city squares. Monuments celebrating Iranian national heroes and the kings—especially the one in power—became popular. Most cities built statutes of Pahlavi shahs at the center of *maydâns,* first of the father and later of the son. The latter practice came to an end in 1979. All statues of the shahs were destroyed during the revolution and were replaced by monuments representing the martyrs of revolution and the Iran-Iraq War. The Shâhyâd Tower, built in 1971 in the middle of a square in western Tehran, came to be a symbol of the city and the greatness of Iran, was renamed as Âzâdi (Freedom) Square. The tower has been associated with many major historical events of the past quarter-century that were initiated from this square, including demonstrations leading to the Iranian Revolution of 1979. The tower is 154 feet high, located in an area of some 5 hectares, and includes a museum, a grand hall, and several art galleries. It combines three architectural designs to a magnificent effect: Iranian (from the Sasanid period), Islamic, and Western.

The second form of Western influence on the Iranian architecture came as a result of Iranian students who had received their education in the Western architectural schools, notably Vartan Havanessian (1896–1982), Paul Akbar (1908–1970), Gabriel Guevrekian (1900–1970), Kayqobâd Zâlâr (b. 1910), and Mohsen Forughi. Forughi's role was crucial both because of his synthetic works and his professional advancement of the field. Following Andre Godard, he became the dean of the Faculty of Architecture at the University of Tehran and funded the Iranian Society of Architects. Another important Iranian architect who has had tremendous impact on modern Persian architecture is Hushang Seyhun. Seyhun's didactic method intuitively synthesized the modern language of architecture with the beauty and fineness of old Persian architecture. When these Iranian architects returned home, each used his intuition about Persian forms and blended them with what he had seen and learned about in the West. The first instances of works of the modernist generation are the Bâshgâh-e Afsarân (General's Club) and Honarestân-e Dokhtarân (Girls' Academy of Arts). Soon, private homes in affluent parts of Tehran, and later in other cities, followed this modernist style. The new pattern was completely new for Iran and had no resemblance to either traditional Iranian forms or neoclassical types. The logic behind this modern architecture was rationalism—a school emphasizing simplicity, pragmatism, functionality, and adaptation to modern technological advancements. Their simplicity made it attractive to speculative developers who replicated these designs without due environmental considerations. Given the large migration of rural poor to the cities and the rise of the middle class, this simple style lent itself to mass-housing production by unprofessional developers without adequate consideration for city planning. Surely, the new style has been responsive to the country's increasing housing needs, but it has also contributed to a congested environment lacking adequate planning and larger social consideration for environmental sustainability. Today, most new high-rise housing in Tehran resembles piled up boxes very much like those found in the inner cities of the West.

A modern phenomenon that has had tremendous impact on the structure and aesthetics of modern cities is roads. Modern roads are wide and often long, cutting through neighborhoods, communities, farmlands, and even markets. With their increasing population, older Iranian cities suffer from lack of adequate roads allowing for movement of passenger cars and shipping trucks. People living in traditional neighborhoods find it difficult to adjust their desire for the modern convenience of mobility with the old fabric of their housing arrangements in which alleys (kucheh) were the major routes connecting their homes to the outside world. To open up some of these closed communities, the government had to buy back some premises in these areas for the construction of roads. But changes in these neighborhoods were not limited to roads and modern lines of sewage and water. Shortage of houses has forced many modern residents to demolish their old flats and replace them with high-rises in very old communities with narrow alleys and limited city services (water, sewer, fire stations, adequate green space, parking, etc.). These reconstructive activities, while beneficial to the city for licensing fees and taxation, have become a major problem when responding to their residents' demands.

Since the Revolution of 1979, Iran's population has doubled and turned Iranian cities, especially Tehran (from 1.5 million in 1956 to 2.7 million in 1966 to 6 million in 1986 and 12 million in 2002) and Mashhad (2,926,000 in 2002), into gigantic communities with congested traffic, crowded streets, high production of garbage, high rates of crime and automobile accidents, a growing underground prostitution problem, and a large number of addicts and street children. The Islamic government has tried to respond the challenges of this growth and to meet the demands of the public for services. In 1999, the Tehran Metro—a project conceived prior to the revolution, abandoned, and again restarted in 1984—began its first service between Tehran and Karaj. Now, electric trains move people to key stations around the sprawling cities. A major challenge in construction of this subway has been the underground wells traditionally used as septic systems beneath private homes all over the city. Today, the cities of Mashhad and Isfahan also have their own urban railways.

With the Islamic Revolution of 1979, Iranian architecture experienced a temporary rupture. The idea was to reject Westernization and go back to elements of Iranian-Islamic architecture. Some revolutionaries were against anything remotely connected to pre-Islamic Iran and were ready to demolish some of monuments and historical sites representing the glory of kings and the kingdom. Partially in fear of such attempts, and partially due to lack of resources during the war with Iraq, the Iranian government had to board up some of the historical monuments for several years. Although cooler heads prevailed and radicals' efforts were stopped, the country was confronted with a new identity crisis. While new Islamic rulers wished to go back to Islamic art, secular elites were more interested in balancing the Iranian and Islamic elements. The result was the emergence of a new nativist trend, emphasizing traditional and Islamic values combined with those Iranian elements deemed appropriate for an Islamic society. This approach has also been applied to restoration of past monuments in need of repair. Some of these monuments are restored in a style commensurate with the new Islamic emphasis. Many of the new buildings and designs combined elements of the past and present. In 1985, the Iranian Cultural Heritage Organization was established in order to coordinate activities of various organizations for preservation, restoration, and promotion of national monuments.

In the past two decades, a variety of highly hybridized cultural forms have appeared on the Iranian urban landscape: Iranian-Islamic, Iranian-Western, Islamic-Western, and Iranian-Islamic-Western. These forms marry Islamic-Iranian motifs and ornamentations to Western traditions. Today, Tehran has become a laboratory of various architectural styles. Modern schools are designed in the format of old *madrasehs* (schools) with domed spaces and geometric designs. Postmodernist styles are adopted by younger architects interested in catching up with the latest Western trends. A number of diverse and conflicting motives play into urban planning, housing design, and decorative culture within the Iranian households. Several high-rise hotels in Tehran have been built with the latest technology and based on the latest technical and safety design but decorated and designed inside with the traditional Iranian styles. Today, the Shah 'Abbâs Hotel in Isfahan represents one of the most attractive hotels in Iran, using parts of a beautiful Safavid building remodeled with the most modern conveniences and technology.

While anxiety about the loss of identity might be a genuine concern, much of this worry originates from nativistic, anti-Western, and ideological tendencies that surfaced after the revolution. Considered one of the richest architectural cities in the world, the city of Isfahan passed legislation recently banning construction of buildings based on Western designs. This type of legislation reflects the anxiety about losing one's cultural identity in face of the Western onslaught. Traditional bazaars are replaced by modern plazas and shopping malls in modern cities. This worries traditionalists who see the bazaar as a major feature of the Islamic-Iranian city. Some communities have tried to build modern shopping malls in the style of a traditional bazaar but with large parking lots around it with modern facilities.

Ancestral technical know-how already has improved and integrated with modern techniques and production. Some of the old styles are simply not economical or safe in a time and age where cement and concrete are basic realities of construction. For a country prone to repeated earthquakes, remaining fully traditional in architectural construction is both unrealistic and anachronistic. Given the increasing urbanization of the country and the vast waves of architectural designs landing on the shores of each continent, Iran will be challenged to expand its urban planning by incorporating new and more convenient modern styles into its desired old structural forms. While the anxiety about the disappearance of traditional forms may be genuine, the growing appetite to become modern by adopting styles and techniques that are less costly and in-line with the norms of modern urbanism permeates Iranian society. Surely, the larger crisis of identity in the Iranian society alluded to in other chapters, surfaces in the embodied architectural forms and practices of the past and the necessity of the modern lifestyle.

Finally, it should be noted that in a country where the housing shortage and lack of city services remain major social issues, attention to architectural sophistication is perceived as a luxury. The lower and middle classes are more interested in constructing adequate shelter rather than worrying about designs. The growing needs of the new rural immigrant population in the cities and the increasing demands that this large population growth has had on city services could not be responded to with architectural finesse. Though elite families play a significant role in the creation of stylish single-family housing, architectural design became a matter of concern for religious and national buildings constructed either by the government or religious foundations. A host of issues relating to government licensing, regulation, and permission, as well as inadequate public resources such as water, sewer, and drainage have also contributed to lack of attention to full implementation of architectural plans and conformity with planned designs.

On December 26, 2003, a powerful earthquake struck the city of Bam in southeastern Iran, killing over 43,000 people, injuring 20,000, and leaving 60,000 homeless. Bam was home to a 2,000-year-old citadel (Arg-e Bam), built primarily of mud brick, during the Sasanid period. Arg-e Bam was one of the most valued architectural sites in the world, some of it surviving from before the twelfth century and some built during the Safavid period. About 60 percent of the buildings in Bam were destroyed, and the old citadel was severely damaged. This devastating earthquake brought fresh attention to the new designs and devices for strengthening old national monuments. It also raised the national consciousness about the structural aspects of housing as a form of national identity and pride. Given the earthquake-prone nature of Iran, and the fact that in the past 1,500 years Tehran, the capital, has been leveled by earthquakes three times, it becomes extremely important to design buildings, roads, and bridges in a way that will not devastate the 12 million inhabitants of this city.

NOTE

1. George N. Curzon, *Persia and the Persian Question* (reprint, London: Frank Cass and Co., 1966), 1:306.

The Citadel of Bam (Arg-e Bam). Bam, located in southeastern Iran, was founded in Sasanid times and rebuilt in the twelfth and sixteenth centuries A.D. The city represented a fine example of architecture using mud bricks, clay, straw, and the trunks of palm trees. In December 2003, a devastating earthquake left this citadel in ruins. Photograph taken in March 2001. Courtesy of Asghar Riahi.

A coppersmith in the Isfahan handicraft bazaar. This city is very famous for its handicrafts, rugs, sweets, and historical monuments. 1995. Courtesy of Ali Akbar Mahdi.

A view looking over Separâw, a remote desert village located north of Nâin in central Iran. 2003. Courtesy of Daryoush Mehrshahi.

A public bathhouse (*hammâm*) in Shahr-e Rayy, south of Tehran, 1995. As indoor water and sewer facilities have become available and people could afford building private baths in their houses, the number of these public baths has declined. Traditional *hammâm*s had elaborate architecture, and in some cities they have been turned into cultural museums. Courtesy of Ali Akbar Mahdi.

A rural man on his porch, north of Iran, 2005. Photograph by Nikrad Mahdi. Courtesy of Ali Akbar Mahdi.

Iranian youth smoking tobacco with a traditional *qalyân* (waterpipe), an old and popular activity. Photograph taken in 2005 by Nikrad Mahdi. Courtesy of Ali Akbar Mahdi.

A poster depicting the Twelve Imams. Of them, Ali and his son Hosayn are viewed with much more passion and devotion, as they are singled out in this poster. Courtesy of Ali Akbar Mahdi.

The Hâfeziyeh is believed to be the burial place of the fourteenth-century Persian poet, Shams-od-Din Mohammad Shirâzi, known as Hâfez. Located in the city of Shiraz in southwestern Iran, this mausoleum is visited by millions of people annually. Photograph taken in 1997. Courtesy of Ali Akbar Mahdi.

The appearance of Tehran illustrates the realities of contemporary Iran: old and new fusing with each other in an unpredictable manner. Recent buildings, like this one located in a square in the western part of the city, imitates modern architectural designs without much consideration for traditional Iranian elements. Photograph taken in 2006 by Parvaneh Mehrabi. Courtesy of Ali Akbar Mahdi.

A villa in Kalârdasht, northern Iran, mixing traditional motifs with modern architectural designs. Photograph taken in 2005 by Nikrad Mahdi. Courtesy of Ali Akbar Mahdi.

A large, hand-carved wooden structure to be decorated and carried by a group of participants in an 'Âshurâ procession. Located in Yazd in central Iran, this particular structure is meant to represent a palm tree (*nakhl*) of Karbalâ, where Imam Hosayn was martyred, and is covered with green and black flags symbolizing the family of the prophet and martyrdom. Many structures like this were lost due to neglect during the Pahlavi era, but this one was kept as a tourist attraction; it is over 30 feet high and said to be over 400 years old. Courtesy of Elton L. Daniel.

A pure silk pile and foundation carpet with a unique hunting scene and epic poems, made recently in the city of Qom. Courtesy of Ali Akbar Mahdi.

A family eating dinner around the traditional *sofreh*, a cloth spread out on the floor in the middle of the room. Photograph taken in 1997. Courtesy of Ali Akbar Mahdi.

Chelow-kabâb (plain rice with grilled meat) is a favorite Iranian food; more restaurants are found offering *kabâb* than other dishes. Photograph taken in 2006. Courtesy of Ali Akbar Mahdi.

The consumption of dried nuts and fruits (*âjil*) is associated with many Iranian festivities. Tavâzo Ajils is the first successful franchise offering this product in stores beautifully decorated with traditional handicrafts. Photograph taken in 2004. Courtesy of Ali Akbar Mahdi.

A pastry shop in Tehran selling an assortment of Persian cookies. Photograph taken in 2005 by Parvaneh Mehrabi. Courtesy of Ali Akbar Mahdi.

A boy carrying freshly baked bread of the type known as *barbari*. Photograph taken in Tehran, ca. 1972, by Keith McLeod. Courtesy of Marta Simidchieva.

Marriages are often officiated in front of a wedding cloth called the *sofreh-ye 'aqd*. Depending on the couple's tastes, religion, economic status, and ethnic background, the *sofreh* may contain any or all of the following items: herbs, spices, sweets, nuts, rice, bread, feta cheese, flowers, needle and threads, burning wild rue, a holy book, and a mirror. Courtesy of Ali Akbar Mahdi.

Female section of a library in Rehnân, Isfahan, 2005. This is a traditional public bath (*ham-mâm*) recently transformed into a library. The short, raised wall separates the female section from the men's section. A sign on the wall says: "A place for cleaning the body then, and a place for cleaning the soul now." Courtesy of Nina Samsami.

Rural to urban migration has been a reality of Iran since the 1970s. This photograph shows three of the older women still remaining in the village of Separâw, north of Nâin, in 2003. Courtesy of Daryoush Mehrshahi.

On the 13th day of the New Year, called Sizdah Bedar, most Iranians picnic outdoors in order to avoid the unlucky aspects of the number "13." One of the activities for unmarried young females, depicted here, is gathering blades of grass or herbs to knot into a charm in the hope of being married a year later. This photograph was taken before the Islamic Revolution, when it was common for women to appear in public in western-style dress. This would not be acceptable today, and the holiday itself is frowned upon by many religious authorities as a vestige of paganism. Photograph by and courtesy of Marta Simidchieva.

Sizdah Bedar picnic in a Tehran park, 2006. Photograph by Parvaneh Mehrabi. Courtesy of Ali Akbar Mahdi.

A Hâji Firuz, a performer who amuses the public prior to Nowruz. The traditional costume has been red clothes with the face colored black. Recently, some have started coloring their face in red, white, and green, the colors of the Iranian flag, as is the case with this one. Courtesy of Ali Akbar Mahdi.

A group of athletes performing group exercises with massive wooden clubs at a "house of strength" (*zur-khâneh*) in Tehran in the 1970s. The activities and exercises of the *zur-khâneh* were guided by a number of rules and rituals intended to instill virtues of chivalry such as humility and modesty. Public performances were accompanied by special music and the recitation of passages from literary works such as the Shâh-nâmeh. These athletic associations and ritual performances thus represented much more than just a sporting activity and were an important part of traditional Iranian culture. Photograph by Keith McLeod. Courtesy of Marta Simidchieva.

The Dastân Ensemble performing traditional folk music. Musicians include (from right): Behnam Samani (*daf*), Pejman Hadadi (*tonbak*), Hamid Motebassem (*târ*), Sima Bina (vocal), Hossein Behroozinia (*barbat*), and Said Frajpoory (*kamâncheh*). Photograph taken November 2004. Courtesy of Ali Akbar Mahdi.

6

Carpets

If there is one thing Iran is known for around the world, it is undoubtedly its carpets. Persian carpets (many of which are actually made by non-Persian peoples in Iran) represent one of the most distinguished and distinctive manifestations of Iranian culture and art. Hand-woven Persian carpets are among the most treasured possessions of homes, offices, palaces, and museums throughout the world. Because of their high market value, these carpets have also been treated as an investments—ones that can actually be enhanced by time and use. To indicate the increasing value of an object with time, Iranians often use the expression, "It is like a Persian carpet: the more it is walked on, the more it gains value."

Many motifs, patterns, and traditional colorations found in rugs that are produced in many countries today have either originated in or been influenced by motifs and patterns used in Persian carpets. In general, Persian carpet designs have been inspired by nature, history, religion, and myths. They may use flowers, trees, natural scenery, historical and mythological characters, Persian poetry and calligraphy, and religious symbols and stories. For Iranians, a carpet with images of Persian kings, legendary or historical, as well as representations of verses from *Shâh-nâmeh* or other books represents an object of identity demonstrating their glorious past. Carpets are not just an item for export or a piece of art, but an intrinsic part of the culture. Carpets are used as floor coverings, prayer mats, and decorations for homes, offices, palaces, and shrines. They have become an indispensable part of the living environment for Iranians.

STRUCTURE, DESIGNS, AND PATTERNS

Persian carpets are famous for their variety in design, color, size, and weave. Moreover, they are known for the uniqueness of each and every rug produced. This uniqueness is the basis on which the quality and value of a rug are determined. The less frequently replicated the design, the more valuable the carpet, demonstrating the originality of the colors, materials, weaves, and circumstances under which it was produced. Another basic factor in determining the quality of a carpet is knot density, or the number of knots per square inch—more knots indicate finer work, better quality, and a higher price.

Throughout Iranian history, the art of carpet weaving has changed, each change further enriching techniques, designs, and the quality of the carpets produced. Handmade carpets have warp (thread running the length), weft (thread running the width), and pile (knots, which may be made of silk, wool, or cotton). Traditional looms are usually made of timber, but newer ones are now sometimes constructed of steel. Although weaving method varies according to the design, in general weaving involves passing the crosswise strings of the weft under and over the lengthwise strings of the warp on the loom. After making several knots, the weaver levels the wefts with a heavy range comb. The threads of warp and weft are generally made of cotton, but sometimes wool and seldom silk. The pile is often colored strings completely woven into the carpet like a basket. Each twisted pile threaded into the warp is called a *knot*. There are two types of knots: Persian (also called Senna) and Turkish (Ghiordes). The names associated with these knots have no connection to geography or ethnicity. Both types of knots are used in carpet weaving in Iran. In the Persian knot, the pile thread forms a single turn about the warp string, while in the Turkish knot, it is taken around two adjacent warp strings. The Turkish knot is symmetrical and works better for geometric designs and is very common in tribal rugs, whereas the Persian knot is asymmetrical and lends itself better to intricate designs found in luxury carpets. Piles are often dyed wool, cotton, or silk. In earlier times, colors were made from flower and vegetable dyes, thus giving carpets unique colors associated with plants existing in each region.

The words *carpet* (*farsh* or *qâlî*) and *rug*, often used interchangeably, need to be distinguished. The major distinction referred to in the literature is the difference in the size and pile. However, according to A. Cecil Edwards, an authority on Persian carpet, this is a European distinction and should not be confused with the American one. In the United States, such distinction is based on the unity of the piece. A rug is a single piece usable in different settings, irrespective of floor size. Carpet is a stripped textile floor-covering matched and cut to the length of the room. As for the size distinction, any hand-woven floor covering larger than 6.5 feet is defined as a carpet and less than that as a rug.

Some *gelims*—another word used in reference to small rugs (in Turkish, *kilim*)—are actually quite large. Another difference distinguishing the two is the absence of pile in *gelims*. *Gelims* are coarse, thin woolen rugs without any pile or knotted fluff. Another term sometimes confused with *gelim* is *zilu*. While *gelim* is made of wool, *zilu* is made of cotton. *Zilu* is a durable and inexpensive floor covering often used in rural town and village mosques. Though the art of *zilu* weaving was strong in Iran, especially in Maybod, it has declined recently, and it is hard to imagine how *zilus* can compete with newer products in the market.

Finally, it should be mentioned that an Iranian household may have several rugs at the same time: more expensive ones for the guest rooms, cheaper ones for the family rooms, and smaller ones for the doorways. In religious families, the one rug that is cared for meticulously is the prayer rug. Small in size, this rug is reserved only for prayer time in order to ensure that prayer is performed on a clean rug. Some families sanctify their prayer rugs by taking them to holy sites such as Mecca, the Imam Rezâ Shrine, etc. Some very dedicated believers even carry their prayer rug while traveling. Traditionally, prayer rugs had simple designs containing flowers, calligraphy, and mosaics. In recent years, there has been a conscious change in the design of prayer rugs incorporating elements from scenes of holy sites, especially Mecca.

Carpets made in different regions and by different tribes often reflect the culture and lifestyle of those people and regions. While carpets produced by small producers in rural areas are often of lesser quality and complexity, those produced by carpet factories or rural people in hire of big producers are of higher quality and more sophisticated designs. Even the availability of botanic resources in an area influences the kind of materials and colors used. One form of simple tribal rug was made more familiar to Western-ers after the 1997 release of the internationally acclaimed film, *Gabbeh*, by Iranian director Mohsen Makhmalbâf. *Gabbeh* was a cinematic poem that truly reflected the beauty of simple tribal designs woven with love, hope, anxiety, and pain. A *gabbeh* is a triple hand-knotted wool rug with deep color, more wefts, and longer fluff. Some dictionaries considered the name synonymous with another Iranian long-plied rug called *khersak*. Such rugs are often woven without a predetermined design by tribal women who incorporate their own taste and imagination into the rugs. Their designs are simple and geometric, containing a few pictures of an animal, bird, tree, or flower. Historically, they were made for personal use in nomadic tents. However, in recent years, they have attracted Western consumers' attention and as such they have become more elaborate, containing scenes of rolling hills and colorful flower fields.

Carpets are generally named after the village, town, or district where they are woven or collected, or by the weaving tribe in the case of nomadic pieces. For instance, carpets known as Baluchi represent those produced by the Baluchi tribes of eastern Iran (or western Afghanistan), and those called Sâruq refer to carpets either made in or with designs originated from Sâruq, a small village in central Iran. These names can also refer to the particular pattern, palette, and weave uniquely linked to the indigenous culture, or to weaving techniques specific to an identifiable geographic area or nomadic tribe. It should be noted that although each of these designs (Afshâri, Bakhtiâri, etc.) started with its own unique features, in the course of time they have come to be synthesized by other elements and innovative variations. For instance, the Bakhtiâri nomads often combine flat weave and pile weaving in the same piece. Or one may find a Kâshân city carpet that uses either material or design elements of Tabriz carpets. The tremendous innovation and creativity found in the industry resists generalities and makes it hard for any description to be taken literally.

Tribal and nomadic carpets are usually smaller and coarser because the looms must be portable as nomads move seasonally from one area to another. Their dyes are also relatively strong and vivid with much broader palettes. Different tribes and nomadic groups have developed different designs and techniques of producing rugs. For instance, typical Afshâri carpets have medallions, either geometric or floral, and typical Bakhtiâri carpets are filled with flower and tendril motifs within geometrical compartments (called *kheshti* design). The styles and designs employed in tribal carpets show many influences. For instance, Shâhsavan carpets are very similar to Caucasian carpets. The Qashqâis make carpets out of wool and, being descendants of the Shâhsavans, decorate their carpets with styles very similar to Shâhsavan designs. The Afshârs use Turkish patterns but also borrow from Kermân city-woven carpets of Safavid style. Carpets made in Lorestân have bronze tones and broken cross patterns. Baluchis borrow largely from Turkoman design, especially in the use of the *gol* (flower) motif. They mostly employ geometric patterns in light colors like light red, blue, and khaki, in contrast to the bright vermilion used by Turkomans. Unlike the other tribes, the Kurds beautifully combine complementary city and tribal designs on wool and other rough materials.

Though many rugs are produced by nomads and villagers without predesigned drawn pattern (known as broken designs), most carpets follow carefully designed curved lines drawn on checkered paper (known as revolving designs). The latter is used as a guide by weavers while making the carpet. Rugs produced by tribal people often lack consistency in color and material. These small weavers can neither afford to purchase all the materials needed for a rug at once nor are they able to devote uninterrupted time to weaving a rug; looms would have to be disassembled should the tribe move from one place to another. Given the conditions under which these tribal rugs are produced, most are usually one of a kind.

Historically, women and children, especially girls, have been weavers, and men have been in charge of the distribution and marketing of the carpets. Given that a carpet is made of millions of knots by unknown individuals whose names do not appear anywhere on the carpet, young female villagers have come to symbolize the pains of carpet laborers. There are numerous works of Persian literature referring to village girls' injured fingers and loss of sight due to making carpets in dark rooms. Fortunately, the situation has changed in the past two decades. As education in rural areas has become more available and the mandatory school attendance for children is better enforced, fewer young girls are working in the carpet industry full time. Although the current labor law forbids the employment of children under the age of 15, the violation of the law in remote areas is common, especially in rural and mountainous areas. In 1992, the official figure for child labor was 286,000, of which 62 percent were girls, mostly working as part-time weavers in the carpet industry.

There are many similarities between designs in carpets and those in Persian tilework and miniature painting. Persian carpet designs can be grouped into at least 17 types. Patterns of well-known Persian designs, many inspired by nature, include *goldâni* (vase), *derakhti* (tree), *Shâh ʿAbbâsi, gol farang* (European flower), *mâhi* (fish, a design also known as *Herât*), *châhâr fasl* (four seasons), *afshân* (scattered), and *shekârgâh* (hunting field). The aigrette design (*boteh*) has its roots in Zoroastrian tradition and consists of the so-called "mother and child" and "friendship and enmity" patterns. The portrait design has been used to depict kings and revered characters. Geometric designs include *qabqabi* (framed), *moharamât* (striped), and *Torkmân* patterns. Used on silk and wool carpets, the triangular citron design (*lachak toranj*) is usually round and sometimes elliptical, with one-fourth of a citron appearing at every angle of the carpet's main body. Designs incorporating historical monuments include *Takht-e Jamshid, Tâq-e Bostân,* and *Tâq-e Kesrâ.*

Designs are also named after the cities or regions that are centers of carpet weaving. These include Kermân, Kâshân, Khorâsân, Isfahan, Tehran, Tabriz, Hamadân, and Nâʾin. Famous for their durability and lush pile, Tabriz carpets usually have a central medallion surrounded by and complimented with flowers and tendrils in a curvature pattern. Typical Hamadân carpets are smaller in size and have strong bright colors, a single weft medallion, and the fringe only on one side. Representing one of the highest-quality Persian carpets, Isfahan carpets are filled with colorful floral designs on an ivory background. Typically, they have a central medallion amid floral twines. Though close to Isfahan, Nâ'in has developed its own distinct carpet design with lighter colors and detailed curvilinear and medallion-and-corner designs. Kermân carpets are most known for their softer hues; detailed curvilinear and repetitive floral patterns; and vase, garden, animal, and medallion motifs. Khorâsân carpets are mostly curvilinear with the single central medallion and corner floral design, and very busy curvilinear floral motifs in the background. They include carpets made in the cities of Mashhad, Birjand, Kâshmar, Torbat-e Jam, Torbat Haydariyeh, Nishâpur, Sabzevâr, Gonâbâd, Quchân, Shirvân, and Bojnurd. To varying degrees, they all employ vivid red, purplish red, and crimson backgrounds. The famous Kâshân carpets have a central medallion with tendrils and vases. During the Safavid period, themes of birds, human beings, and mythical figures were common in Kâshân carpets. Kâshân is known for producing luxurious carpets made of silk and velvet.

THE HISTORY OF CARPET WEAVING IN IRAN

It is difficult to be certain about the early history of carpet weaving in Iran. Given the fragile nature of the materials from which a carpet is made, not many carpets have survived. Indeed, most old carpets found in museums today date from the sixteenth century onwards However, the carpet tradition is no doubt much older than that. In 1949, Russian archeologist Sergei Rudenko found a pile carpet in a tomb in the Altai Mountains of Siberia; the carpet was dated to the fourth or third century B.C. Known as the Pazyrk carpet, and now in the Hermitage Museum in Leningrad, it has two wide borders, one with images of yellow-spotted deer, and the other depicting men either riding or standing by horses. Some of the designs are thought to be similar to shapes found on carvings at Persepolis, but this has been disputed; there is no clear evidence of either Iranian origin or influence in the case of this carpet. The earliest remains of carpets from Iran itself date to the Sasanid period; the art historian Arthur Pope thought that the production of carpets as we know them today was established at that time.

Most of what can be said about the earliest Iranian carpets comes not from artifacts but from historical writings describing courts, battles, and economic exchanges. The classical Greek historian Xenophon, for example, mentioned luxurious carpets made by the Medes. Reports about Alexander's campaigns indicate that he had found a carpet in Cyrus's tomb. Some believe that a phrase in the *Avesta*, the Zoroastrian scripture, indicates that ancient Iranian carpets may have been woven with golden threads. The Byzantine emperor Heraclius apparently took a sumptuous carpet from a Sasanid palace after he sacked the city of Dastjerd in A.D 628. Also, among the spoils taken from the Sasanid capital Ctesiphon by the Arab army in A.D. 637 was a magnificent carpet made during the reign of Khosrow I. Called "the Carpet of the Spring Garden" (*farsh-e bahârestân*), this 90-foot square carpet, had a flower design and precious gems in its warps and wefts and covered the great hall at the Ctesiphon palace. Huan Tsang, the Chinese world traveler of the seventh century also wrote about the artistry of Iranians in weaving carpets and silken cloth.

In the spirit of Islamic egalitarianism, the early Arab caliphs viewed carpets as a luxury and thus did not show much interest in them (the caliph 'Omar, on the advice of 'Ali, supposedly had the priceless Baharestân carpet cut into small pieces to distribute to people as charity). However, with the rise of Umayyads and Abbasids, carpets became objects of desire for decorating the court. Palaces of both dynasties were filled with magnificent Persian carpets. During the Saljuq period, the art of carpet weaving expanded and was further enriched by the skillfulness of women who made extensive use of the Turkish knots, especially for carpets made in Azerbaijan and Hamadân. A number of carpets currently preserved in the Alaeddin Mosque and Mevlevi Museum in Konya, Turkey, closely resemble carpets produced in this period.

After the initial devastation of the Mongol's invasion of Iran, the production of carpets grew and new rulers began to fill their palaces with Persian carpets. Ghâzân Khân's palace in Tabriz was reportedly filled with precious Persian carpets. Tamerlane's son, Shâh Rokh was also a patron of the arts and encouraged the elevation of the Persian carpet industry by establishing court-subsidized looms. Although reports indicate that carpets of this period had simple motifs in geometric designs, there has apparently been a great deal of exchange between carpet and architectural designs. Medallion forms and certain arabesque borders are reported to have been very popular. Most Persian carpets of the fifteenth century are described as being decorated in miniatures with geometric patterns. With the Herât school of miniature illustration in the late fifteenth century, curved lines also began to be used in carpet designs.

During the Safavid period, the court became a major sponsor of Iranian arts and commerce—two necessary ingredients of the carpet industry. Workshops were even set up for producing carpets exclusively for the court. Safavid gardens, architecture, and monuments all became sources of inspiration for designing the carpets during this period. Both Shah 'Abbâs and Shah Tahmâsb are reported to have encouraged the industry and used Persian carpets as gifts to foreign leaders and dignitaries. The best known carpet of this period, which is currently in the Victoria and Albert Museum in London, is the Ardabil carpet (alternatively called Shaykh Safi or the Mosque of Ardabil carpet) made in 1539 by the master weaver Maqsud-e Kâshâni. A new feature of carpets in this period was the use of gold and silver thread, culminating in the great coronation carpet—a piece with perfect velvetlike pile and a gleaming gold background now held in the Rosenborg Palace in Copenhagen. Also, most luxury carpets of this period were woven with silk.

Luxury carpets and finely woven quality textiles were marketed in Europe and soon became items of attraction for European courts and aristocracy. Many Europeans visited Iranian carpet factories and wrote about the high quality of materials and designs found in Persian carpets at the time. E. Kaempfer visited Isfahan workshops; D. Garcia de Silvia y Figueroa wrote of his visit to Kâshân factories; and Pedro Teixeira spoke of rugs from Yazd, Kermân, and Khorâsân. John Baptiste Tavernier, a famous French jeweler, and Jean Chardin, a French traveler, both visited Isfahan factories and described Persian carpets as the best-quality carpets, as did Adam Olearius about carpets from Herat.

The quality of Persian carpets attracted the attention of European kings, who even sent their own merchants and craftsmen to either acquire Persian carpets or to learn the art of making them. Louis XIV, king of France, sent several craftsmen to Iran to learn how to weave carpets like Persians. Sigismund III Vasa, king of Poland, sent a merchant to the city of Kâshân for purchasing Persian carpets in 1601—some currently preserved in the Presidentz Museum of Warsaw. Two such early purchases, with the royal arms of the king woven into them, still survive—one in the Textile Museum in Washington, DC, and the other in the Bavarian Museum in Munich, Germany. Since April 1700, when Frederick IV and Queen Louise of Denmark were crowned, a Persian carpet has been used in the anointing during the coronation ceremony of every Danish king—a carpet "woven with gold," which was given as a gift to a Danish king's wife by the Dutch in 1666 and preserved at the Rosenborg Palace. Carpets like this are among many more found in Europe. Over 1,000 carpets from this period have been located in various museums and private collections around the world. Those made in the early 1600s are often referred to as Polonaise carpets because they were made to the specifications of the Polish king—silk carpets often made in Isfahan and Kâshân, with gold and silver warps and wefts.

The Afghan invasion of Iran in 1722 started a long period of political and economic instability, resulting in the fall of the ruling Safavids. Nâder Shah's short rule could not reverse the economic decline, which was compounded by a general decline in world trade due to wars in Europe, rising insecurity in sea and land routes, and European abandonment of posts in the region.

Carpet production in this period was limited to local markets supplied by nomads, rural women, and craftsmen in small towns. During the time of the Zand dynasty, Kermân became an important center of carpet weaving, and the highly valued goat wool from this city was exported. While the export of Iranian carpets declined, the industry imported new design elements from India, and new colors such as light pink, green, and blue were added to white backgrounds on Persian carpets.

During the reign of the Qâjârs, the carpet industry flourished. Qâjâr rulers encouraged the production of some beautiful carpets in Khorâsân and Tehran with small patterns of scrolls, arabesques, and floral designs. Nâser-od-Din Shah was an active promoter of the industry in Europe, offering beautifully-made carpets as gifts to European leaders. He presented Queen Victoria with 14 new Persian carpets from Kurdistan and Khorâsân in 1876 and many more to the Vienna Exhibition in 1891. Khorâsân and Kurdish designs from this period gained tremendous popularity in Europe, the former for their glowing colors and higher quality, and the latter for their mixed-fish and triangular citron designs. During the Victorian Era, Farâhân carpets, which had a light green color with tiny knots, became very popular among British families. In this period, Tabriz also became a major exporter of Persian carpets to Europe through Turkey.

By the late 1800s, when Europeans had become exposed to and interested in Persian carpets, and Western palaces, museums, and rich homes had begun collecting them, American, British, and German companies began investing in Persian carpets, thus ensuring a steady flow of these carpets to their countries. Foreign investors organized the commercial production of carpets in Mashhad, Tabriz, Kermân, and Soltânâbâd. Export of commercial-style carpets soon supplanted the export of luxury carpets and silk materials during the late eighteenth century. By 1914, Ziegler and Company, P. Hotz and Company, and Oriental Carpet Manufacturers of London had operations in Iran and were marketing Iranian carpets abroad. Foreign interest in Persian carpets provided a badly needed boost to the industry. These companies encouraged mechanization and standardization of many procedures that were often left to the whims and wishes of small producers and middlemen in the industry. However, such interest was not without its detrimental effects. Synthetic aniline dyes were introduced and used widely since they provided bright, even garish, colors that were more attractive to Europeans. This reduced the durability and overall quality of carpets in which this material was used.

The rise of Rezâ Shah to power began to curtail foreign investment in the carpet industry. On February 3, 1936, the Pahlavi government ordered the closure of the Eastern Carpet Manufacturing Company (ECMC), which had operations in Kermân, Arâk, and Hamadân, and transferred its assets to the newly established Iran Carpet Company. The government banned the import of synthetic aniline dyes, established carpet factories, and encouraged the use of the finest materials and methods of manufacturing. Although graduated taxes were introduced in order to discourage the use of synthetic dyes, the practice did not subside since it provided the industry a wider and more flexible range of colors. As the government centralized, the Iranian economy and industry were modernized, international trade was expanded, a middle class was formed within the Iranian society, and the demand for Persian carpets increased both at home and abroad.

Taking advantage of foreign interest in Persian carpets, as well as the strong artistry associated with this product, Mohammad-Rezâ Shah Pahlavi continued to promote the carpet industry as both an art and an important source of foreign exchange for Iran. With the rise of the middle class around the world and the ease of communication and transportation, the Persian carpet became a globally known and desired object. The Iranian government responded to this demand by passing supportive legislation for the industry and the export of carpets abroad. Locally, more shops were established by government subsidies, and rural cooperatives were established as a way of helping the small producers. The establishment of the Tehran Carpet Museum provided a forum for organizing various exhibitions and educational seminars about the industry.

After the Iranian Revolution of 1979, it was hoped that the Iranian carpet industry would expand and become stronger due to the revolutionary government's espoused aim of improving Iran's nonoil exports. In reality, however, the Iranian carpet industry began to decline. First, influenced by Marxist ideas, the revolutionary leaders shunned luxury carpets as bourgeois items. Second, the war with Iraq took a toll on the economy, resulting in further decline in industrial and economic production. Third, lack of experience and knowledge on the part of the newly established government created confusion in policies and procedures related to the carpet industry. Policies and affairs of the industry were assigned to four different ministries: Agriculture, Commerce, Jihad for Construction, and Industries and Mines. Unfortunately, each acted without coordination. Fourth, the economic nationalization policies implemented by the revolutionary government caused capital flight and deprived the industry of needed investment. Low productivity, imbalance in distribution, and alarming inflation in the postwar period led to further deterioration in the industry. Finally, in 1987, political conflict between Iran and the United States resulted in a ban on the import of Iranian carpets to the United States, further contributing to erosion of Iranian market share in the West.

The 13-year-old U.S. import embargo on Iranian carpets opened the opportunity for Asian countries to take over Persian markets. India, Pakistan, Turkey, China, Egypt, and even Nepal increased their production of handmade carpets and filled the vacuum left by Iran's absence. In 1980, Iran supplied 40 percent of the Western carpet market—which decreased to 16 percent by 1985. Many of these countries, especially China, produced carpets with Persian designs at prices cheaper than those produced in Iran— a practice that has continued even after the ban on Persian carpets was lifted in 2000. These imitation carpets usually cost less than those produced in Iran, mostly due to cheaper production costs. Some of these non-Persian imitations are of high quality and even more attractive because of the variety of new colors introduced to the market. To mass consumers today, the design and color are more important than the country of origin—the latter still being a factor in the antique market. Though Iran still has its own niche in the global carpet market, it has never been able to recover the market share it had prior to the revolution. The only area where Iran still has a market advantage is Europe, which gets 62 percent of its 1.2 billion dollars worth of imported carpets from Iran. Given the strong competition, especially from China, Iran is now faced with the challenge of innovation in design and productive technology.

Another challenge to the Persian carpet industry comes from the widespread availability and acceptability of machine carpets with Persian designs. These mass-produced and nonartistic rugs have lower prices and are marketed more aggressively. As the size of educated middle classes around the world has increased, so has their desire for affordable handmade carpets. Making handmade carpets available to this ever-increasing market has forced producers to use synthetic rayon instead of silk or cotton, giving the consumers handwoven products of lesser quality.

7

Food and Dining

CUISINE AND CULTURE

Cuisine, in terms of both the preparation of food and the social aspects of dining, is an essential part of any culture; indeed, some fundamental aspects of a culture may be more readily apparent in its culinary arts than in other traditions. Certainly, many observations that might be made about food in Iran reinforce those that can be deduced from other facets of its culture. There is a mainstream culinary tradition primarily associated with the urban, Persian-speaking population that can be taken (as it will be in this chapter) as essentially the common national cuisine, but the country also has a very rich array of local, regional, and ethnic dishes.

Persian cooking has many features in common with Indian, central Asian, Turkish, and Middle Eastern cuisines, yet it has its own particular characteristics and is unmistakably different from any of its counterparts. For instance, while many ingredients of Iranian and Indian food are similar, Indian food is spicier and uses pepper very generously. Likewise, many of the ingredients used in Persian cooking would be familiar to Americans, but Americans would be surprised at the unique ways the ingredients are used and the flavors they produce. A good Persian cook has an almost miraculous ability to turn simple ingredients into dishes of great subtlety and beauty. This Persian style of cooking is sophisticated and refined enough to hold its own with any of the world's other great cuisines, but it is relatively little known and appreciated outside the region. However, that is changing as the recent emigration of Iranians and their settlement in other countries, especially Europe and the United States, has resulted in the appearance of Persian restaurants in major cities like Paris, London, New York, Washington, Chicago, San Francisco, and Los Angeles.

Food and dining has a public face in Iran, but its fullest development and greatest glories are to be found in the private setting of the home, among relatives and friends. Especially in social gatherings, the variety and abundance of foods, as well as the conviviality and generosity of the host, are remarkable. Sharing food is an important mechanism of socialization and social bonding. A traditional proverb states that a way to win someone's favor is to share your food with them: *namakgir kardan*, which means "having someone to have a taste of the salt in your food" (i.e., to become bound by hospitality). Food is not an end itself but a means of family solidarity and social exchange, especially in the traditional world of the past when families were extended and eating was a communal affair within the extended family.

The culinary tradition in Iran has certainly been affected by the influence of modernity and Western customs, be it in the way of New World ingredients like tomatoes or potatoes, eating habits, or the appearance of fast-food shops. Indeed, the fastest growing restaurant type in Iran today would probably be pizza shops with delivery service. Yet on the whole, Iranian dining has proved remarkably resilient in preserving its essential character and distinct identity. Even pizza produced in Iran is not exactly the same as that found in the United States or Europe. Both the sauce and cheese used are closer to Persian flavors than American or Italian ones.

In general, culinary practices in Iran have been affected by several important cultural factors. The most obvious, of course, are the requirements of Islamic dietary law since the vast majority of the population are Muslims: meat should come from animals that have been ritually slaughtered; pork and certain other foods are forbidden; and wine or other alcoholic beverages, though certainly used by some people at various times, are illegal under Islamic law and have been strictly prohibited since the establishment of the Islamic Republic. Prior to the 1979 revolution, alcoholic drinks and pork meat in the form of ham and hot dogs were available in modernized sectors of major cities, even though these foods were avoided by the majority of people. Secularized Iranians, especially educated ones, are not much concerned about religious dietary restrictions.

There is also a kind of basic philosophy to Iranian cooking that has its sources in ancient Zoroastrian tradition and concepts perhaps derived ultimately from Galenic medical theory. Foods are regarded as being either "hot" (*garmi*) or "cold" (*sardi*) in their nature and in the effects they have on the consumer, inducing either excitement or lethargy, for example. For instance, while yogurt is regard as a cold item, red meat is classified as hot. Individual dishes and meals as a whole seek to balance these two qualities; spices are used in moderation, and ingredients often emphasize contrasting flavors like sweet and sour. Of course, the younger generation, educated in modern sciences, tends to be neither familiar with these traditional concepts nor to find them particularly relevant when it comes to modern food items like pizza.

BASIC FOODS

Wheat and rice are the two main cereal crops grown for human consumption in Iran, and one or both of these provide the staples found at virtually every Iranian meal. In earlier times, the national diet tended to be divided between areas where wheat or rice was produced and eaten exclusively, but today both products are grown and used throughout the country.

Grain crops such as wheat or barley are well suited for cultivation in the arable areas of the Iranian plateau and have been grown there since ancient times. Some, such as barley, are used mostly to feed livestock, but wheat is of course produced to make the variety of breads that form an important part of the daily diet. In towns and cities, it is customary to buy bread freshly made from one of the many neighborhood artisanal bakeries. That is why bakeries cook their bread three times a day: in the early morning, at noon, and in the evening. Scenes of crowded bakeries during these times are very common, not only in Iran, but all over the Middle East. Since most people come to purchase bread at the same time, bakeries have long lines at rush hours, and families prefer to send a male member, especially a teenager, to buy bread. Although mass-produced breads like those now found in Europe or the United States are not appealing to Iranian tastes, the fast pace and stretched nature of social life in big cities like Tehran are forcing some families to adjust to products of a number of Westernized bakeries.

Bread in general is known as *nân,* but there are several distinct varieties of bread produced at the bakeries. Two of the most common are *tâftun* and *lavâsh;* they are both baked in very thin, flat sheets pressed against the wall of the oven and differ primarily in the type of wheat (whole wheat or white) used to make them. *Lavâsh* bread offered in bakeries is usually soft. In rural areas, many families bake their own bread on a weekly basis and produce a hard *lavâsh,* which is softened at the time of use by sprinkling a little water on it. Another popular flat bread is *sangak,* which gets its name from the process of baking it on a bed of heated pebbles instead of the wall of the oven, which gives the bread a very crisp and irregularly surfaced texture. Finally, *barbari* is a special type of leavened bread that seems to have been introduced to Iran fairly recently and under the influence of European-style bread. It comes in a long, relatively narrow loaf about half an inch thick and 2- to 3-feet long and 8- to 12-inches wide. It is often slightly perforated before baking to give it added crispness and sprinkled with sesame seeds. It needs to be eaten soon after baking as it does not keep well and is often used as a breakfast bread. Each of these breads has its own typical shape: *tâftun* is round, *sangak* is oval in shape, *barbari* and *lavâsh* are rectangular. Religiously speaking, bread is treated with respect, and Muslims are taught to avoid dropping bread under the feet or dumping it in a disrespectful place. Unused bread is often used as a feed for birds.

The types and quantity of bread found at Iranian meals can to some extent be understood as an artifact of traditional dining habits. In earlier times, the custom was to eat sitting on the floor. A large cloth, called *sofreh,* would be spread out, and the bowls and platters containing the various dishes put on it. In the older times, there really weren't any individual plates or cutlery. Instead, the sheets of thin, flat bread served both as plates and eating utensils for holding or scooping up morsels of food. (The art and etiquette of dining in this fashion is frequently described in books by early Western travelers to Iran.) More recently, under the influence of European habits, the use of chairs, tables, forks, spoons, and so forth has become more common, especially in urban areas. In rural areas, villages, and among the lower social classes, it is still not unusual to find the traditional practices in use.

It might be thought surprising that rice would be a major crop in a country as arid as Iran, but certain areas, especially the relatively warm and humid shores of the Caspian, can support rice production. It is not known exactly when or how rice came to Iran, but it was almost certainly first grown in the Caspian region, and then its production and use spread to other parts of the country. In the plateau areas, rice was a fairly expensive food used mostly for luxury dishes at court and among the wealthy as late as the Safavid period. As production and transportation improved, it became an important element of the ordinary diet throughout the country, so much so in fact that the demand for rice has far outstripped the production capacity and necessitated its import. Long-grain rice is now used in a great variety of ways, from main dishes to breads and puddings and even as a breakfast food in some regions. Well-to-do families like to use an aromatic variety known as *bâsmati* rice, which is more expensive.

The simplest type of rice dish is known as *kateh*. The rice is washed and cooked until the water (slightly less than twice the volume of the rice) is absorbed. A good deal of butter is then added on top of the rice, which is covered and kept over low heat until done. The result is a fairly sticky kind of rice cake, which can be further compressed and molded if desired. *Kateh* is used mostly for a quick or a casual meal at home; it would never be served to a guest, because it lacks delicacy.

When cooked mixed with other ingredients such as meat or vegetables as a main dish, the rice is called a *polow*. Such *polow*s include those made with lentils (*adas-polow*), fava beans (*bâqela-polow*), sour cherries (*âlbâlu-polow*), barberries (*zereshk-polow*), or orange peel (*shirin-polow*), as well as many others.

Rice cooked as an accompaniment to another dish such as a stew or grilled meat is called *chelow*. The preparation of a *chelow*, however, is not a casual matter and actually requires a good deal of time and effort. The rice has to be washed and sometimes soaked overnight and then partially cooked in boiling water. It is then drained and rinsed before being returned to a pot with clarified butter and water to be steamed. The rice is heaped in a cone-shaped mound in the pot, which is covered with a special fabric top to prevent the steam from condensing and dripping back down on the rice, and kept warm until time for serving. This process gives the rice a wonderful taste and fluffy texture that is not at all sticky. It also creates a crunchy, buttery layer of rice at the bottom of the pot (called *tahdig*) that can be served alongside, or broken up over, the rice and is regarded as a choice delicacy. Before serving, some rice is colored and flavored with saffron and sprinkled on the top of the dish. This gives a beautiful look to the dish and adds a delicious taste to the rice.

A *chelow* served with grilled meat is known as *chelow-kabâb*. This is virtually the national dish of Iran and is a mainstay of restaurants all over the country. The meat may be a special type of lamb fillet (*barg*) or ground meat (*kubideh*). It is usually served with grilled tomatoes; butter, an egg yolk, red onion, and sumac can be mixed into the *chelow* according to one's taste. A stack of flat bread and a plate of fresh herbs (*sabzi*) round out this tasty, nutritious—and very filling—meal. Fresh herbs are used regularly and may serve the same function as a salad.

Chelow served with a stew is known as a *chelow-khoresh*. Almost all the stews, like the grilled meats, are based on either lamb or poultry (beef is not a common ingredient in Iranian cooking; fish may be used in some regions). The most highly regarded *khoresh* is undoubtedly *fesenjân*, chicken or duck cooked in a sauce of pomegranate and ground walnuts. A good *fesenjân* is considered the hallmark of an accomplished Iranian cook. It is but one, however, of a great variety of stews that showcase the many ingredients and considerable ingenuity in Iranian cooking: different stews feature vegetables (*qormeh sabzi*), green beans (*lubiâ*), okra (*bâmyeh*), peaches (*hulu*), quince (*beh*), eggplant (*bâdemjân*), spinach and prunes (*esfenâj o âlu*), split peas (*qaymeh*), or other ingredients.

A full Iranian dinner, especially on a social occasion, might include not only *chelow*, a number of different stews, and a copious amount of bread, but also an assortment of appetizers, soups, salads, side dishes, and desserts.

Only a sampling of these can be mentioned here. Typical appetizers include *mast o khiâr* (a mixture of yogurt and grated cucumber), *mâst o mosir* (a mixture of yogurt and minced shallot), and varieties of pickles (*torshi*), mostly prepared with vinegar and unlike the salty ones found in the West. A popular side dish might be *kuku,* a thick, spongy kind of soufflé (there are numerous varieties made with ingredients such as spinach, eggplant, peas, potatoes, herbs, or meat). Special cookies, puddings, candies, or cakes might be offered for dessert, but the finest desserts may well be the fresh fruits for which Iran is famous, especially the indescribably sweet and succulent Persian melon.

Snack foods constitute another rather important element of Iranian cuisine. These are typically called *âjil* (a mix of nuts and dried fruits). Iranians love to snack, so they munch on *âjil* not only before and after meals but also throughout the day, such as when out for a stroll. Ingredients of *âjil* may vary according to occasions, like *âjil-e Chahârshanbeh suri*, used during the celebration of the last Wednesday of the calendar year; *âjil-e shab-e yaldâ*, consumed on the longest night of the year; and *âjil-e moshkel-goshâ*, literally meaning "problem-solving mixed nuts and dry fruits" consumed during the New Year holidays in the hope of unraveling one's problems. Some of the more popular elements of *âjil* include pistachios, abundantly produced in Iran and known as one of the most important Iranian exports; roasted chickpeas (*nokhod*); and roasted seeds of pumpkins, melons, or sunflowers. Breaking the shell and retrieving the kernel of the seeds by teeth is an art Iranians demonstrate during their pastimes.

Soups (*âsh*) are a fundamental part of Iranian cuisine (in fact, the generic term for cooking, *âshpazi,* literally means "soup making"). Like stews, soups come in a number of varieties, each named for its main ingredient (beans, barley, yogurt, etc.). One of the most common soups is *âsh-reshteh,* made of vegetables, kidney beans, and thinly made flat noodles. Another widely used soup, which might also be regarded as a kind of stew, is *âb-gusht* ("meat broth"). Like many Iranian dishes, it is not prepared according to a fixed recipe so much as designed to take advantage of ingredients that are in season and readily available and to use them as economically as possible. The meat broth is prepared and then cooked with beans (typically garbanzo beans) and various other vegetables, herbs, or fruits. After preparation, the solid ingredients are typically strained out and mashed to a puree; the broth and puree are served separately along with flat bread. *Âb-gusht* may also be prepared and served in an individual pot, in which case it is customary to toss in some pieces of bread and mash it all to a pulp with a pestle. For poor and working class Iranians, *âb-gusht* is a mainstay of the daily diet. It is also a popular dish with more affluent classes on outings or picnics; for example, shops specializing in the dish can be found along hiking trails in the mountains north of Tehran.

As for beverages, tea can be regarded as the national drink of Iran. It is served hot and plain, usually in small, clear glasses. The traditional custom is to sip the tea through a hard lump of sugar (*qand*, or sugar cube) held in the front teeth. Many people now use samovars to keep a pot of brewed tea and hot water to mix with it before serving. Other traditional drinks are made from fruit juices, either freshly squeezed (*afshoreh*) or from prepared syrups (*sharbat*), and served with ice; *dugh* is a drink made from yogurt, mint, and either still or sparkling water. *Dugh* is often served with food. In recent years, of course, bottled sodas and similar drinks have also become common.

8

Family, Women, and
Gender Relations

Family is one of the most central and important social institutions in Iranian life. The family gives individuals social status, determines their life chances, protects them against all threats, and ensures their emotional health. Social life also revolves around the family and its kinship. Elders are the backbone of the family and garner the most authority and respect. Children, especially sons, are responsible for protecting and caring for their parents in their old age. Sending an ailing parent to a nursing home is a new concept and is not accepted by most Iranian families. Recently, a few nursing homes have been established in Tehran for elderly people without children or with children unable to care for them.

Family gatherings are the most important aspect of social life. As Iranians face strict limits on entertainment under a theocratic government, family gatherings have become extremely important, not only as a means of performing various rituals, sharing food, and so forth, but also as the safest and most protected site for entertainment. The Iranian family, like most other Middle Eastern families, used to be an extended family where new couples lived with their parents and siblings, either in the same compound or adjacent to one another. However, with increasing urbanization and social mobility, the number of extended families has declined; most new couples form their own households away from parental compounds.

To understand the Iranian family and the norms governing its operation, it is significant to start with a historical view of gender roles and women's status within the society.

HISTORICAL EVOLUTION OF WOMEN'S STATUS AND GENDER RELATIONS

The dominant view of women in postrevolutionary Iran, often reinforced by the mass demonstration of women in government rallies, is that they are all alike, all oppressed, obedient to their male counterparts, overly traditional, and shrouded in the veil (*châdor*). This could not be further from the truth. Though Iranian culture remains patriarchal, women in Iran are diverse, belong to different subcultures and social classes, and follow different traditions within the overall patriarchal culture. Women are ordered by the Islamic government to have appropriate *hejâb* (veil), but Iranian women demonstrate a great deal of diversity in their physical appearance as well as their behaviors. Some women are very modern, even more modern and more feminist than some of their counterparts in Western countries. Many women are traditional but not necessarily passive or even submissive to their partners or fathers. Though Islam and traditional Iranian culture command women's obedience to their husbands, not all women comply. Nor do all women put up with their husbands' dominance. Even in traditional households, where sexist attitudes might abound, women find many subtle ways of resisting these attitudes and even on occasion turn the tide in their favor. The reality of women's status in Iran and gender relations is complex and subject to change and diversity.

Although there is no such thing as a typical woman in such a geographically and culturally diverse society, cultural rules and religious regulations shape the lives of women in various communities in Iran. The most important cultural norm affecting a woman's life is the prevalent cultural association of a married woman with family honor. Women must be conscious of their public behavior and be constantly chaperoned by male relatives outside of the home. As involuntary guardians of society's moral contract, many women feel unduly restricted and held responsible for appropriate standards of behavior, lest they malign the patriarchy's honor. In many cases, privacy, freedom, and individuality are subsumed by the interests of family, husbands, or parents. Tribal and religious traditions also influence women's rights and obligations. For instance, among the Lurs, men retain absolute control over women, whereas among the Qashqâis, women have more freedom.

The gender relationship in Iran has gone through a sea change in the last century. Up until the early twentieth century, Iran was a segregated society in which urban women stayed home and the public arena was filled by men. Public places like bazaars were filled with men, and few women were seen roaming for shopping or traveling between destinations. A walk in the streets of Tehran today shows another picture. Women have an overwhelming presence in the public arena as shoppers, sellers, passers-by, police, drivers, and even spectators.

At the beginning of the twentieth century, women were denied the opportunity to pursue schooling, trades, politics, and even the arts. They had no visible presence in the public arena. The Iranian educational system was still traditional as male teachers and students met in private schools or even homes, known as *maktab-khâneh*. The few women who excelled in arts and education were the daughters or wives of aristocrats or politically influential elites who could afford private mentors. Even these educated families did not expose their wives or daughters to the public, as this would have damaged the reputation of the family.

The first efforts in educating girls began by a few educated women who had observed missionary schools in Iran and wished to create similar opportunities for Iranian women. At the close of the nineteenth century, a few schools emerged, where teachers taught modern curricula using a blackboard and chalk. Slowly, women activists succeeded in opening a few schools for girls. By 1913, some 2,500 girls were being taught in 63 girls' schools in Tehran. Urban women began breaking their traditional role by learning how to read and write. As demands for labor increased, women began working in silk-weaving and wool-spinning factories, fisheries, and the textile industry. Soon, this demand for labor was expanded to include different educational and service-oriented institutions.

As Rezâ Shah began his modernization of Iran in the 1930s and expressed an interest in breaking away from the tradition of secluding women, more and more women were educated and hired in government offices. Educational expansion and urbanization offered educated and willing families the opportunity to send their daughters to schools. The Pahlavi government viewed women's participation in the educational system as a sign of modernity and progress and encouraged families to send their daughters to school. In 1936, following Turkish leader Kemal Ataturk's earlier abolition of the veil in his country, Rezâ Shah banned the use of veil in public places, alienating a large segment of the population who viewed such a practice as an assault on their dignity and their religious beliefs. Although this policy could not be followed thoroughly and had to be relaxed, its impact of encouraging young women to participate in national life was drastic. The education of women went hand in hand with the expansion of opportunities for women's presence in the public sphere. After the establishment of universities, women were accepted at universities, and as they gained more education and skills, they began to take government jobs, especially in hospitals and schools.

A number of legislative and political developments during the Pahlavi rule increased women's chances of overcoming traditional obstacles in gaining civil protection and political participation in society. The first was women's enfranchisement as a part of the White Revolution in 1963. Although opposed by some segments of the religious community, the act resulted in women's participation in civil and political affairs. In the decade that followed, several women were elected to the parliament, and a woman was appointed as the minister of education. The second most important legal development affecting the lives of women during the Pahlavi era was the Family Protection Act (FPA) of 1967, which was revised in 1975. This legislation was meant to improve conditions for women; it changed existing practices regarding the legal age and conditions of marriage, a woman's right to divorce, and the practice of temporary marriage (*sigheh,* discussed in an earlier chapter); it also altered the legalities surrounding women's rights in the domestic sphere.

In 1966, the High Council of Iranian Women's Associations, which was established in 1959, was renamed as *Sâzmân-e Zanân-e Irân* (The Women's Organization of Iran [WOI]). Although the WOI actively campaigned for legal reforms, it was not able to mobilize women in any effective way. Its efforts often focused on urban, educated women; the majority of women from traditional sectors of society never connected with the WOI. Despite legal changes and gains in education and political participation, male attitudes toward women did not change much, and the majority of girls were socialized to become good wives and mothers rather than to seek education for future employment. There was a weak relationship between increased education and women's domestic attitudes. Girls married at a young age, and if they chose a career, it was often due to economic necessity and was always of secondary importance to that of their husbands.

The more Iran modernized, the more pressure was felt by the traditional sector, resulting in a polarized society with two separate cultures living side by side: one in which women stayed home and another where women studied and worked in public; one in which male-female interaction was limited to intimates and relatives alone, and another in which men and women interacted openly and attended schools, theaters, and parks. The traditional sector, being the larger segment, included most women in rural areas and small towns, and religious populations in urban areas. The modern sector included the educated segment of the population, mostly working in modern industries, government bureaucracies, and private businesses dealing with companies in foreign countries. The male-female interactions in the traditional sector remained relatively unchanged: arranged marriages, female housewives, male breadwinners, family travels only to religious destinations, attending mosques with some regularity, obedient children following parental choice of occupation, separate schools for boys and girls, and so forth. The modern sector looked into the Western lifestyle: marriages based on individual love with ceremonies in modern settings, both couples holding jobs, educating children with a higher expectation for social mobility, family vacations at beaches and resort towns, travels abroad, attending theaters and modern cultural centers with some regularity, living in modern houses and apartments, and so forth.

This polarization ended with the Iranian Revolution of 1979, in which both traditional and modern Iranian women came together in opposition to the shah's regime and participated in a revolution that opposed much of the shah's modernization programs. In the late 1970s, the political opposition to the shah brought secular women together with traditional women in massive demonstrations in Iranian cities to overthrow the Pahlavi regime. Women of all classes and ideological persuasions participated in anti-shah's demonstrations. Some young female members of underground political organizations even engaged in a few armed confrontations with the army. Since the demonstrations were sanctioned by the clerics, traditional women felt comfortable appearing in public. Traditional husbands also were disarmed of their religious reasons to disallow the public appearance of their wives. Scenes of revolution in the streets of Tehran, with millions of Iranian men and women of all stripes demonstrating together in defiance of the shah, seemed both unprecedented and miraculous.

The alliance did not last long. After the success of the revolution, secular women realized that their veiling in political sympathy with the traditional women was here to stay, as Âyatollâh Khomeini demanded that women dress "properly" and abolished the Family Protection Act. As the revolution succeeded and an Islamic Republic was established, women in government offices faced new restrictions on their movements and interactions with male colleagues, and many were asked to leave employment in order to open up the opportunities for men. Public places such as universities, schools, and government offices were segregated again. Women were barred from the legal profession as judges and were also denied entrance to certain fields in the universities. Prior to the revolution, women's public appearance and social interactions with men were regulated by tradition and religion. No civic law dictated the form and the extent of their interaction in public. However, since the revolution, male-female interaction has come under strict codes, both in public and private spheres. Nonrelated males and females are forbidden from having contact with each other, and the sexes are strictly segregated in public and even in private. Narrowly defined Islamic laws put in effect after the revolution are a constant reminder to men and women as they interact in various public arenas. The morality police are never far from people's minds during the course of their everyday lives. But the problem is not just the law but how these laws are interpreted differently by different men (father, husband, son, and unrelated males), religious authorities, and government officials. Furthermore, where the laws are specific, they are arbitrarily applied as different punishments are meted out in different circumstances, seemingly at the will of the police.

The measures introduced by the government created a divide between the secular women, who did not wish to veil, and the then dominant and powerful religious women, who had massive support from the government for religiously sanctioned employment and political activism. Demonstration against new restrictions was harshly suppressed, and women's demands for choosing one's dress, the preservation of the Family Protection Act, and the right to work in legal professions were denied. The war with Iraq gave the regime ammunition to suppress political dissent and push for a policy of Islamization of social and gender relationships. By and large, the government succeeded in having its way in the 1980s, and gender-relations in the country became much more segregated. The restrictive policies against women, coupled with the economic recession caused by the Iran-Iraq War, contributed to a notable decline in women's participation in the labor force, especially in the industrial sector. Yet, nonsecular women's participation in social and political life increased. Religious women were recruited for political offices and for supportive roles on the war front. In a religious environment, traditional men felt comfortable supporting their wives' employment and daughters' demands for higher education, music lessons, and English classes.

The increasing participation of women in education and the social arena caught up with the restrictive laws of 1980s. As the war ended and many female activists returned from the war front, they began to push for the gender equality promised by religious authorities. Arguing within the religious tradition, these women demanded the removal of discriminatory and restrictive policies that denied them equal opportunity and respect in society. These new Islamic feminists did not demand open male-female relationships, abolition of mandatory *hejâb* (veil), and elimination of the *Shari'a* as the basis of women's rights—demands that have been consistently made by secular women. These women saw to it that they have a say in the interpretation of the *Shari'a* and argued that genuine Islam is supportive of women's rights. This nonconfrontational and insider strategy made it easier for traditionalists to allow for a more flexible interpretation of religious edicts in the area of dress, women's participation in politics, and their mobility within educational and social institutions—as long as it did not contradict the Islamic law. This has dramatically changed the appearance of Iranian society since the early 1990s. Women's participation in the job market and education increased, and technical and engineering fields, once closed to women in the 1980s, were opened in 1993. The socioeconomic profile of women within the society increased and allowed them to obtain professional status in many fields. Despite the institutional barriers put in place by the Islamic Republic in cultural and male-female interactions, women have pushed the imposed boundaries farther out and made concerted efforts in penetrating various professions in the public arena, especially in the film industry, literary works, and mass media.

Today, public places are filled with women, women's dress has become more colorful and stylish, and young girls often try to interact with their male partners with more courage and a sense of rebellion. Though the morality police are still a reality of Iran's public arena, young women have been able to develop new gender relationships that are much more liberal than those experienced by their parents. In 2005, it was not unusual for an 18-year-old in metropolitan Tehran to have a boyfriend, even though this relationship may not have involved any physical intimacy.

Despite all these changes, studies dealing with the effect of traditional gender roles on women reflect a very challenging situation. The suicide rate among women has been high in several provinces due to the stress of high expectations put on women inside and outside the family. In recent years, runaway girls, usually escaping parental restrictions and physical harassment, have become a major challenge for the current government. Prostitution has increased, mostly due to restrictions put on the interactions between an increasingly large, young population, and it has now extended to young girls. Drug addiction is spreading among young females as well. Yet, the negative impact of gender roles is not limited to women alone. There are tremendous disappointments with the social imposition of traditional roles for both genders. The effect of socialization cannot be overestimated in placing men and women in unhappy patterns of domination and submission. Considerable pressures exist for many men, too, whose lives are defined as being the sole breadwinner, with pressure to protect the family honor. Not being able to provide for one's family is a serious threat to a husband's claim to manhood.

For women who stay home, housework is a full-time job and is therefore a significant deterrent to taking a job outside of the home. Although in recent years the number of women in workplace has increased, many educated and capable women remain excluded from traditional male domains. Although working women make significant contributions to the economy, particularly in rural areas and the heavily agricultural northern areas where women are essential to cultivating rice and raising livestock, women comprise a small percentage of the workforce. Women have difficulty securing jobs in management positions, especially in industry and services. Labor laws are not clear about equal pay, and where there is a clear mandate, it is largely ignored. Working outside of home is an issue for women in urban areas because rural women have always been engaged in family work or farmwork. Historically, the job market in urban areas has been restricted by gender. But recently, several factors have contributed to the gender neutralization of many occupations, which are thus becoming available to women as well. These include recent changes in the global economy, increasing female education, changes in the public's attitude about female work, economic necessity, and new legislation supporting female work.

While most traditional women in urban areas are content to remain housewives and forego outside work, most educated women are unhappy, and many resist the strict female roles imposed on them as mother, wife, housemaid, and nurturer. Women pursue work outside the home for several reasons: direct contribution to the family income, autonomy, personal needs, or fulfillment of educational capabilities. Women's wage-earning capabilities are sometimes perceived as a threat to their husbands' masculinity. Women who do have income feel that their contributions are underappreciated relative to the primacy of men's work.

In most cases, once a woman bears children, she ends her wage-earning work. As a mother, her devotion and energy are expected to return to the domestic sphere to raise the children. Still, the superwoman complex of the so-called career mom, so prevalent in Western industrialized countries, does have an Iranian counterpart as well. Many working women are bound to raise their children, attend to their husbands' needs, and still pursue their careers with excellence. Many working women with young children often experience guilt for not being able to fully attend to their children's care or resentment by others for not giving priority to their children's welfare.

MARRIAGE

Marriage in Iran, as everywhere else in the world, is a contract guided by individuality, religion, culture, and politics. Although Islam is the dominant religion and its impact is universal, when it comes to marriage requirements, procedures, and ceremonies, different ethnic and religious groups might have their own special considerations and arrangements. Today, Islamic Shi'ite laws are the basis of personal and family law in Iran, but their influence has never been absolute or universal. Non-Muslims and non-Shi'ites are allowed to follow their own religious practices in such matters. Starting from the 1930s onward, civic laws were established governing marriage, custody, and male-female relationships. The basis of these laws was religion, various ethnic and cultural traditions, and modern Western laws. While government attempts to register marriages were relatively effective, the attempt to implement uniform family laws was not always successful, especially among pastoral groups, ethic minorities following their own traditions, and religious minorities who married according to their own religious rules. More importantly, what is written down in Islamic law is not what is actually practiced by all Muslims. There is always a gap between the real and ideal culture. Prior to the Islamic Revolution of 1979, family interactions and conflicts were subject to civil laws. As mentioned before, after the revolution, the Family Protection Act was annulled and the *Shari'a* became the source for decisions about marriage, divorce, and custody. This book discusses only dominant laws and norms emanating from Islamic tradition. Readers are advised to look elsewhere for the specifics of marital rules and norms among ethnic and religious minorities.

The first requirement of marriage is a legal contract stipulating the conditions of the marriage and its dissolution. Islamic law requires the consent of the woman at the time of the contract and that the contract be witnessed by two men, or one man and two women, of the groom's family. Women marrying for the first time, thus being virgins, require parental permission for marriage. Both Islamic law and the cultural tradition give the father ultimate say over whom his daughter is allowed to marry. A previously married woman is free to consent to marriage to her suitor, even if her parents might not agree. Going against a parent's wishes would be difficult because parents often bear much of the economic burden of marital ceremonies; without their cooperation, it would be nearly impossible for a woman to proceed, unless she was wealthy and willing to cope with the consequences of her family's dissatisfaction.

In many cultures, the marriage union is accompanied with various forms of exchanges: goods, money, and favors. The essential component of a marital contract under Islamic law in Iran is the bride price, or *mahriyeh*. *Mahriyeh* is stipulation in a prenuptial agreement signifying the bridegroom's right to his bride's sexual and reproductive organs in return for a monetary commitment to her. Though the woman has a right to ask this amount at any time in marriage, it is customary that *mahriyeh* is only asked at the time of divorce or the husband's death. In the latter case, the amount is deducted from his estate before the inheritance is divided according to religious law. Some families perceive *mahriyeh* as a form of insurance against a man's arbitrary decision to dissolve marriage, thus demanding a higher sum in cases where the family senses a higher degree of unpredictability about the groom's character and future plans. Though the amount of *mahriyeh* reflects the social status of the bride's family, it varies depending on a couple's social class, educational level, tribal customs, kinship traditions, and regional norms. Some families treat *mahriyeh* as a status symbol, demanding a higher amount as a sign of high status for their daughter. In recent times, to protect against inflation, *mahriyeh* is specified in valuable fixed objects such as gold. For instance, a girl's *mahriyeh* might be 250 gold coins. Since these coins have a fixed weight, they will appreciate in value as inflation devalues the national currency. Prior to the revolution, the Pahlavi Coin, now called the Âzâdi (Freedom) Coin, is the denomination used.

Another outdated and rarely practiced custom is the giving of money by the groom to bride's family, known as *shir-bahâ* (nursing fee). This was a tradition among poorer families where the groom's family offered the bride's mother a mutually agreed upon amount as compensation for her having nursed the bride. In fact, the money was a form of financial assistance to the bride's family in order to be able to fund the dowry (*jahâz*), thus maintaining the ability to support their daughter with some means of living as she started her new life—a very important practice for maintaining one's social status in the community as well.

Mahriyeh is also tied to the dowry (*jahiziyeh*) or household items brought into marriage by the woman. The wealthier the woman's family, the higher the probability of demanding a higher *mahriyeh* and offering a more extensive *jehâz*, as it is often called. The responsibility to provide *jehâz* at the time of a daughter's marriage is a major financial burden for parents. People jokingly offer sympathy to men who happen to have more girls or only girls in their families.

In classical Islamic law, another requirement of marriage is that both the bride and the groom have reached puberty. Although the law technically defined puberty as age 12 for boys and age 9 for girls, this was not often used in practice for determining a suitable age for marriage except perhaps in remote rural areas and among very poor religious families. But even in those cases, prior to the revolution of 1979, such marriages were not recorded formally because the official marriage age set by the Family Protection act was 20 for boys and 18 for girls. After the Islamic Revolution, these ages were reduced to 9 for girls and 14 for boys. The reformists in the Sixth Majles introduced a bill to raise these legal ages, but it was rejected by the Guardian Council—an official body of religious experts who oversee all the laws made by the parliament. Still, the legal age does not reflect the realities of the actual marriage age. In 2004, the average age of first marriage was 26.7 for men and 23.9 for women (up from 24 for men and 20 for women in 1986). As a general rule, rural, less educated, and poorer families usually marry off their children sooner than educated, middle- to upper-middle-class families. A major factor contributing to the increase in marriage age is the financial burden of marriage in an economy with a high rate of unemployment. It should be noted that the age differential between the man and woman has also been declining. Traditionally, men married women much younger than themselves. The rise of public awareness about the negative impacts of such marriages has made both parents and young women hesitant to accept suitors much older than the woman.

Though polygamy is recognized by the Koran (up to four wives), and it has been an ancient tradition predating Islam, it is not widely practiced, and Iranian society generally does not approve of it. The instances are rare and mostly limited to traditional, wealthy men and poorer and widowed women. Traditional Islamic law states that the wives must be treated equally, and current laws require that existing wives agree to their husband's new marriage. A man who is determined to marry a new wife, especially when he does not have convincing reasons for asking permission of his first wife, often fabricates her permission or marries the new wife without declaring his first marriage. These cases are often the subject of television shows and comedy films.

Homosexuality, although it exists underground, is illegal; those found in such a relationship, male or female, are severely punished as adulterers since the Koran forbids same-sex intercourse. Although not all religious scholars agree on the type and extent of punishment, in Iran, homosexual partners found in actual intercourse, with the testimony of four witnesses, would be sentenced to death. Since 1980, Iran has executed many individuals charged with homosexual acts.

Though Islam allows a Muslim man to marry a non-Muslim woman as long as she believes in one of three religions recognized by Islam as "religion with a scripture" (Christianity, Judaism, and Zoroastrianism), a Muslim woman is not allowed to marry a non-Muslim man unless he converts to Islam first. Given the fact that the number of Iranians marrying non-Muslims has increased due to the postrevolutionary emigration of over 3 million Iranians to foreign countries, the the law has become hard to implement and has not been enforced with regularity.

Modern marriage is supposed to be based on love. However, not all marriages are based on individual love. Although arranged marriages occurred more in the past, still there are reasons other than family arrangements or personal love influencing the decision to marry. Criteria used for selecting a wife vary depending on social class, level of education, and religious devotion. Although physical attraction, personality, chastity, and decency are primary factors, wealth, family obligations, ethnic considerations, and religious devotion play a role in many cases. Marriages also stem from curiosity or a desire to escape a restrictive family environment and achieve a modicum of status and autonomy in society.

In general, premarital sex and intimate relationships are prohibited. However, this rule is often applied to girls rather than boys, and socializing between boys and girls is not uncommon among middle- and upper-class families, especially in major cities. Historically, dating has been taboo in Iran by most standards. Even today, where women have the chance to meet their prospective husbands in college or at work, a combination of social and administrative restrictions basically negate one-on-one cross-gender socialization. Women's autonomy in making marriage choices is significantly dependent on socioeconomic class and education. Uneducated women with no income are economically dependent on their parents and in most cases live with them, thus having no choice but to agree to their wishes regarding timing and the suitability of a prospective husband.

In a gender-segregated society, it is no exaggeration to say that most women are naïve about men, relationships, courtship, or even how to interact with potential suitors. Women's perspectives on arranged marriage range from complete resistance to complete acquiescence. Having married as a way to escape from an unhappy home environment, some women do not know the personality and temperament of their husbands until they live under the same roof. The same is sometimes true of men in arranged marriages in traditional settings. Most divorces are reported to be based on personality incompatibility.

Marriage requests are always initiated by the groom's family. A woman might be interested in a man and make her wishes known to him privately if the two have premarital contact at work or school. However, a formal request for marriage comes from the groom's side. Women do not lose their surnames by marriage. There is no social or legal requirement to change their names after marriage. Even those women who use their husbands' last names do so symbolically because the legal change of names is almost unheard of. Those women who do use their husbands' last names are often married to high-ranking officials or well-known public figures. Also, legally, and by religious laws, women are allowed to maintain their own wealth and continue to add to it if it generates profits or income. However, in reality, most women of the lower and middle class come to their marriage with little assets, except their *jahiziyeh*. In recent years, modern, educated working women with independent occupations have acquired better social and legal status in keeping their own earnings for themselves.

Once married, a woman is expected to bear children and be loving, loyal, trustworthy, tender, giving, and gracious. She is responsible for raising children, preparing food, and taking care of the primary needs of the whole family (hygiene, clothing, family gatherings, etc.). Rural and nomadic women have the additional tasks of taking care of animals and helping with farming. The husband is also expected to respect his wife and her family. However, given the patriarchal and patrilocal nature of the family, it is the man's family that demands a lot more from the new daughter-in-law than the bride's family from the son-in-law. Iranian mothers-in-law have often been stereotyped as being controlling and demanding. As time has passed and women have become educated and economically independent and often do not live with their in-laws anymore, the mother-in-law has lost her power over the daughter-in-law. In case of infertility, in most cases women are confronted with the choice of either divorce or acceptance of their husband's decision to marry a second wife (known as *havu*). Women and children are not permitted to leave the country without the father's or husband's permission.

A wife's power or influence within the family depends on a host of factors: her personality, parental status, education, occupational skills, and age. In addition, a married woman's power over a lifetime is variable. Educated and professional women often do not settle for a traditional arrangement in which men make all decisions. While some women remain submissive and relatively powerless for their whole lives, others become the more influential spouse over time, especially when buffered from a husband's authority by adult children. Generally, having children gives women more say in the family, and as children grow and develop strong bonds with their mothers, women gain more leverage over their husbands. While having children adds to a wife's responsibilities, for traditional women, it gives them more power over their husbands' arbitrariness and unpredictability. Having children often obligates a husband to a family, thus preventing him from possible infidelity since men are expected to provide for their family and protect their children.

Although infidelity is not tolerated in Iranian culture, it does happen, and it is found more among men than women. Women found in extramarital affairs are severely punished and often denied social standing. Men who have extramarital affairs or who keep concubines have to go through many efforts to conceal their infidelity, because, when exposed, it would bring them shame and in some cases severe punishment.

MARRIAGE RITUALS AND CEREMONIES

When a man's family makes his wishes known to the woman's family and the proposal is accepted, numerous formalities, ceremonies, and rituals follow. The couple has to go for a blood test and receive a clearance certificate from designated health agencies for blood compatibility and related diseases. Islamic law does not absolutely require any specific arrangements for the marriage ceremony, and most are determined by cultural variables. Though no part of these ceremonies should violate Islamic norms, minor deviations from these norms, particularly in the area of entertainment associated with the wedding, are often tolerated. The number of parties and events associated with marriage ceremonies varies depending on the ethnic and regional subcultures and the economic status of the families involved. The following is a breakdown of some of these ceremonies. While in some families these events are conducted separately, in others they are combined and often indistinguishable. Social class, family status, circumstances surrounding the wedding, the couple's autonomy or dependence on their parents/family, and other factors determine the variation in wedding ceremonies.

Preparation Events

In most cases, especially in modern times, the bride and groom have known each other and might have even talked about their plans, then informing their parents of their intentions. If so, the families proceed to the next stage. In most arranged cases, which were typical of past and even some current traditional families, the groom's family makes several unobtrusive efforts to have a close assessment of the prospective bride's personality and behavior, if she is not already intimately known by them. A groom's mother or sisters may visit the prospective bride in social gatherings or talk to her friends and acquaintances.

Engagement

The engagement process involves the *Khâstegâri* (marriage request) and *nâmzadi* (engagement) ceremonies, either independent of each other or combined. *Khâstegâri* is a meeting during which the groom's family visits the bride's family and formally asks for a union between the young couple. The groom's family takes different types of gifts with them for this occasion. Sweets are the most common gift for urban families. During this meeting, the bride's family requests her to come into the guest room, thus allowing all members of the groom's family who might not have been involved in the earlier screenings to have a brief view of her. After this ceremony and engagement, where the ring is exchanged and the conditions of marriage are negotiated (the amount of *mahriyeh,* where they plan to live, whether the daughter should be allowed to continue her education, etc.), the couple may begin dating each other. Among traditional families, this might be a supervised date, where an adult will accompany the couple. In modern times, especially in the cities, girls and boys have often dated each other prior to this event, and *khâstegâri* is simply a way of formalizing their desire to marry.

The 'aqd Ceremony

Modern marriage is a civic contract that needs to be registered with government officials. In traditional Islamic law, marriage is a contract between individuals and does not require the involvement of any government or religious agencies. However, to be valid, the contract (*'aqd*) must be witnessed; customarily, witnessing takes place at a ceremony presided over by a religious authority. In the presence of the witnesses, a religiously sanctioned text is read prior to finalization of the marriage. While the cleric reads the text, two women hold a fabric above the couple's head, while a third woman rubs two pieces of rock sugar against each other over the fabric as a way of symbolically sweetening their life. When the marriage is officiated and vows are exchanged, the couple starts their life together by feeding each other spoonfuls of honey or fruit jelly. Among religious conservatives, no kisses are exchanged in front of the guests—a tradition enthusiastically abandoned by Westernized, urban, educated youth. During this ceremony, the amount of *mahriyeh* is specified, and the new couple is asked to sign the marriage documents (*aqd-nâmeh* or *qabâleh*). In recent times, especially in the past decade, many educated or wealthy women request a prenuptial agreement in which the man is obligated to grant the woman certain rights: guaranteeing the woman and her children the right of travel without further permission from the husband, the right to initiate divorce, the right to custody of their children, the right to family property beyond what is designated in the *Shari'a*, and so on. *The 'aqd-nâmeh is to be notarized by authorities and registered.*

The *'aqd* procedure itself is fairly simple. However, it has historically been a festive moment for the family, involving the participation of close relatives of both families, music, dancing, and an elaborate arrangement known as the *sofreh-ye 'aqd*. Literally, the *sofreh* is a tablecloth spread out on the floor, with various objects placed on it. The *sofreh-ye 'aqd* is the occasion of the marital vows. Rooted in pre-Islamic Zoroastrian symbolism, containing vital elements in one's life, it is used in most marriages regardless of religion. The items placed on the *sofreh* vary according to region, ethnicity, religion, and the family's economic status. A typical *sofreh-ye 'aqd* includes some of the following: various herbs and spices, representing something or guarding against evil spirits; salt; rock sugar (*kaleh qand*); rice; an assortment of sweets and pastries; bread; cheese; jam; honey; eggs; nuts; flowers; needle and threads; and a holy book, depending on the religion of the family. A mirror is always placed on the *sofreh* right in front of the new couple. Many people also put a book of poems by Hâfez on the *sofreh*, either in addition to or in place of the Koran.

The Wedding Celebration (*jashn-e 'arusi*)

This is the largest and most public aspect of marriage. Once the couple is engaged, they will have a wedding party in which families, relatives, and friends are invited. The wealthier the couple, the larger, fancier, and more elaborate the party becomes. Traditionally, wealthier families held the wedding party in their own home since it was large enough to accommo-date all the guests. Poorer families often arranged for their parties at a large house owned by a relative or acquaintance. Nowadays, the Western model of having the ceremony in a party hall with facilities is followed, and many hold their wedding in hotels, rental party halls, and picturesque outdoor facilities. Traditionally, the groom's family is responsible for the expenses associated with this party. Some modern families have started dividing the costs between the two families. In the past, it was not unusual for a man to engage and wed later, thus separating the *aqd* ceremony from the wedding. In most cases, these days the '*aqd* ceremony and wedding celebration are either combined or are sequenced to occur on the same day.

CHILDREN AND SOCIALIZATION

Socialization of children is based on a host of norms and values drawn from Iranian traditions, Islamic morality, and historical communal ethics. Relation-ships between children and parents are framed within social ethics known as *adab o ehterâm* (discipline and respect). Although the rules of *adab o ehterâm* are vague and fluid and might vary by subcultural values, parents are often clear as to their expectations from their children in specific situations. Good ethics are seen as a basis for strengthening family cohesion, communal solidarity, and the collec-tive conscience. These ethical values often cut across ethnic and religious divides, thus influencing all, regardless of their communal or religious orientation.

Although the Iranian culture is patriarchal, and men are granted much legal power over their wives, in the household, authority is shared between husband and wife, even though unequally. In recent times, children have gained more influence over urban parents than they ever had in the past. Traditionally, men had authority over the decisions related to the economic status of the family and the place of residence, and women over the living conditions, children's affairs, household consumption, and the daily interactions with relatives. Although professional men are becoming more helpful to their wives with respect to child care since their work hours allow them late afternoon presence at home, women still play a much bigger role in child care than men do. Women who do not work outside of home spend a lot more time with their children than those who work. Men's interactions with children remain limited to emergencies, evening hours, and holidays. In smaller towns and rural communities, women also depend on their relatives and other women in the community for help with child care and household work. Tasks requiring extra help are shared through a reciprocal relationship neatly woven in kinship and community networks.

The traditional Iranian culture requires that once a girl reaches puberty, or starts menstruating, she must cover her body and hair when in the presence of males outside of her immediate family. While for traditional Muslims this means wearing a *châdor* (head-to-toe cover), more modernized Muslims require that their daughters wear a head scarf, a loose tunic, and long pants. In older times, the onset of female puberty would also prohibit young girls from interacting with their male friends—a practice still found in rural areas and among traditional families.

In earlier times, when schooling was not prevalent and the major influence on children's lives came from the family, parents had a tremendous impact on the lives of their children. Parents imposed many restrictions on their children's activities. Children were not permitted to initiate any major activities without the consent of their parents. These activities might include the choice of play or a friend, and at older ages, an educational major or even a spouse, especially by girls.

Although the relationships between parents and children have been subject to change in the course of time, children are taught at an early age that they are to remain obedient to and respectful of their elders in all places and at all times, related or not. They are to initiate the greeting to their parents and elder siblings and relatives—a rule pretty much observed in interaction with acquaintances, friends, colleagues, and neighbors. Older people are to be respected in all situations, and priority should be given to them in initiating eating at the table, entering a room or house, speaking in public gatherings, and other settings.

These restrictions were particularly stifling for young people and often, in educated families, led to subtle manipulations, resistance, or even rebellion, by children. As schooling has become prevalent and the media's influence has become global, parents find it difficult to impose these restrictions. In most cases, they have become counterproductive as more young people in today's Iran make their own selection of careers, friends, and partners. The postrevolutionary period, especially since the 1990s, has seen a sea change in youths' behavior. Despite increasing autonomy asserted by the youth in recent years, young people still face considerable pressure from their parents and society to conform to religious and social values. Many parents try to control their children into adulthood, and girls must endure especially intense scrutiny.

Parental involvements in child raising and child training varies in different families, depending on social class, age, occupation, and children's gender. Generally, mothers have tremendous influence in the upbringing of children at an early age because fathers are working outside the home and are often absent during the day. Lower-class fathers have less time and inclination to be engaged in taking care of their children's affairs. As children get older, slowly the father's influence on his children, especially boys, becomes more salient. In lower classes, especially farm families, boys are taken to work alongside the father, thus engaging them in work as well as influencing their behavior by exposure to the father's personality. Fathers remain the real role models for boys, especially in traditional families. More modernized and educated families often raise their boys with a more idealized model in mind. Most fathers want their sons to achieve what they could not achieve in their own life. Most middle-class parents expect their sons to be engineers and medical doctors. In fact, one of the major complaints of youths is the imposition of career choices by parents.

Daughters remain predominantly under the influence of their mothers because they are generally at home, unless they have reasons to be outside (schooling, shopping, visiting relatives, etc.). This is more the case among the poorer, less educated, and more traditional families in which mothers are predominantly housewives. Girls' lives are undeniably connected to their mothers' experiences and perceptions about gender roles, marriage, and social expectations of propriety. The mother-daughter bond occupies a spe-cial place in the family because the mother can provide a unique ally for her daughter as she has the shared experience of being in the same family with similar expectations, duties, responsibilities, and honor. Moreover, this relationship can buffer the husband's influence over female children. This relationship often is one of mutual dependency because as most women's mothers have been young mothers, the eldest daughter is often her mother's closest friend and confidant. A mother's tribulations are often wholly passed onto her daughters, who serve as de facto therapists. This causes many girls to carry the burden of their mothers' woes, a damaging psychological condition experienced by most women.

Fathers' interactions with and influence on their daughters are very complex and quite significant. There is diversity in father-daughter relations, indicating that the nature of their interactions is not solely dictated by an unwaver-ingly stern patriarchy. Some fathers are very involved with their daughters, especially those whose occupation and education allow time for more family involvement. These fathers provide genuine love and positive support for their daughters' career growth and maintain constructive relationships within the family. Others are aloof and limit their role to breadwinning. Yet there are fathers acting like despots, whose constant surveillance and restriction of their daughters' activities causes them to run away from home in order to escape total patriarchal domination.

DIVORCE

Although Islamic law allows for divorce, social norms neither encourage nor easily accept it. Courts also do not approve requests for divorce without ade-quate counseling and reconciliation efforts. The current Islamic government has instructed judges to slow the process so that couples may find enough time to overcome the initial disagreements that had led to a request for separation.

Many women in distressed marriages are under immense social pressure to remain married no matter how destructive the marriage is to the couple or their children. This pressure comes from their husbands, relatives, and peer groups. Social and economic support for divorced women is often negligible in the face of, at the least, basic economic stability from a wage-earning husband. Many women are effectively trapped in marriage, because of their own economic marginalization and concerns for the welfare of the children.

According to the *Shari'a,* men have the right to divorce at will, and women cannot initiate a divorce that their husbands oppose unless they can prove the husbands' sexual impotence, drug addiction, incarceration for life, or other conditions specified by religion. One protection given to women after the revolution is the authority to write a prenuptial agreement stipulating the conditions under which the couple may initiate a divorce. This has been a no-starter for women for several reasons. First, in traditional families in rural and small towns, most decisions about marriage are made by parents based on family status, economic concerns, and community obligations. Second, large numbers of eligible women do not find themselves in such a social and economic position to be able to raise the specter of divorce at such an early stage in their life. Third, men generally perceive such a demand as a sign of assertiveness—a feature still unattractive to prospective male suitors. Finally, even when such a contract is signed, it has to be implemented by a male-dominated court—a system negatively biased toward divorce.

According to Islamic law, once divorced, women are prohibited from remarrying for three menstrual cycles in order to determine the paternity of any unborn child. Similar waiting periods apply to women who have lost their husbands by death. After a divorce, men often retain a remarkable amount of control over their ex-wives, largely due to custody laws, which generally grant custody to the mother only until the children reach the age of 7 and only if she has not remarried. Moreover, divorced women face an especially powerful stigma and are often pressured to remarry. In most cases, being widowed or divorced makes it very difficult for a woman to find a suitable husband, unless she is rich, young, or physically attractive.

Despite all the misgivings and negative attitudes about divorce, the number of couples divorcing has been increasing steadily. This increase is pronounced among younger couples without children and living in major cities, especially Tehran, in which more than a quarter of all divorces take place. As the population has migrated to cities and become more educated and more mobile, traditional norms holding couples together in hard times have given way to convenience, autonomy, and higher expectations of family life. As women have become more educated, employed, and financially independent, they have become more reluctant to remain in bad marriages. According to government statistics, 80 percent of requests for divorce are filed by women.

Sample Costumes from 2000 B.C. to 1900 A.D.

1. 2000 B.C. Elamite man.
2. 700 B.C. Median soldier.
3. 400 B.C. Achaemenid noble.
4. A.D. 800 Hypothetical Abbasid official.
5. A.D. 1100 Saljuq man.
6. A.D. 1100 Saljuq woman.

7. A.D. 1600 Safavid.
8. 1780 Lotf-'Ali Khân Zand.
9. 1740 Afsharid man.
10. 1831 Âghâ Mohammad Qâjâr.
11. 1890 Zoroastrian woman.
12. 1870s Qâjâr courtiers.

Prepared and provided by Ali Akbar Mahdi.

Sample Costumes from 1900 to 2005

1. 1900 Woman outdoors.
2. 1904 Qâjâr elite.
3. 1920 Aristocratic politician.
4. 1924 Foreign minister.
5. 1929 Parliament deputy.
6. 1958 Writers, Dâneshvar, and Âl-e Ahmad.
7. 1968 Education minister.
8. 1970s Traditional and modern females at the beach.
9. 1980–Present, government official.
10. 2000 Vice president.
11. 2004 Female Islamic militia.
12. 2005 Woman in Tehran.

Prepared and provided by Ali Akbar Mahdi.

A Sample of Traditional Costume of Different Ethnics in Iran

1. Abyâneh, female.
2. Armenian woman.
3. Azerbaijani woman.
4. Baluchi woman.
5. Kurdish woman.
6. Qashqâi woman.

7. Zoroastrian woman.
8. Baluchi man.
9. Khorâsâni man.
10. Kurdish man.
11. Qashqâi man.
12. Turkoman man.

Prepared and provided by Ali Akbar Mahdi. Drawings 3–12 are based on the Sketches in 'Abdolhosayn Sa'idiân, *Sarzamin va mardum-e irân* [The land and people of Iran], Iran: Tehran, 1372 [1994].

9

Holidays, Festivals, and Annual Events

Iranians tend to be enthusiastic observers of holidays and festivals, and Westerners are likely to be struck by the very large number of occasions they have for celebrating them. Indeed, even some members of the Iranian parliament (Majles) have complained that the country has so many declared holidays (as many as 145 nonworking days in a year, with about 26 official public holidays) that it is adversely affecting the development of the country. There are what might be called civil holidays, general Islamic holidays, specifically Shi'ite holidays, and national holidays, as well as events particular to specific religious and ethnic minorities in the country. Some are quite joyous and festive in tone, others somber and reflective, and still others amount to little more than days on which government offices and some businesses are closed. The focus in this chapter is on those holidays and festivals that have an official or quasi-official status affecting the country as a whole.

IRANIAN CALENDARS

Before attempting to review the major holidays and festivals celebrated in Iran, it is necessary to explain some features of the various systems of dating in use there. The Gregorian calendar familiar to Westerners and now used in many countries around the world is known in Iran, but it has no official standing (in fact, at times its use has even been outlawed). Dates from that calendar may be given on newspapers or various documents, especially those involving non-Iranians, but this is purely for ease of reference. Instead, Iranians use two other calendar systems for official purposes: the Islamic lunar calendar (*qamari*) and the Iranian solar calendar (*shamsi*).

The lunar calendar was introduced in Iran following the Arab conquest and the spread of Islam. For many centuries it was the only calendar in general use, and it still serves as the only system for dating Islamic religious holidays. It was based on an era (*hejri*) beginning with the year of the Prophet Mohammad's emigration from Mecca to Medina (the Hegira [*hejrat*] in A.D. 622). The year consists of 12 months, each of which begins with the sighting of a new moon. The Arabic names of the months are used, but most are pronounced somewhat differently in Persian: Moharram, Safar, Rabi'-ol-Avval (I), Rabi'-ol-Âkher (II), Jomâdâ-ol-Ulâ (I), Jomâdâ-ol-Âkhereh (II), Rajab, Sha'ban, Ramazân, Shavvâl, Zu'l-Qa'deh, and Zu'l-Hejjeh (in colloquial Persian, the latter two are often pronounced as Zi-Qa'deh and Zi'l-Hejjeh or Zi-Hajjeh). Since a lunar cycle takes just over 29.5 days, and the sighting of a new moon depends greatly on local conditions, it is possible any given month might have 29 or 30 days. As a matter of convenience, printed calendars assume the months will alternate between 30 and 29 days, with the last month having one or the other. This enables one to estimate fairly closely when a holiday or other event should occur, but the dates may be off a bit depending on the actual astronomical observations.

Long before the coming of Islam, Iranians used a very sophisticated solar calendar, usually referred to in its classical form as the New Avestan Calendar, that was closely tied to the beliefs and practices of the Zoroastrian religion. The year began at the moment of the vernal (spring) equinox, and consisted of 12 equal months of 30 days. There were no weeks, and each day had its own name. Since the tropical year (the time to complete the cycle from one spring equinox to the next) is actually 365.2422 days, intercalary days were added as needed to make up the difference. Other adjustments were to be made every 120 and 1,440 years in order to keep the calendar in sync with the actual position of the sun.

A key difference between the two calendar systems is that dates in the solar system correspond consistently to seasons, while those in the lunar calendar do not. Since the lunar year (354.367 days) is shorter than the solar year, dates gradually cycle backward through the seasons: For example 1 Moharram 1400 fell on November 21, 1979, but now, in 2006/1427, 1 Moharram has moved all the way back to January 31. Even in the Islamic period, variations of the old solar calendar thus continued to be used, especially for fiscal and administrative purposes (since it worked better for assessments tied to the agricultural season). The most technically advanced and widely accepted of these solar calendars was the Jalâli calendar, devised by a committee of celebrated mathematicians and astronomers in 1079.

In 1911, during the course of the Iranian Constitutional Revolution, the Majles made a version of this solar calendar the official one. It used the names

of the 12 signs of the zodiac for the names of the months, but this was modified by a new law in 1925 that restored the use of the names from the Jalâli
calendar. These are still in use today: Farvardin, Ordibehesht, Khordâd, Tir,
Mordâd, Shahrivar, Mehr, Âbân, Âzar, Dey, Bahman, and Esfand. The year
begins at the exact moment of the vernal equinox. The first 6 months have 31
days, the next 5 months have 30 days, and Esfand may have 29 or 30 days.
Like the lunar calendar, this solar calendar uses an era beginning with the
Hegira, but the difference in the length of the respective years means that
the lunar and solar *hejri* years do not correspond: for example, the current
(A.D. 2006) *qamari* year, 1427, is 1384 according to the *shamsi* calendar.

The result of all this is that certain holidays are determined on the basis
of the national or solar calendar, while Islamic religious holidays follow the
lunar calendar (somewhat like the way Independence Day is a fixed date in
the civil calendar of the United States, but the dates of Easter or Yom Kippur
vary according to a different religious calendar). Converting the lunar dates
to the equivalent in other calendars also involves a certain amount of impreci-
sion and variation from year to year, but the Iranian solar dates can be given
an equivalent date in the Gregorian calendar quite easily. The only complica-
tion is that the start of the year on the vernal equinox always corresponds to
1 Farvardin but in the Gregorian calendar may be March 21 or March 20
(in leap years). Thus the Gregorian equivalents given in the following discussion would be advanced one day in leap years (e.g., Islamic Republic Day, 12
Farvardin, usually falls on April 1, the Gregorian date on which the event it
commemorates actually occurred, but in 2004, a leap year, it was celebrated
on March 31).

CIVIL HOLIDAYS

Like all countries, Iran has holidays that commemorate special days in
the history of the nation-state. It really cannot be said, however, that these
holidays are deeply rooted in the culture. They are political in nature and
as such tend to be ephemeral, going in and out of fashion according to the
dictates of the time, and rather formless, with few if any clearly defined ways
of observing them. Those currently being celebrated are thus all of rather
recent vintage, replacing the set of such holidays observed during the time of
the Pahlavi regime. Most are linked to the events of the Islamic Revolution
and the life of Âyatollâh Khomeini: the anniversary of Khomeini's arrest for
leading the protests of 1963 (15 Khordâd/June 5); the "Magnificent Victory
of the Islamic Revolution of Iran" commemorating Khomeini's return to
Iran and ascension to power in 1979 (22 Bahman/February 12); the plebiscite establishing the Islamic Republic (12 Farvardin/April 1). There is also a

holiday commemorating the day on which the Anglo-Iranian Oil Company was nationalized in 1951 (29 Esfand/March 20). Perhaps as part of the effort to reduce the number of official holidays, several similar observances no longer seem to be included on the official list (e.g., holidays commemorating the martyrs of the revolution on 17 Shahrivar/September 8 and the assassination of Âyatollâh Beheshti in a bombing of a meeting of the Islamic Republican Party on 7 Tir/June 28).

Of all these civil holidays, the one that seems to have acquired a truly substantial and popular place in the culture of the country is that held in observance of the "Heart-Rending Departure of the Great Leader of the Islamic Republic of Iran" on the day of Khomeini's death (14 Khordâd/June 4). In this case, the civil and political aspect of the holiday has merged with two typical aspects of Shi'ite religious holidays in Iran—the special significance attached to mourning the death of an individual (as opposed to celebrating his or her birth) and the ritual visitation of shrines. On other holidays, people might do nothing more than take a day off from work to enjoy themselves, but this is meant to be a real day of grief. Black flags symbolizing mourning are displayed everywhere, and a somber demeanor is more or less mandatory. Many people take the opportunity to spend the day at some place connected to Khomeini: the village of his birth, the city where he received his religious education (Qom), or the massive mausoleum built over his tomb near the entrance to the famous Behesht-e Zahrâ cemetery south of Tehran. For the holiday, literally hundreds of thousands of people visit the Khomeini shrine to observe mourning ceremonies and to listen to sermons of remembrance. Of course, those Iranians who have been disappointed in the outcome of the revolution and who oppose the Islamic government are not interested in participating in any of this. Most activities associated with the holiday are official ones and organized by the government.

MUSLIM RELIGIOUS HOLIDAYS

Muslim religious holidays and festivals have long been an essential component of Iranian cultural life. As one would expect in the Islamic Republic, in contrast to the more secular Pahlavi regime that preceded it, these religious occasions have effectively become important national holidays as well. Even if the non-Muslim minorities do not participate in them, they certainly respect them and adjust their own activities around them accordingly. These holidays can be divided into two main groups, one of a general Islamic character and one specific to Shi'ite Islam.

General Islamic holidays include Friday as a special day of prayer, the month of fasting during Ramazân, the celebration marking the end of the

Ramazân fast (*'Id-e Fetr,* 1–3 Shavvâl), the holiday marking the end of the time for the ritual pilgrimage to Mecca (*'Id-e Qorbân,* 10 Zi'l-Hejjeh), and days connected with the life of the Prophet Mohammad. The nature and observance of these holidays in Iran, though in many ways similar to other Muslim countries, do have some unique characteristics. For instance, in Iran, as elsewhere, the *'Id-e Fetr* is a joyous holiday, marked by almsgiving and feasts, but the celebration is quite restrained in comparison to the mood of jubilance, with musical performances and festivities, that prevails in south Asian and Arab countries.

The *'Id-e Qorbân,* also known as *'Id-ol-Azhâ* in other Muslim countries, is a somewhat more somber occasion. It takes its name ("Holiday of Sacrifice") from the custom of offering an animal (usually a sheep) for ritual slaughter on that day. Ideally, the meat should be distributed to feed the poor, but in practice many families take the opportunity to provision their own larders with it. The sacrifice is essentially a private and individual observance, but in earlier times in Iran it also had a public dimension. Many cities, towns, or government officials would offer a camel as a kind of communal sacrifice; the camel would be decorated with mirrors, flowers, and other objects and led on a procession through the community before being killed. Meat and hair from the camel was regarded as having special or even magical properties. During the Pahlavi period, this colorful if violent practice was regarded as inconsistent with the image of the country the ruler wanted to project, and it was eventually outlawed and has not been revived.

Friday is both a religious and secular holiday in Iran. While the day has a religious significance, for working people it is a day of rest from work. The religious establishment attaches great significance to this day, organizing Friday collective prayers in mosques and/or public places. The strong public and congregational nature of the Friday noon prayer, which unlike the other five daily prayers includes a sermon, has made it a particularly important—and politically sensitive—occasion throughout Islamic history. Today, most Muslim countries, including Iran, treat Friday as a holiday (much like Saturday and Sunday in the Jewish and Christian traditions). In the Islamic Republic, this has acquired an almost official and formal status, as it is expected that a major public religious figure will deliver the sermon (and often address pressing social and political issues) at the heavily attended prayer service at the mosque of the University of Tehran. Prior to the Revolution of 1979, fewer Friday prayers, limited in scope, were conducted in seminaries and selected mosques. After the revolution, the Friday prayers have been administered by the government, and the prayer leaders are appointed by an organization of Friday Prayer Leaders controlled by the Office of the Leader of the Islamic Republic.

Holidays associated with the life of the Prophet Mohammad, notably his birthday, are observed in many parts of the Muslim world, but they are subject to some controversy among conservative Muslims as they tend to be a vehicle for the expression of popular folk religion. In the case of Iran, the Islamic Republic has taken to promoting three such official holidays: the birthday of the Prophet, the ordainment (*mab'as*) of the Prophet (corresponding to what many Sunnis regard as his miraculous Night Journey from Mecca to Jerusalem to the Seven Heavens and back), and the death of the Prophet. The prominence now given these holidays seems intended to solidify Iran's ties to other Muslim countries and to defuse criticism that Shi'ism ignores the Prophet in favor of the Imams. Even so, the holidays are ambiguous since they are determined on the basis of Shi'ite tradition (giving, for example, 17 Rabi'-ol-Avval as the Prophet's birthday instead of 12 Rabi'-ol-Avval as in Sunni areas) and overlap with more established Shi'ite holidays (the date of the Prophet's birth is also the birth date of the Sixth Imam, Ja'far Sâdeq, and the date of his death corresponds to that of his grandson Hasan, the Second Imam).

Shi'ite holidays, or more properly holy days, are of course also observed in more or less similar ways by Shi'ite communities outside Iran, but the unique status of Iran as an officially Twelver Shi'ite country gives them a special significance. These holidays are divided into two categories: *marâsem-e shâdi* (happy occasions) and *marâsem-e 'azâ* (mournful occasions). On happy occasions, the idea is to celebrate a religious leader's birth or an important event in his life; at the heart of *marâsem-e 'azâ* is the concept of lamentation (*'azâdârî*), which can be regarded as a fundamental aspect of not only Shi'ite but also Iranian culture. In many contexts, Iranian culture emphasizes politeness (*ta'rof*) and concealment of one's true feelings, but the unrestrained, even dramatic, outpouring of grief, weeping, and mourning—at a funeral, for example—is viewed very positively. In Shi'ism, this has acquired a formal and ritual aspect that, it has been suggested, may have assimilated even more ancient and deeply imbedded cultural traditions going all the way back to lamentation cults in Mesopotamia and central Asia.

In any case, the core idea of these mournful holidays is to remember the suffering and martyrdom endured by the family of the Prophet through the display of pity and sorrow for their fate. This grieving, and especially weeping, is believed to secure the sympathy, blessing, and intercession of the Imams for the faithful. This also has a cathartic value, establishing the believer's solidarity with those victims of the evil at work in the world. According to Shi'ite dogma, literally scores of Mohammad's descendants and relatives suffered martyrdom at the hands of their enemies, so there is certainly no shortage of days that could be adopted for this purpose. In practice, the most important of such observances are those associated with the deaths of the Prophet's daughter Fâtemeh, his son-in-law 'Ali, Imam Ja'far Sâdeq, Imam 'Ali Rezâ (the only Imam whose tomb is in what is now Iran), and, above all, Imam Hosayn and the members of his family killed at the Battle of Karbalâ. The typical and traditional way of observing most of these days is through the practice of visiting shrines (*ziârat*) and listening, in private or public gatherings, to orations about the martyrs (*rowzeh-khʷâni*), both of which have been discussed in an earlier chapter. Sometimes, ritual dinners may also be held (the affluent providing meals for the poor, for example).

The most impressive by far of all these observances are those held over the first 10 days of Moharram in commemoration of those martyred at Karbalâ, culminating on the 9th (Tâsu'â) and 10th ('Âshurâ) of the month. There are many customs associated with these observances, and as with most Iranian festivities, they vary considerably from one locality to another. The most common and important, however, are the processions and passion plays held in connection with Tâsu'â and 'Âshurâ. In cities and towns of any size, the processions are organized and conducted by religious fraternities (*hay'at*s) or groups of men (*dasteh*s). Men in the fraternities regularly practice the chants and rituals they will perform beginning on the first of Moharram and culminating in the 'Âshurâ processions. They take great pride in these activities and not infrequently try to outdo other *dasteh*s in the fervor and dedication they bring to the task. In addition to chants, they typically practice some type of rhythmic self-flagellation (usually with a flail made out of chains bundled together, but sometimes with knives or swords). Other members of the *hay'at*s may make large, symbolic structures to carry in the procession, somewhat like floats in a parade. In some cases, these are known as plates (*tabaq*s) and used to carry portraits of the Imams, replicas of their tombs, and so forth; others are huge wooden edifices (called *naql*) draped with black banners and meant to symbolize Hosayn's coffin. Other participants may carry black flags or large iron hands (representing the hands of 'Abbâs, Hosayn's half-brother, which were chopped off after his death in battle). The processions are accompanied by chanting and religious music and may include other reminders of Karbalâ (such as a riderless horse commemorating the fallen Hosayn, or horses and camels carrying children, women, and men acting as the martyrs and captives taken away to Syria after the battle). Large crowds turn out to watch the processions and can display great emotion upon observing the spectacle. In cities where there is a shrine, public processions begin from the neighborhood and end at the shrine as the destination. There are two important observances related to the commemoration of Hosayn: one known as *shâm-e gharibân*, or the first night after the day of 'Âshurâ, when Hosayn's remaining family members had to wander in the dark desert in search of a home; and the other known as Arba'in, held 40 days later on 20 Safar, commemorating the time when the decapitated head of Hosayn, which had been carried off to Damascus, was reunited with his body (for that reason, the day is also sometimes called *sar-tan,* "head-body," in Persian). A ritual *ziârat* to Hosayn's tomb in Karbalâ is regarded as the appropriate way to observe the day. On *shâm-e gharibân,* various *dastehs* and *hay'ats* carry candles and proceed in the streets praying and singing lamentation songs. In all ritual activities associated with the commemoration of the martyrdom of Imam Hosayn, children and young adults are major participants. These occasions provide an important social opportunity for young people to socialize and do team work with each other.

The custom of having passion plays (*ta'ziyeh*) during Moharram that recreate the story of the events at Karbalâ is a very original and distinctive feature of Iranian Shi'ism. Like the 'Ashura processions, the practice of *ta'ziyeh* is based on the idea that imitating and representing the suffering of Hosayn, or expressing grief for it, establishes a reciprocal bond of affinity with the family of the Prophet and wins forgiveness of sins. *Ta'ziyeh* became very popular in the nineteenth century and was subsidized by the Qâjâr rulers, especially Nâser-od-Din Shah. During the Pahlavi period, public performance of *ta'ziyeh* declined for two reasons. First, some of the religious leaders opposed it because it involved *shabih-sâzi,* or image making (Muslims generally do not approve of making portraits and especially not statues or sculptures, because of the association with idolatry). Second, the secularizing Pahlavi governments saw the practice as a low-class folk custom not worth promoting. However, the Iranian Revolution brought this traditional performance into a new light. Artists took note of *ta'ziyeh* as an important native theatrical production. With efforts by the Islamic government in reviving native traditions, modern production of *ta'ziyeh* in varied forms became the focus of theater and movie producers and reached the international scene. In 2002, the world famous Iranian filmmaker 'Abbâs Kiârostami produced a new presentation of *ta'ziyeh,* shown at several European film festivals. In early 2005, Nâser Taqvâ'i made a short film about *ta'ziyeh,* named *Tamrin-e âkhar* ("The Last Rehearsal"), on commission by the United Nation's Educational, Scientific, and Cultural Organization (UNESCO) for officially recognizing *ta'ziyeh* as a religious tradition and cultural heritage in the UNESCO World Heritage List.

Unlike the lamentation processions, *ta'ziyeh* are held at a fixed location, and the performers act out the story of Karbalâ—the events leading up to the battle, the battle itself, the slaughter of the family of the Prophet, and the plight of the widows, orphans, and captives after the battle. They may be somewhat improvisational, or they may follow a well-established script. Popular *ta'ziyeh* productions may be quite simple in terms of costuming and scenery; those financed by the religious foundations or now by the government can be quite lavish. They all make heavy use of convention, such as having the villains dress in red, and those about to be martyred in white. Some are held in open squares or courtyards; others are performed at special theaters (community ones known as *Hosayniehs* or large, state-financed ones known as *takiyehs*). In either case, there are no real boundaries to separate the stage and actors from the audience—all are participants in the drama. Although the *ta'ziyeh* looks very much like a play, the audience is not there simply to observe and certainly not for entertainment; it is a ritualized mourning ceremony in which all participate, either through imitation in the case of the actors or lamentation on the part of the audience. The emotions unleashed by the *ta'ziyeh* can be more intense than those of the processions, even to the point where the line between re-creation and reality is blurred—as has often been noted, this can result in real peril for the actor who has the unenviable task of playing Shemr, the merciless chief villain of the story who bars Hosayn and his thirsty followers from water and ultimately kills the Imam.

As mentioned earlier, not all the Shi'ite holidays are connected with mourning. The birthday of Imam 'Ali (13 Rajab), the birthday of Imam Rezâ (11 Zi'l-Qa'deh), and the birthday of the Twelfth Imam (15 Shabân) are all official holidays and can be fairly festive occasions. The day on which Shi'ites believe Mohammad made a speech at the Pool of Ghadir confirming 'Ali as his successor is also a major holiday (*'Id-e Ghadir,* 18 Zi'l-Hejjeh), although in practice it involves mostly official receptions for members of the clergy. In earlier times, there was also a very raucous and colorful, almost carnival-like, holiday on 26 Zi'l-Hejjeh (or alternatively, 9 Rabi' I) celebrating the murder of the caliph 'Omar (regarded by Shi'ites as a special enemy of 'Ali; he was also the caliph under whom the Arabs conquered Iran, so there were national as well as religious reasons for hating him). The highlight of the day was making an effigy of 'Omar to be cursed, insulted, and finally burned. These rituals started with the establishment of Shi'ism as the state religion during the Safavid period. As relations between Iran and Sunni countries have improved, the holiday is now regarded as inappropriate and is no longer observed.

NATIONAL HOLIDAYS

The last category of events to be discussed here can well be described as national holidays for several reasons. They are deeply rooted in the history and tradition of the country, unlike the civil holidays tied to recent political events of transitory significance. Although they reflect traces of ancient cults of sun worship and were (and are) part of Zoroastrian tradition, they have become essentially secularized and are no longer tied to any particular religion. At the same time, they have been accepted by essentially all ethnic groups, not just Persian speakers, and are enthusiastically celebrated not only all over the country but also in many neighboring countries. They include four important occasions: Chahârshanbehsuri, the last Wednesday of the solar year; Nowruz, the New Year's Day; Sizdah Bedar, the 13th day of the year; and Yaldâ, the night of the winter solstice.

On the evening before Chahârshanbehsuri (colloquially pronounced Chârshambeh-suri), people gather whatever type of kindling is common in their locality and make bonfires in their yards, the streets, or the open country. Whoever wishes and is able—men, women, children—jump over the flames while singing, "Your redness to me, my pallor to you"; the ritual is intended to ensure good health and fortune for the coming year. Traditionally, there are various rules that apply to how the fire is tended and how the ashes are dealt with subsequently (reminders, perhaps, of the sacredness of fire in Zoroastrianism). Many other supplementary or local customs are practiced in connection with the holiday. The most common include setting off fireworks; "banging spoons" (qâshoq-zani), when young people go door-to-door banging a spoon on a plate and receiving little gifts, in some ways similar to Halloween door-to-door visits; social gatherings where people stay up most of the night snacking on fruits and nuts and burning rue seeds to ward off misfortune; making a special dish known as the soup of Abu Dardâ to give to people who have been chronically ill; and smashing an old pot or jug after jumping over the fire (another omen of good luck, as is the general practice of spring cleaning and refurbishing the house that follows the holiday). Despite, or perhaps because, of its popularity, conservative Muslim religious leaders view this holiday, and indeed most of the others in this category, with a good deal of suspicion as non-Islamic and pagan in character and have occasionally tried to suppress or constrain it, but without much success. It can be a particularly sensitive issue when the holiday falls at the same time as Moharram, as happened recently.

Nowruz is one of the most celebrated and important Iranian holidays. It is observed not only in Iran but also in Azerbaijan, central Asia, Afghanistan, Pakistan, parts of India, and among the Kurds. Officially, the New Year's holiday lasts for four days, from Nowruz itself on 1 Farvardin to 4 Farvardin. Unofficially, the holiday season typically lasts much longer; it is the most popular time by far for people to take trips and vacations, given that schools close longer than government offices. It is also an important time for renewing social relationships and putting household and financial matters in order. People clean up their houses (like spring cleaning in the United States), buy new clothing and furniture, and often hope for a new beginning. New Year's resolutions are as common in Iran as in the United States. People may begin celebrating 10 days or so before Nowruz and continue until the Sizdah Bedar holiday on the 13th day of the year. Children, employees, and various acquaintances also expect to receive a cash gift, *'idi,* for the New Year. Nowruz is a very joyous time, with lots of special foods, visits to friends and relatives, performances by street entertainers, and so forth.

The central event of the Nowruz holiday, however, is the laying out of the *sofreh,* a special holiday tableau, on New Year's Eve. Iranians take great pride in the preparation of the *sofreh,* a practice that is rich in tradition, meaning, and symbolism. By custom, this consists of an especially attractive dining cloth spread out on the floor (or in more recent, somewhat Westernized usage, a table) and decorated with the *haft sin,* seven objects whose names in Persian all begin with the letter *s.* There is some variation in the choice of the *haft sin,* and there may in fact be more than seven *s* objects on display. They will almost certainly include sprouted seeds of grain (*sabzeh*), *samanu* (a kind of paste made out of minced green wheat, oil, almonds and other ingredients), apples (*sib*), vinegar (*serkeh*), garlic (*sir*), and coins (*sekkeh*). Seeds of wild rue (*sepand*) may be placed in a dish and burned (something commonly thought to ensure good luck). Hyacinth (*sonbol*), fennel-flower (*siâh-dâneh*), sumac (*somâq*), jujubes (*senjed*), green herbs (*sabzi*), or other items might also be used, either as part of the *haft sin* or the overall display. The *sofreh* should include a mirror; lighted candles, which should not be extinguished before they have burned out; a Koran or other sacred or valued book (non-Muslims or the secular-minded might use the *Shâh-nâmeh* or a book of poems by Hâfez or Rumi); coins; fish (usually a goldfish in a bowl); a bowl of water with a pomegranate leaf or bitter orange floating in it; pitchers of milk, rose water, and so forth; and foods such as yogurt, cheese, bread, and other delicacies. There will also be a number of colored eggs, specially cooked and dyed for the purpose: This is probably the most ancient custom incorporated into the *sofreh* (as well as one distantly related to the custom of Easter eggs in Christianity). The egg, like the leaf in the bowl, is a symbol of the universe; most of the objects on the *sofreh* are meant to represent the earth and its place in the cosmos, the particular auspiciousness of the moment of the vernal equinox, charms for good fortune and the warding off of evil, the forces of rebirth and regeneration, and the good things of life one hopes to enjoy over the coming year. Foods associated with the New Year have varied by region, period, and ethnicity. In recent times, in Tehran and many other cities in central Iran, eating *sabzi-polow mâhi* (herbed rice with fish) on the New Year has become customary.

Another important feature of the New Year celebration is a character known as Hâji Firuz. Hâji Firuz is a man dressed in red clothes with his face colored in black. A couple of weeks prior to New Year, Hâji Firuz comes along with tambourines, kettle drums, or trumpets, dancing and singing in the streets and cheering people, especially kids, in preparation for New Year. His songs are comical, and his performance very theatrical, causing laughter and cheer.

The transition from the New Year's celebrations to regular life is marked by the observance of Sizdah Bedar (13 Farvardin/April 2; official calendars have recently taken to referring to this as Nature Day). The idea is that 13 is an unlucky number, and any quarrels or problems on that day portend misfortune for the whole year. Everyone should thus try to ward off the bad luck by having as good a time as possible, traditionally by spending the day outdoors on a picnic in a park or open area (always a popular activity with most Iranians). Traditional foods for the occasion vary in different regions and among various ethnic groups. However, many consume a noodle soup and lettuce leaves soaked in a homemade syrup called *sekanjebin* (a mixture of sugar and vinegar). It is also customary to dispose of the sprouts used for the *sofreh* on this day, the last formality of the New Year's celebrations. The task is often assigned to young unmarried girls; in a more general practice suggestive of the fertility aspects of the New Year's celebrations, they may also tie together blades of grass and throw the bundles in running water while singing, "Sizdah Bedar! Another year! Husband's home! Baby on the lap!" (expressing their wish for marriage and children soon).

Yaldâ, like Chahârshanbehsuri, is not an official holiday but is nonetheless observed quite widely among Iranians. In Zoroastrian tradition, the winter solstice, with the longest night of the year, was a particularly inauspicious day, and the practices of Yaldâ reflect customs intended to protect people from any evil occurrence at that time. One should stay up most or all of the night and keep a fire burning in the fireplace if possible. Having small parties or social gatherings to eat, talk, and tell stories (or dance and listen to music if one is not of a conservative bent) is a common way of passing the time. Traditional practice was also to eat the last available fresh (as opposed to dried) fruits of the year for Yaldâ; today, fresh fruit is of course available throughout the year but is still used for Yaldâ. Grocers will often have spectacular displays of a variety of fresh fruits for people to buy for this occasion, especially watermelon, which has become associated with this night. Consuming *âjil,* exchanging jokes, and playing games are common activities of the night.

10

Music and Dance

Music is a cultural expression reflecting national feelings, social moods, and state of mind. These elements are inevitably tied to a nation's values, historical experiences, and politico-social conditions. In Iran, music and poetry are very closely linked, both in form and in structure. There is a close relationship between the rhythmic patterns in poetry and music, each serving as a basis for the other. Classical Persian music was based on the memorization of melodic segments linked by kinship to the poetry.

Persian music is an ancient art utilizing numerous instruments, established vocal styles, and rich musical traditions—traditions that have been passed down for thousands of years in the region and are recognized and cherished by the inhabitants as a part of their cultural identity. It is a skilled, expressive, and emotional art with beautiful mystic and oriental melodies in which the vocalists and instrumentalists perform with intense passion. Persian music is based on original and natural recognition of consonances in musical intervals. Inner melodies in lyrics are often combined with musicians' own emotions to produce a mesmerizing flow through traditional musical instruments.

While it is easy to identify Persian music and its constituent elements today, it is very hard to identify one or more stable musical forms performed and preferred by everyone who has lived in historical times in various parts of the Iranian plateau. One can more comfortably talk about a distinct music as Iranian up until the Abbasid period. However, with the political decentralization after this period, Iranian music became localized by cultural and communal entities which emerged in the Iranian plateau. The many cultures and people who have been exposed to Persian music have influenced it in some way. Some of these contacts have enriched Persian music, some have limited its scope, and some have generated alternatives and competition to it. As one of the more notable cultural centers of the Middle East, Iranian music has both influenced and been influenced by musical traditions of countries in the region as well, especially Iraq, Egypt, Syria, and Lebanon. What has remained constant is a strong tradition of maintaining continuity and perfecting those diverse traditions.

RELIGIOUS INFLUENCES ON PERSIAN MUSIC

Throughout the centuries, Persian music would periodically flourish and decline as different religious and governmental restrictions were imposed on it, especially after the adoption of Islam as a religion in Iran. Since music was an important part of religious rituals prior to the arrival of Islam in Iran, Persian music has been influenced by pre-Islamic religious traditions. With the arrival of Islam in Iran, Persian music experienced periods of decline and growth in a discontinuous manner. Still, despite the controversial status of music in Islam, which had a restrictive attitude towards music, the country has produced music, musicians, and musical lyrics in almost all her historical periods. In modern times, those restrictions have changed the character of Persian music but have not been able to prevent its growth and popularity both inside and outside the country.

The status of music in Islam has been surrounded by controversy; several statements attributed to the prophet Mohammad and Shi'ite Imams forbid Muslims from engaging in singing and listening to songs. Although the subject of music is not discussed directly in the Koran, some religious scholars have interpreted the words *lahv* (corrupting entertainment), *zur* (vain words), and *laghv* (inappropriate words and idle tales) in the following verses of the Koran as a reference to music: "And of mankind is he who payeth for mere pastime of discourse [*lahv-ol-hadith*], that he may mislead from Allah's way without knowledge, and maketh it the butt of mockery. For such there is a shameful doom" (Koran 31:6); "So shun the filth of idols, and shun lying speech [*zur*]" (Koran 22:30); "Successful indeed are the believers; Who are humble in their prayers; And who shun vain conversation [*laghv*]" (Koran 23:1–3). Religious scholars have often opposed music for one or more of the following reasons. First, Islam does not show an unconditional positive attitude towards music. Second, music has a morally corruptive nature as it elevates emotions and enslaves one to his/her passions. Third, musical activity is a "waste of productive time" since it takes the individual away from useful activity and diverts his/her attention to sexual themes.

These reservations have not prevented all Muslims from listening or performing music, especially in Iran where a strong musical tradition has been part of pre-Islamic religious and cultural rituals. Moreover, many Sufi rituals rely on the use of music and dance. For example, the instrument known as *daf* came to be regarded as a spiritual drum played in *khânqâhs* (Sufi monasteries) of Iran, particularly Kurdistan. Many Shi'ite religious scholars would permit music that supports religious rituals (prayer music), music that motivates and mobilizes believers in the defense of Islam (martial music), and music in passion plays (*ta'ziyeh*) that expands on religious themes (or that helps believers to achieve spiritual transcendence (*erfâni*, meaning "mystical or Sufi").

The recitation and chanting of the Koran has also been an important tradition in Islam. The monophonic aspect of Koran recital easily spilled over into classical Persian music. Sufis and mystical characters have often used musical instruments to enhance recitation of the Koran. They have often relied on vocals and instruments in order to attain an ethereal status of the soul. This practice has been approved by some religious leaders and rejected by others who see it as a practice contrary to *tajvid* (the proper and authentic way to chant the Koran).

Prayer music has three versions: solo songs, choral music, and a dialogue between solo and choral singers. Their melodies have hymns with little cadence. Though most melodies are in Arabic, Persian and regional dialects are not uncommon. The music is meant to create a solemn mood and is customized to the religious text, the occasion, and the environment. This kind of music utilizes different texts: Koranic verses, prayer texts, and mystical poems in praise of the God. It is performed in mosques, shrines, religious halls (Hosayniyeh), and public places.

Mystical music (*erfâni*) is based on poems from great mystics like Jalâl-od-Din Rumi (A.D. 1207–1273); Shams-od-Din Mohammad Shirâzi, known as Hâfez (ca. A.D. 1310–1388); Farid-od-Din 'Attâr (A.D. 1119–1230), and so on. "Love" as a subject of this kind of music has both temporal and divine connotations to be interpreted by listeners to their own liking. When mystic followers or devotees (*morid*) engage in dancing and whirling in presence of their leader or devoted (*morâd*), this kind of music is played. Music performed in this manner is called *samâ'*—a music believed to be a heavenly creation for preparing the devotees to gain transcendence. In Iran, which has its own brand of mysticism, Sufi vocals and musical performances are often combined in order to attain ecstasy and generate an atmosphere for contemplation.

Âshurâ music involves melodies of elegies and lamentations performed during elaborate rituals involving beating or flagellation of the back or shoulders with chains, stones, or daggers. These rituals are often performed in the Hosayniyehs (religious halls), *takiyehs* (temporary places designated for commemoration ceremonies), mosques, shrines, and streets. Lamentations often involve Persian, Turkish, and other local texts, though Arabic texts are sometimes used. Numerous instruments are involved in Âshurâ music, depending on the size, elaboration, and the location of the ceremony. These include *damâm* (a large double-sided drum), *karnâ* (trumpet), *kârb* (cymbal), brass and shell horns, oboe, and *naqâreh* (kettledrum).

The controversial status of music in Islam, combined with the traditional cultural attitude that regards music and dancing as immoral activities, has affected the status of musicians in society. Until recently, musicians did not have the kind of status, reputation, and income that they enjoy today. In the past, most trained musicians performed in the court. Status and rewards came from court patronage. Starting in the late nineteenth century, a more liberal attitude developed toward music, especially among the secular educated population. In the twentieth century, professional musicians without court patronage appeared in Iran. During the Pahlavi reign, the establishment of radio and television provided some musicians with a steady source of income. This kind of support and employment did not vanish with the establishment of the Islamic Republic in 1980. In late 1979, many predicted that the emergence of a theocracy in Iran would result in the banning of all music. Not only did this not happen, but in fact the establishment of the Islamic Republic created a more receptive environment for classical Persian music. During the revolution, religiously sanctioned popular songs were produced in order to encourage participation in the revolution. In fact, several pieces praising Âyatollâh Khomeini were played on the Iranian radio and TV regularly. The fate of entertainment music, especially that following Western pop music, was certainly different. As the Pahlavi regime collapsed, all female musicians were banned from performance. Cabarets and bars were closed. Public performances of music were banned, even during marital ceremonies and cultural events. Many top pop musicians left the country. The most respected and popular pop singer, known as Gogoosh, was briefly arrested and then released on the condition that she not sing any more. The pop star agreed and remained in seclusion for some 20 years. In 2000, she was allowed to travel abroad and came to North America to restart her musical career.

In the second decade of the Islamic Republic, as the regime became more established and pressures built up on clerical rulers to adapt to the changing environment and popular demands, women were allowed to perform only for female audiences. Since most female musicians had left the country or retired, there were not enough musicians available or willing to take up the regime on this offer. Also, many secularly minded musicians opposed this offer as a form of gender apartheid. Two popular singers who performed for all female audiences were Fâtemeh Vâezi, known as Parisâ, and Pari Zangeneh. Under pressure from competition by Iranian pop music from abroad, which was widely smuggled and listened to within the country, the government allowed some musical performances in public and encouraged a new genre of pop music with religiously-approved lyrics. Female instrumentalists and vocalists were allowed to perform in public as part of a group but not as solo singers. Official support was granted to musicians involved in folk music. Iranian vocalists and musical groups began to tour European and North American cities offering their music to Iranian diaspora and foreign audiences. Limited entertainment opportunities increased public reception for Persian classical music and enhanced the status of Iranian musicians. In a gesture of defiance as well as the demonstration of a new attitude toward music, private music classes have increased and a large number of urban youth participate in these classes.

Therefore, it can be concluded that the Islamic regulations imposed on music after the revolution did not diminish the growth of Persian music, but instead increased its appeal. While the clerical rulers have generally remained skeptical about music, the cultural agencies under their control have provided incentives for targeted musicians in line with the cultural policies of the Islamic Republic. While secular musicians have often had to fight hard to maintain their profession and the type of music they deem appropriate, they have invented creative ways of getting around religious regulations and reaching their audiences.

STRUCTURE AND INSTRUMENTS

Classical Persian music is generally modal and is not always based on the traditional major and minor scales of music. It is also generally monophonic, (mostly consisting of a single vocal part). Musical pieces consist of melody and rhythm, and, when a singer is involved, the melody is repeated with some variation. Melodic patterns are called *gushehs* (literally meaning "corner") and generally reflect the rhythm or the melodic pattern of the poem being used. Traditional melodies are ordered in a *radif* (literally meaning "rank" and "series"). *Radif* is a sonic space identifying the movement of the melodies, and, as such, it groups a large number of sequences or melodies (*gusheh*) in a mode. The procedure for melodic invention with a mode is called *mâyeh* (basis) and "includes rules for cadences, a hierarchy of tones," and an appropriate "melodic pattern."[1]

In the late nineteenth century, the above system was restructured and the modes were reconstituted in twelve *dastgâhs* (literally meaning "system"). A *dastgâh* is very similar to the Indian Raga or Arabic *maqâm* system. Each *dastgâh* has a related eight note scale and its own repertoire of *gushehs* (such as *kereshmeh, chahâr pardeh,* and *suz-o godâz*). Seven of these *dastgâhs* are considered primary modes (*shur, navâ, mâhur, chahârgâh, homâyun, segâh,* and *râstpanjeh*) and five as secondary (*Abu 'Atâ, dashti, bayât-e turk, afshâri, bayât-e Esfahân*).

The compositional structure of Persian music includes three instrumental forms and one vocal form. The instrumental forms are called *pishdarâmad* (prelude), *châhâr mezrâb* (a solo piece based on the melody that precedes it), and *reng* (a dance piece played at the end of a *dastgâh*). The vocal form (*tasnif*) is sung based on the melody. The rhythm is usually "in duple, triple, or qua-druple time,"[2] and the melodies are derived from the *gushehs*. The initial *gusheh* in a *dastgâh* is called *darâmad*. The lyrics are often mystical selections from the classical Persian poetry. Recently, modern poetry, which often is devoid of traditional rhythmic structure, has been used as well.

Performers are expected to develop their own compositions by selecting items that would make a "suite." Ornamentation, decorating a piece of music without changing the context, is widely used and is an important feature of delivery. Performers expand upon the composition either through careful preparation or spontaneous improvisation (*bedâh-e navâzi*). Ornamentation and improvisation add excitement and creativity to the pieces by allowing both instrumentalists and vocals to improvise "within a single mode for the duration of the performance."[3] Relatively similar to yodeling in the Western music, vocal ornamentation (*tahrir*) is often dense and the tempo rapid. Poems are often sung within the context of a suite and without a time signature (thus rhythmically free). Long pauses are also common in musical performances. Rhythms and melodies are freer and there is slurring between the notes.

The various schools of music in Iran are often named after the region in which they were originally developed (i.e., *Gilaki, Kordi, Shushtari,* and *Esfahân*). Traditionally, master musicians teach their students individually, offering them tailored education. Reading biographies of Persian musicians, one notices a clear distinction from Western ones: each musician identifies the master under whom s/he has been trained. This is very similar to the traditional education in the seminaries where each teaching *âyatollâh* devotes himself to a few students, making sure to pass all the relevant knowledge to them. While following a guideline of general rules, each musical master often has his own interpretation of *gushehs*. The *radif* is transferred orally because there are no written symbols. A student learns by observing the master's performance, memorizing the piece, and practicing it in his presence. The *radif* takes a student about four years to learn, since it is the entire repertoire of Persian music which has been passed down. It takes about ten hours or so to perform the *radif*. As these *radif* collections have been passed along, the number of *gushehs* within them has increased since new master musicians often add new elements to their collection.

Persian music is usually performed in a small chamber ensemble, rather than in an orchestra, consisting of different instrumentalists accompanied by a vocalist. Musicians sit on benches or carpets spread on the floor, with some decorated pillows behind them. Instruments used would vary but invariably two or more of the followings are involved: *kamâncheh, târ, setâr, santur, tonbak,* and *nay.* The *kamâncheh* is a bowed lute with a small, hollowed hardwood body and a thin stretched skin membrane. The *târ* is a six-stringed long-necked lute ranging about two and a half octaves. The *dutâr* has two steel strings and is tuned in fourth or fifth intervals. The *setâr* has four strings, even though its name means "three strings." Its delicacy and intimate sonority has made it a favorite instrument for Sufi music. The *santur* (hammered dulcimer) is a zither-type stringed instrument with 72 strings arranged over two sets of nine bridges on each side. It has a range of a little over three octaves. The *tonbak* (also called *dombak* or *zarb*) is a kind of goblet-shaped drum and is used as the chief percussion instrument. The *nay* is a flute with finger holes, which has a range of two and a half octaves, producing a nasal and thin sound. The *daf* is a frame drum often used in spiritual Sufi music. Recently becoming very popular, this instrument has been integrated into all genres of music in Iran. For a period of time the violin overshadowed the *kamâncheh*, but recently the latter has gained a new popularity. Although each of these instruments has distinct sound, they maintain a monophonic texture.

FOLK MUSIC

Folk music (known as "regional music" in Iran) has probably existed as long as people have lived on the Iranian plateau. It has resisted formalization and, until recent times, its lyrics were preserved by the word of mouth and collective memories. Folk musicians were generally amateurs within rural areas. There are many distinct traditions and styles of folk music practiced throughout the country and its diverse regions. Some of these styles and methods are specific to an individual region or a distinct ethnicity. Kurdish, Turkish, Baluchi, Qashqâi, Gilâni, and Bandari music are some of the regionally specific music. Another example of locally established and recognized musicians are the Bakhshis in Khorâsân. (Bakhshis are also found in neighboring countries of Turkmenistan, Tajikistan, Afghanistan, and Uzbekistan). The word means instrumentalist, singer, and storyteller. However, Iranian Bakhshis believe that it is derived from the word *bakhshandeh*, meaning a donor or a generous person. Bakhshis usually perform in village ceremonies and weddings. They play the *dutâr,* narrate stories (*dâstâns*), and sing variously in Persian, Turkish, or Kurdish.

Depending upon its needs, folk music calls for the use of one or more of the above-mentioned instruments. Instruments used are sometimes made by the musicians who play them. Some lyrics are reflective of historical tragedies. For instance, in Mâzandarân, there is a vocal known as *"sut."* *Sut* recants the pain of harms and destruction imposed on the community by the rebels and outlaws of the late nineteenth century. Some other lyrics are so specific that they are only relevant to specific rituals, such as child rearing, harvest collection, birth and marital ceremonies, and even burial traditions. The merry ones are generally accompanied with folk dances and the sad ones often reflect hardships and sufferings experienced by people or communities. This kind of music remains vibrant and adaptable, allowing its various forms to be reinvented within popular culture and manifested in modern media. It has also gained the attention of ethnomusicologists and educational institutions. The latter have become actively involved in preservation and collection of unrecorded lyrics in remote areas. In the past half a century, folk music has become professionalized and performers are trained and specialized in distinct folk traditions. Several modern folk singers have acquired international recognition. Two such singers who have performed in many European and American concert halls are Pari Zangeneh and Simâ Binâ. Hâj Qorbâni from Khorâsân and Morâdi from Lorestân are two male singers who have also represented the music of their respective regions to Western audiences.

HISTORY OF PERSIAN MUSIC

In some archeological remains from ancient Iran, one can sometimes see depictions of singers, accompanied by musicians playing harps, large tambourines, and long necked lutes and double-flutes. Music was an important aspect of court life, cultural celebrations, religious rituals, and military operation. Religious music consisted of vocals drawn from Zoroastrian scriptures, the Gathas and Yashts, and was performed by priests in major tone without instruments. Courtly music involved musicians, singers, and dancers. Musicians, known as *gosân* and *khonyâgarân*, most often performed and sang at the same time. A bereavement song called *sug-e Siâvoshân*, which had developed to mourn the death of soldiers in this period, is believed to be a predecessor to the Shi'ite mourning in commemoration for Imam Hosayn during the month of Moharram.

Music flourished under the Sasanids because many of their rulers were patrons of the arts and some were even artists themselves. Ardashir, Bahrâm Gur, Khosrow Anushirvân, and Khosrow Parviz established measures protecting musicians and promoting their works. Foreign musicians were recruited to teach and perform music. Minstrels, or popular entertainers singing and reciting poetry, traveled from one community to another. Several musicians, like Râmtin, Bâmshâd, Bârbad, and Nagisâ became so masterful and popular that their popularity and influence surpassed their own time and place. Both

Bârbad and Nagisâ contributed to the development of a musical system known as *khosravâni*. There were many instrumentalists and players at the court of Khosrow Parviz. Viewing music as a source of entertainment rather than art, Bahrâm Gur was skillful in offering elegies (*chekâmesarâi*) and encouraged a series of changes in tones and scales similar to today's "*shirin-navâzi*" (rhythmic and happy tones) in party music.

As noted earlier, the Arab invasion of Iran and spread of Islam posed a new challenge for musicians as some conservative Muslims challenged the propriety of music on religious grounds. Yet music continued to to be patronized at the courts of the Umayyad and Abbasid caliphs. Mutually enriching exchanges gradually developed between Iranian and Arab musicians, contributing to the development of a more systematic approach to music during the Abbasid period. Hârun-or-Rashid's court hosted so many musicians that they had to be grouped into competing camps. Ebrâhim Mowseli (742–804), whose family was Persian by origin, was one of the favorite musicians of the time and helped develop what became known as the "classical" style of music; he is known to have tried to imitate Bârbad. A young and innovative musician named Ebrâhim, son of an the Abbasid caliph Mahdi, played a crucial role in introducing Persian instruments to Arabic music. The interaction of Persian, Arab, and Byzantine music in this period laid the foundation for changes that took place in musical schools in the thirteenth century.

Music continued to flourish under the various regional dynasties in Iran, though at different paces and to varying degrees. Taherid rulers, like both Tâher b. Hosayn and his son 'Abdollâh, were musicians and strong patrons of this art. The rise of the Buyids changed the restrictive environment towards music that the increasing influence of the conservative Hanbali religious tradition had created. The Samanids returned Iranian music to its pre-Islamic roots, revived many of the old traditions, and in some regions made music a special field in the school curriculum. Greek, Indian, and Arab musical traditions were fused into Iranian compositions. A new musical *pardeh* ("mode," "interval," or "fret") system, known as the *Khorâsâni* school and connected to a literary school with the same name, emerged in Khorâsân and central Asia. Daqiqi, a poet and harpist of the Samanid period, is believed to have invented an instrument known as "*shahruz*." Most Saljuq rulers were also supportive of the arts. Sultan Sanjar (d. 1157) loved music, and his court musician Kamâl-oz-Zamân was very well known.

There were also efforts to establish music and music theory as formal fields of scholarship and philosophy. This tradition was pioneered by the famous philosopher Kendi (ca. 801–866) and continued by others such as Fârâbi (d. 950), Ebn Sinâ (known in the West as Avicenna; d. 1037), and Safi-od-Din Ormavi (1294). The famous astronomer Nâser-od-Din Tusi (d. 1274) also wrote on music theory and is said to have even invented a kind of flute. His student Qutb-od-Din Shirâzi (d. 1311), in addition to being a distinguished astronomer, was also an instrumentalist and wrote an important treatise on modes and rhythms in a chapter of an encyclopedia he authored.

In the Mongol and post-Mongol period, Iranians submerged themselves deeper in Islamic devotion and Sufism—a trend replicated in the growth of ghazal-khʾâni in the fourteenth century. Earlier happy themes of the Persian music were replaced by sorrowful themes of foreign domination. This development increased the role of the ghazal (a poetic form generally romantic in nature, with limited stanzas and recurring rhymes) in Persian vocals (âvâz) —a development signaling the decline of the Khorâsâni musical school. Under the Safavids, the increasing influence of conservative Shiʿite religious thought affected music as well as other areas of Iranian cultural life. New restrictions were placed on musical performances and musicians; Shah Tahmâsp even banned music at the court and ordered punishment for practicing instrumentalists and vocalists. This generally negative environment, however, did not prevent some musicians from working on their skills in private and passing it to a new generation. Two new musical instruments, shish târ and chahâr târ are reported to be invented during this period. After the fall of the Safavids, the tolerant Zand rulers accorded new respect to music; Iranian musicians who had left the country previously were invited back, and foreign musicians were invited to perform in Iran. Karim Khân's support helped veteran musicians to pass along their skills to a new generation and promote a form of popular music known as bâzâri—music that was good for dancing, with a happy tone and rhythmic lyrics. During this period, many Jews in Iran were attracted to music as a profession.

Despite the generally negative economic and political developments during the Qâjâr era, Persian music gained new life, especially during the reigns of Mohammad Shah and Nâser-od-Din Shah. Demand for musical performance in aristocratic private parties increased, and a form of music known as majlesi (private party) became very popular. Qâjâr shahs surrounded themselves with musicians, many of Turkish origin. As has been mentioned earlier in this book, upon his return from a foreign trip Nâser-od-Din Shah attempted to introduce some cultural developments he had seen in Europe. In 1873, he founded the Takiyeh Dowlat, a kind of state theater, in which taʿziyeh was regularly performed. Later, during the Constitutional Revolution new opportunities for artistic developments arose. A public concert was organized and the performances were recorded in the first gramophone imported to the country.

What is known today as "classical Persian music" is rooted in the developments of the Qâjâr period. Classical music was distinguished from light music (motrebi) by adding new melodies and modal patterns to existing *radifs* (repertoire). The old modes were restructured and the *dastgâh* system practiced today was developed. New nomenclature and designations to songs were created. While *târ* and *setâr* became prestigious instruments, several others like *'ud* (lute), *robâb* (a string melodic instrument like violin played on the ground), and *chang* (harp) became popular. The man behind many of these developments was Mirzâ 'Abdollâh —a virtuoso artist whose *radif* is the source of much of modern music in Iran. Ethnic minorities made distinct contributions to Iranian music, especially Armenians who were famous and masterful in making most musical instruments. Persian melodies absorbed many popular melodies from ethnic stock, especially those from Fârs, Bushehr, Azerbaijan, Kurdistan, and Lorestân.

As more Western instruments were imported and more Iranians became familiar with the Western music, Persian music came under Western influence. A Frenchman, Alfred Jean-Baptiste Lemaire, was invited to Iran to help teach music at the Dâr-ol-Fonun. Mirzâ 'Ali-Akbar Khân Naqqâshbâshi translated Lemaire's lessons into Persian as the first introduction to European music. Later, the music department at Dâr-ol-Fonun was transformed into an independent music college whose graduates were trained in Western martial music, rather than in Persian classical music.

In early years of Rezâ Shah's reign, music teaching became institutionalized, and Persian music was modernized by efforts of 'Ali-Naqi Vaziri. Having traveled to European countries and studied at numerous schools, Vaziri was the first person to write an instruction book for Iranian music in the form of notes. In the course of his career, Vaziri directed the Music College, established a music club, organized large orchestras and regular concerts, published a music magazine, and recorded music albums. Vaziri's efforts were followed by Parviz Mahmud, who founded the Tehran Symphony Orchestra in 1937. Later, the National Music Department and the National Academy of Music were founded. The establishment of Iranian Radio gave a boost to music industry and the need for training, promoting, and helping musicians became a national concern for the government.

During the Pahlavi period, exposure to a broader range of music encouraged musicians to debate the modernization of the classical music system. In order to facilitate the composition of polyphonic pieces within traditionally monophonic Persian music, Vaziri proposed a 24 quarter tone scale while Mahdi Barkeshli suggested a 22 tone scale. Hormoz Farhat regarded octaves and scales as foreign to Persian music and suggested going back to the earlier system of *mâyeh* or melodic type. He believed that melodic formulas were more articulate for imparting improvisation.

The establishment of the Iranian Television in 1958 and the expansion of the movie industry helped the growth of music industry. As the coverage of radio spread throughout the country and the number of cinemas increased, music became more accessible and in high demand. The establishment of a music department in the University of Tehran in 1965, the Iranian Center for Preservation and Dissemination of National Music (ICPDNM) in 1968, and the Institute of Musicology in 1973 boosted the demand for better and more qualified musicians in schools, radio and television, cultural centers, national ceremonies, and even private parties of affluent classes. The ICPDNM soon became a power house bringing together some of the masters of Persian music in the twentieth century.

PERSIAN MUSIC IN CONTEMPORARY IRAN

The latter part of Mohammad-Rezâ Shah's reign had a disastrous impact on Persian classical music, one with significant political implications for the Pahlavi regime itself. With the shah's fast pace of modernization and importation of everything Western, classical Persian music became a victim of Western and Western-style pop music. As Westernized pop music became dominant, traditional music lost its appeal. Viewed as a sign of Western penetration and "illicit" activities, pop music was rejected by the religious and traditional sectors of the society. After the revolution, the clerics banned pop music and replaced it with revolutionary music. Pop music went underground. Old cassettes of popular music were sold on street corners illegally, and pop musicians had to either retire or flee the country. The majority of those who left the country ended up in Los Angeles, a city with the largest concentration of Iranians outside of Iran. Soon, artists in Los Angeles began producing tapes smuggled back to Iran. Iranian pop music imported from Los Angeles was labeled *muzik-e los angelesi*—a form of pop music with happy themes geared for dancing and partying.

As the clerics consolidated their power, they found certain kinds of music helpful in promoting ideological unity and nationalism, especially during the mobilization for the Iran-Iraq war. The Ministry of Culture and Islamic Guidance began promoting revolutionary and epic songs as well classical Persian music with mystical themes. Islamic arts were encouraged and promoted throughout the society. A new cadre of musicians and singers more comfortable with the new Islamic culture emerged. Some of the old musicians, who had adjusted their expectations to the new situation, started to produce new works. The Fajr Festival of Music was established, new music halls were built, and public musical performances by male musicians were encouraged.

In the past two decades, hundreds of new educational and analytical books on scientific music and music instruction have been produced and published. Attention to music, both by professionals and the public, has been phenomenal. Numerous private music schools have sprung up in most major cities and young people, including women, are rushing to these schools to learn various instruments. As for professionals, their productivity has been quite extraordinary: numerous concerts are offered to the public, thousands of CDs and cassette tapes of new music are produced, and many books on music are published annually.

Like many other aspects of life in twentieth-century Iran, classical Persian music has been under pressure by the modern Western music and musical instruments. The larger tension of modernity and tradition has influenced this art and divided many musicians and their followers to opposing camps: those who continue to produce music by traditional musical rules and instruments, and those who favor music produced by the modern instruments. The classical music often attracts cultural elites and educated segment of the population who views music as an art. The popular music is more successful among the younger generation that treats music as entertainment.

While music scholars are engaged in a debate about "tradition" versus "modernity" in music, younger generation of musicians are already bridging the gap between the two. Many do not see a need for viewing these two as mutually exclusive. Though traditional musicians were averse to using modern poetry, recent albums by master vocalists like Mohammad Nuri, Mohammad-Rezâ Shajariân, and Shahrâm Nâzeri have lowered this resistance. A genre of music combining both traditional and classical instruments has also emerged.

Today, Persian music is widely listened to in neighboring countries like Tajikistan, Afghanistan, Turkmenistan, Azerbaijan, Uzbekistan, Pakistan, and some Arab countries in the Persian Gulf. For some time, it has gained some popularity in the "World Music" scene as well—a development not unrelated to the presence of large communities of Iranian immigrants around the world, especially in the Western countries. Children of Iranian immigrants abroad have begun experimenting with newer, richer, and more diverse forms of music mixing Iranian themes with the modern Western musical genres.

DANCE

Dance in Iran represents a mixture of elements drawn from diverse sources, some similar to those in neighboring countries, some uniquely related to cultures and customs of people living within a specific region in Iran today, and some synthesizing both foreign and native influences. For instance, ethnic dances found among Iranian Kurds and Turkomans are very similar to those practiced by these ethnic groups beyond current borders of Iran. Or what is known as "*Tehrâni* dance" contains elements of various Iranian dances, and even Arabic dance. Therefore, it is important to emphasize that the cultural borders of dance forms in Iran go far beyond current geographical borders and may have to be traced to neighboring Arab and non-Arab countries, especially Tajikistan, Afghanistan, Uzbekistan, Azerbaijan, and even Armenia and Georgia.

Some define dance as the rhythmic movement of the body for various purposes: prayer, self-expression, celebration, pleasure, etc. Others argue that since some of these activities are not intended as dance by performers, and are not conducted with the goal of either pleasure or demonstration of artistic movement for others, then they should not be considered dance. In Iran, there are activities classified commonly as "sports" or "rituals" and yet some art historians consider them as dance. For instance, the self-flagellation and the rhythmic movements of body and hands during the procession of Moharram might have derived from dances from pre-Islamic Zoroastrian practices. Or sports activities performed in the *zur-khâneh* (the "house of strength" or sports center) may be continuations of pre-Islamic military dances.

Many forms of dance are found in Iran: ethnic/tribal, ritualistic/spiritual, therapeutic/healing, ceremonial, athletic, and recreational. Some are specific to ethnic groups, some to men, some to women, and some to both. Some are specific to certain occasions and some are performed wherever the conditions have demanded. Some dances were performed in the past but are no longer practiced.

Except for Sufi dances and folk/ethnic dances associated with certain events like weddings, seasonal festivals, and national holidays, dance is not an integral aspect of social life in Iran. It is an occasional entertainment heavily dependent on the circumstances and context. Since the arrival of Islam, recreational dance, like music, has acquired a paradoxical status in Iranian society. On the one hand, it has had a relatively steady presence, with variation in the form and frequency, in privacy of the royal court and some homes. On the other hand, it has been condemned religiously and not recognized as a legitimate form of performing art. As a result, until recent times, recreational dance in Iran has not been subject to the kind of systematic codification and organized transmission through formal study and instruction that can be seen in the history of other Asian and Western dances.

Dances in rural areas are often of the folk type and are not viewed negatively. Folk dances are marked by intricate hand, arm, and feet movements along with shimmering costumes. Though most folk dances are conducted in group, by both men and women, there are folk dances involving only solo dancers.

Though no touching is involved in these dances, if conducted collectively, participants may hold each other's hands in a chain format. If they do not hold hands, individual dancers perform the same movements in unison. Collective dances may involve performing in circle or in line-up. They are often guided by a dance leader who signals the steps at the end of the line or in the middle of the circle. It is common to use an object, like a handkerchief, for signaling the change in the movements. These dances are often performed as a community matter and involve both young and old. Some tribal folk dances are associated with seasons and certain produce, like the "dance of rice" and the "dance of winter." These dances involve body movements demonstrating activities associated with the occasion. For instance, women in Gilân perform the "dance of rice" during the harvest season. While holding a tray, dancers move their hands and body in a coordinated manner to demonstrate collection, cleaning, and preparation of rice. Some dances involve the use of objects like a short stick, handkerchief, or sword. Some of the latter are more systematic and might have originated from combat, and others are less systematic and the object serves either as a symbol or an expressive tool for enhancing the effect of the performance. For instance, in some Turkish dances, performers carry a sword. In a popular folk dance known as *chub-bâzi* (stick dance, also called *tarkeh-bâzî* or twig dance among Bakhtiâri tribes), the dancer performs with a stick in hand. In some dances, hitting two sticks together is part of the music and rhythm of the dance. The use of an object may follow either a definite rhythmic pattern or instantaneous improvised movements.

Modern Iranian folk dances can be broken into four categories: (a) those in their traditional form without much change, often performed among the ethnic groups and in rural areas; (b) those which have been slightly modified and are performed by trained dancers on the stage; (c) artistic folk dances studied and taught systematically by dance schools; and (d) those choreographed and composed with modern techniques. All four types are still performed in Iran, though the third and fourth types are receiving attention by Iranian immigrant artists working in the West. While some of folk dances are ethnic and some religious, there are also those representing both.

Mystical or Sufi dance (*samâ'*) is spiritual in nature and is performed by dervishes in their *khânqâhs* (retreats), often in presence of a master Sufi or *shaykh*. It is accompanied by music and poetry reading, mostly from Hâfez, Rumi, and other mystic poets. To Sufis, God resides not in books and words but in the flow, rhyme, and sound of objects, material or non-material. Sufi dances, like music, rhythms, soulful melodies, poetry, and spiritual instructions, help the person to achieve ecstasy and unity with God. Qâderi Sufis of Iranian Kurdistan are well known for their spiritual dancing during which, in the frenzy of movement and ecstasy, some men even cut themselves. It should be noted that many Sufis do not refer to *samâ'* as a dance because of the ambivalent attitude and religious concerns about dance in Islamic societies. *Samâ'* also has been a source of inspiration not only for practicing Sufis but also for non-Muslim choreographers who see it as one of the most delicate form of spiritual dance. *Samâ'* dances are not limited to Muslims. Zoroastrians also practice a form of mystical dance involving violent shaking of the body and chanting in order to achieve ecstasy.

Somewhat related to mystic/religious dances are also healing dances, like the dance of *shafâ'* among Baluchis. In these dances, the person is believed to be possessed by an evil spirit. To get rid of the spirit, the afflicted shakes her or his body in certain manner until falling into a trance—manifested in shivering, cries, tears, and intense movements. In southern Iran, females believed to be afflicted by jinns are covered with a veil and asked to dance for 30 to 45 minutes to the beat of a drum, in order to rid their body of the evil spirit.

Recreational dance is closest to what one may call "Persian dance"—not very different than what others have called "*Tehrâni* dance." It involves the rhythmic movement of the shoulder, simultaneous curving of arms and hips, and coordinated facial expressions. The latter is extremely important because the dance is often done either for or in front of others, thus without emotional conveyance, not much is delivered. Foot movement is not as essential as it is in Western dances. Foot movements are slight and often in coordination with body movements. This type of dance does not follow any rule in terms of the number of people involved, the order of movements, and the extent of improvising. It emphasizes the agility of the upper body parts and face. At times, depending on accompanying music, occasional clapping and/or snapping of fingers are performed too. If conducted collectively, two or more performers many dance in unison. These collective dances reduce improvisation and shift the emphasis from facial expressions to body positions and footwork.

During the Qâjâr period, this recreational dance became an integral part of *bazms* (parties) and was performed purely for pleasure. As it evolved in the decades later, it became the major source of entertainment for private gatherings in urban areas and even weddings in some rural towns. Forms of this dance include those known as *motrebi, ruhowzi, Bâbâ Karam, shâteri and Tehrâni;* a style known variously as *lâti, jâheli,* or *kolâh makhmali* is one of the most popular dances in cabarets and Film Fârsi. Another version of this dance, with a strong focus on hip movements is called *qer Kamari* (*qer* means "movement" and *Kamar* refers to the hips). *Qer dâdan* is often used as a reference to body movement in dance from.

In the Qâjâr period, and even in the early Pahlavi period, recreational dance was performed in sex-segregated settings: female dancers or boys dressed as women danced for men-only parties and women for female parties. After the 1960s, some modern families began mixed dancing, and nowadays it is a common practice in confines of the private home among Westernized youth in urban areas. Mixed dancing was also more common among religious minorities, especially non-Muslims. Since there was no formal instruction, or even schooling, for this kind of dance, men and women learned it by watching others doing it. Young girls are often taught by their mothers, other family members, or peers.

Unlike the Sufi dance of *samâ'*, which serves as a religious practice, recreational dances are situational and are performed in occasions where the right conditions, performers, and audience are present. Situations in which people engage in dancing are varied and until the conditions are right, participants may not initiate dancing. Merry situations and happy times are the most common occasions when this kind of dance is performed. While dancing is common during weddings, not all weddings are accompanied by dancing. Generally, religiously oriented Muslim families reject dancing as sinful activity all together. Yet, at some religious weddings, dancing takes place in areas reserved exclusively for women.

Recreational dance is improvisational in nature. Even the most skillful dancers rely on their own determination and creativity rather than on a systematic set of rules and practices. The lack of fixed rules provides dancers the opportunity to be creative and improvise according to the mood and context of the performance. In fact, this improvisational aspect has introduced flexibility and spontaneity as two most important features of Persian recreational dance—features more adapt to informal settings rather than formal dance halls in Western countries. As this dance became a desired form of entertainment for emerging middle classes, it became a standard feature of new nightclubs emerging in northern Tehran in 1930–40s. Its popularization was related to the growth of theater and cinema. It was this close association with entertainment that preserved this form of dance in a vulgar format until the time of Mohammad-Rezâ Pahlavi, when formal dance schools began to approach it more professionally.

Dance in Iranian History

In some ways, the history of dance in Iran parallels the history of music, albeit in a much more restricted manner, especially in the case of recreational dance. In other words, in any period when music is forbidden, so is dance. If music is highly encouraged, then dance is more tolerated in society. This is more or less the case from the Arab invasion until the late 18th century. The ebb and flow of disapproval of dance continued afterwards, but in shorter cycles and with less intensity. Historically, some rulers have favored dance and even recruited dancers for their own court and some have not. Some were poets or musicians themselves and treated dance favorably either for artistic purposes or for entertainment. But the recorded history of Persian dances between the time of the Arab invasion and the rise of Karim Khân Zand to power remains very thin and often sporadic. This on-and-off negative attitude towards dance in Iranian history has made this art the least institutionalized form of performing arts until the twentieth century.

Based on archaeological remains found in Iran, dance in pre-Islamic Iran appears to have been practiced since the emergence of Mithraism. A ritual ceremony in which Mithra sacrificed a bull was followed by a dance performed by men. Writing about the Achaemenid period, Greek historians make reference to dancers of Persia such as Zenon, a talented female dancer at the court of Artaxerxes II. Achaemenid kings used to participate in an autumn festival, known today as Mehrgân, during which Mithra was worshiped by dancers. Zoroastrian worships also involved ritualistic dancing. The Parthians adopted Greek theater and dance to their own taste, and the Sasanids developed a form of military dance in which their soldiers utilized their weapons rhythmically while riding on horseback. Decorative mosaics left from the palace of Shâhpur I show female dancers. An adventurer in hunting and love, Bahrâm Gur had many female entertainers in this court. Three of these entertainers were sisters, one playing harp, one singing, and one dancing.

With the Arab invasion and rise of Islam, the performing arts came under severe restrictions and dance was perceived as an immoral and sinful activity. However, as mentioned before, with the passing of time new rulers revived the practice of entertainers for the court. Reportedly, Hârun-or-Rashid had hundreds of female dancers his court. Courtiers and nobility also employed young boys dressed as women for dancing. Women entertainers were viewed as morally lax and socially low in status. As Arab rulers indulged in luxury, corrupt practices, and worldly ambitions contrary to the egalitarian spirit of early Islam, Sufism emerged as a revolt against both this worldly orientation of the state and the establishment of formal orthodoxy in a society built on unequal distribution of wealth and power. Sufis integrated devotional dance into their worship of God. Mystic poems by Rumi, Saʻdi, and Hâfez reinforced this positive attitude toward devotional dance.

Attitudes of different Mongol rulers towards music and dance were contradictory. Some, like Timur, did not have a positive attitude towards dance and others are known to have frequented parties with dancers. The Safavids could not have openly endorsed dance as a legitimate activity, no matter what the true feelings of various rulers might have been in private. Given that their founder Safi-od-Din belonged to a Sufi order, Shiʻism was their state ideology, and the ʻolamâ were very influential in their courts, dance was not viewed as morally acceptable. This especially became the case when Mohammad Bâqer Majlesi, one of the most respected religious scholars in the late Safavid period, developed a close relationship with the court and his opinion often affected the official policy. Majlesi regarded dancing, even Sufi dancing, as a sinful activity. Yet, Shah 'Abbâs, who ruled prior to Majlesi's rise to prominence, had more tolerant attitudes towards worldly activities and reportedly there was a dance school in Isfahan during his reign.

Supportive of the arts, Karim Khân Zand made the city of Shiraz a center of poetry, music, and dance. A form of dance accompanied by rhythmic and happy music became very popula—a precursor to recreational dance popular among secular urban middle classes in the twentieth century. The Zands' supportive attitude continued during the Qâjâr period as well. Some Qâjâr kings had their own *motrebs* (a generic term used for musicians and dancers whose job was to entertain) in the court. Fath-'Ali Shâh is known to have had a group of female dancers and male musicians in his court. His grandson Mohammad Shah also hired many dancers for court entertainment. It is from this period on that dance becomes an integral part of *bazm*s, which had been a gathering for poetry reading and Sufi dances in previous times. *Motrebi* dance became very popular, especially when incorporated into the *ruhowzi* theater and Nowruz celebrations.

During the political instability associated with the Constitutional Revolution, dance lost its significance and did not gain much attention until the rise of Rezâ Khân to power in 1920s. It is during the reign of the Pahlavis that dance came to be viewed not just an entertainment but also an art. As such, it started to be approached professionally. Modern education was used to teach various forms of dances. Traditional and folk dances were discovered, studied, and developed. Given the clerical opposition to dance, as well as negative public attitudes, teaching modern dances had to start gradually, on a small scale, and often in private sessions.

Yelenâ Avedisiân opened a dance school first in Tabriz in 1927, and then in Tehran in 1928. These schools taught ballet lessons to children of upper classes. Most early teachers were either foreigners or non-Muslims. As time went by, the state protection and encouragement resulted in attraction of able dance teachers, especially for ballet. Two other important ballet teachers who had significant role in dance education in Iran, in addition to Avedisiân, were Madame Cornelli and Serkis Jânbâziân. Although dance was still viewed negatively by the public, Rezâ Shah's order to abolish the veil in 1936 served as an important catalyst for public performances by female dancers, first in the films, then in theater halls, and later in nightclubs. In the 1940s, more resources were devoted to preservation of traditional dances. The government hired an American, Nilla Cram Cook, to lead dance education. Cook helped to found the Iranian Ballet Company (IBC). Soon, IBC ensembles began touring foreign capitals offering Iranian dances and promoting Iranian cultural heritage.

In the 1950s, Mohammad-Rezâ Shah showed a more positive attitude toward dance education, and again dance was integrated into the official ceremonies. In 1958, the Ministry of Culture and Fine Arts established the National Folkloric Music, Song and Dance (NFMSD) in order to revive Persian old songs and dances. The NFMSD's ensembles were routinely invited to perform in national ceremonies and for the guests of the state in the royal court. In subsequent years, they also performed and represented Iran in various international festivals.

In 1962, Avedisiân expanded her activities and founded the Song and Dance Ensemble in Tehran. In 1967, the Iranian Folk Society (IFS) was established in order to, among other things, gather information and resources on various ethnic and folk dances in the country for promoting them both at home and abroad. The IFS worked on Iranian folk dances and ballet renditions of Persian classical epics. The government sent Iranian experts abroad for visiting opera houses, inviting foreign teachers, and preparing resources for expanding artistic forums in Iran. Tâlâr-e Rudaki (now renamed Vahdat Hall) was established for opera and other musical performances. The Pars National Ballet was established for attracting foreign dancers to teach and perform in Iran. In 1969, a new ballet department was established at the Music College in Tehran. In 1972, Hâydeh Changiziân, a former student of Avedisiân was appointed as the prima ballerina of the Iranian National Ballet. Classical and contemporary ballets, inspired by the Iranian history and literature, were written and performed with Persian musical compositions. Three such works included *Shahrzâd* ("Scheherezad"), *Afsâneh-e khelqat* ("The Myth of Creation"), and *Bijan o Manijeh*.

During the Pahlavi period, efforts by the government, artists, and interested citizens, helped to institutionalize dance within the educational system and to elevate dance from a lowly means of entertainment to a respectable art form. Furthermore, dance was no longer viewed as an activity for the court or upper class families. Middle classes became interested in dance, nightclubs began to have regular dancers to entertain their customers, and several stylish restaurants with dance floors emerged as a hub for university students. In most wedding parties, even traditional ones, some kind of dance took place. If families were modern and affluent, they either arranged their own music or hired a musical group whose performance engaged guests in dancing. In traditional families, such parties were sex-segregated: men in a hall separate from women. But even in these traditional ones, in women's section there was always some form of dancing in which mostly younger girls participated. Even in some traditional male parties, where dance was not favored in general, at times younger men still engaged in dancing as soon as conservative guests and elders had left the party.

A dancer who contributed the most to the popularization of Persian dance among the middle classes is the talented and legendary Iranian woman who performs under the name Jamileh. She is a skilful dancer who started her career in the nightclubs as a belly dancer and in the course of a long career became, according to Robyn C. Friend, "the Goddess of Persian dance."[4] As Jamelih became more practiced professionally, her performances became a staple of *Film Fârsi* movies.

Once the revolution overthrew the Pahlavi regime in 1978 and the Islamic Republic was established, all dance related institutions and activities were abolished. Dance and ballet were banned as corrupt, perverse, and sinful activities. Some professional dancers quit, some went underground, and most left the country. Though dancing disappeared from the public scene throughout 1980s, starting in mid-1990s, folk dances performed by men were occasionally offered in public halls and television programs. Yet, dance did not disappear from people's lives. As all un-Islamic forms of entertainment were banned, secular and even some conservative families used dance in private parties as a means of lifting up their spirits and warming up their gathering.

Another person who has had a significant role in the promotion of Persian dance is a young Iranian who migrated to the United States after the revolution. Mohammad Khordâdiân established Sabâh Dance Company in Los Angeles and succeeded in turning Iranian dances to aerobic forms. Videotapes of Khordâdiân's flashy choreographies of folkloric and stylish Iranian dances, as well as his workout dance instructions, are imported to Iran illegally and widely viewed by both men and women. In major cities, his tapes are found in most houses where people engage in dancing. In 2002, while on a trip to Iran for visiting his ailing father, Khordâdiân was arrested and convicted of "corrupting behavior." He was barred from giving dance classes for life and leaving Iran for 10 years. Furthermore, he was ordered to avoid public celebrations or weddings of nonrelatives for three years. Later, Khordâdiân managed to leave Iran and now resides and performs in Turkey.

Finally, a few words about Western dances in Iran are in order. Western dances were introduced in Iran by secular Iranians who had traveled to the West or by Westerners who came to Iran. They were performed only in private settings. In the 1970s, as television and cinema exposed Iranian youth to Western dances, they became a choice for secular urban youth in their private parties. Later, as Tehran became metropolitan and more Westernized, a few Western-style restaurant bars with dance floor opened and the upper and upper-middle class youth frequented them for dancing the tango, rock 'n' roll, and other Western dances. Most recent reports by the Western journalists indicate that nowadays Western dances are widely performed by Iranian youth in their private parties.

NOTES

1. This description here follows that given at a useful Web site dealing with Persian music, accessible at http://www.duke.edu/~azomorod/dastgah.html. This Web site includes many photographs of musical instruments and sound clips of music that readers may find useful to supplement this chapter.

2. "Compositional Structure" at http://www.duke.edu/~azomorod/persian2.html.

3. "The Dastgah" at http://www.duke.edu/~azomorod/dastgah.html.

4. See http://home.earthlink.net/~rcfriend/jamileh.htm.

Glossary

Âkhund Though historically used as a title for a very accomplished Muslim religious scholar, in the past century the term usually refers to a religious student who failed to master the advanced curriculum and has been accredited only to run a mosque. People opposed to the current theocratic government in Iran use the term pejoratively in reference to all clerics.

'Âshurâ The tenth day of the Islamic month of Moharram, when Shi'ites commemorate the slaying of Hosayn, grandson of the Prophet Mohammad, and his family in a battle with the Umayyad army at Karbalâ on this day in A.D. 680.

Âyatollâh Literally meaning "sign of God," it is a title for a religious scholar whose advanced training in religious studies is confirmed by demonstrated publications and his superior teachers.

'Azâdâri The processions and ceremonies associated with mourning the death of religious figures in Shi'ite Islam.

Azeri Term for both the Turkish language and people of Azerbaijan.

Châdor A name, also meaning "tent," for the loose, formless, usually black garment worn by women to cover the body, head, and perhaps face when they go out in public.

Chahârshanbehsuri The celebration on the last Wednesday of the calendar year during which individuals jump over a fire.

Dastgâh Literally meaning "system," it refers to a set of musical notes, scale, and the associated repertoire of melodies.

Fatvâ A binding legal pronouncement issued by a religious jurisprudent.

Ghazal A lyrical form of Persian poetry.

Gusheh Literally meaning "corner," it refers to melodic patterns within a set of notes in Persian music.

Hadith Traditional reports about things the Prophet Mohammad said. Shi'ites use the term to refer also to statements from the Imams.

Hâji Firuz A character with black-colored face and red dress with a kettle drum in his hands dancing and singing in the streets during the Persian Nowruz festivities.

Harâm Anything forbidden by religion, as opposed to *halâl* or licit.

Hayât The courtyard in a house, traditionally containing a small pool and garden.

Hejâb A term referring to religiously appropriate dress for women in public arenas.

Hezbollâhi A term that came to use after the revolution for individuals belonging to the "party of God." Although Hezbollâh in Lebanon is an established political-military force, in Iran the term is loosely used for supporters of the Islamic Republic working in various governmental units.

Hojjat-ol-Eslâm Literally meaning "proof of Islam," it is a title for a midranking religious scholar who has completed advanced training in religious studies.

'Id The Arabic word for "celebration." In Iran, it is used for both religious and national holidays.

'Id-e Fetr A celebration marking the end of the Muslim month of fasting.

'Id-e Qorbân The usual Persian name for the Muslim holiday known in Arabic as 'Id-ol-Azhâ, the day an animal is sacrificed in commemoration of a similar sacrifice by Abraham for the sparing of his son. It is part of the rituals of the pilgrimage to Mecca but is performed on the same day by Muslims everywhere.

Imam For Sunni Muslims, it refers to the leader of the congregational prayer. Shi'ites use the word for the twelve charismatic religious leaders they recognized after the Prophet Mohammad. After the Islamic Revolution of 1979, the term has been used as a title for Âyatollâh Khomeini as well.

Madraseh Originally a term referring to an institution to teach Islamic law, it is now used in Iran generically to denote any school or learning center, whether religious or secular.

Mahaleh A neighborhood or community.

Mahriyeh As the bride price and a part of the Muslim marriage contract, it refers to an agreed amount of money to be paid to a woman by her husband. Though she can demand it anytime during the marriage, it is often asked for at the dissolution of marriage.

Majles Generically, a term for any planned assembly, thus *majles 'arusi* (wedding party) or *majles 'aza* (a funeral). In politics, Majles refers to the Parliament or the Islamic Consultative Assembly.

Marja'-e taqlid Literally meaning "source of emulation," the term refers to a religious scholar of independent judgment. In the absence of an Imam, Shi'ites are supposed to recognize and follow one of these as their religious guide.

Masjed Mosque or the place of prayer.

Moharram The first month of the Islamic lunar calendar and the month in which Shi'ites commemorate the martyrdom of Imam Hosayn at Karbalâ.

Mojtahed A religious scholar who has acquired the skill and authority to interpret religious texts and laws. *Ejtehâd* is the ability to independently arrive at God's rulings.

Molla⁻ Like *âkhund*, a generic and informal term used in reference to low-ranking Muslim clerics.

Mostaz'afin Gaining currency after the Islamic Revolution, it is a term used by religious leaders in reference to the poor and helpless segment of the society. During the revolution, the word effectively was used as a substitute for proletarians.

Mot'a Arabic term for "temporary marriage" or what in Iran is commonly referred to as *sigheh*.

Naqqâli Dramatic recitation of stories in teahouses or sports centers, with or without a drum.

Nowruz Persian New Year holiday, celebrated at the beginning of spring.

'Olamâ Plural of *'âlem*, meaning "a learned person." It refers to individuals with extensive education in the Koran and Islamic law.

Qanât A network of underground channels to carry water by gravity feed from highland water tables to fields at lower elevations.

Qasideh Elegy, a poetic form similar to *ghazal* but with a strict theme and no limit in length.

Qezelbâsh Literally meaning "red heads," it refers to Shi'ite Turks who helped found the Safavid Dynasty in Iran.

Radif Literally meaning "rank" or "series," in music it refers to a specific sonic space identifying the movement of the melodies in a mode.

Rowzeh The recitation of stories about the sufferings of the Imams and other Shi'ite personalities. The actual practice is called *rowzeh-khʷâni*.

Ruhowzi Literally meaning "over the pool" and also called *siah-bâzi*, it is a type of comic folk drama often performed at weddings on a board covering the small pool in the middle of a yard.

Sofreh Literally meaning "dining cloth," this refers to different ritualistic arrangements of food and nonfood items Iranians make for different occasions. *Sofreh-'aqd* refers to items set up for a wedding occasion and *sofreh-haftsin* refers to items set up for Nowruz festivities.

Ta'ârof An attitude among Iranians expressing politeness in a variety of contexts by concealing one's true feelings in order to be gracious or to avoid offending someone.

Takiyeh Structures built for commemoration of the martyrdom of Imam Hosayn through performances of *rowzeh-khʷâni, 'azâdâri,* or *ta'ziyeh.*

Ta'âiyeh Theatrical passion plays recreating the tragic events leading to the suffering and death of Imam Hosayn.

Velâyat-e Faqih The term devised by Khomeini for the concept of rule by the most eminent Shi'ite legal scholar; now used as the formal title for the supreme leader of Iran.

Ziârat The practice of visiting Shi'ite religious shrines. A special text (*ziârat-nâmeh*) is usually prepared for each saint or religious leader to be recited during the visit to their shrine.

Zur-khâneh Literally meaning "house of strength," it is the name of a traditional Iranian sports center.

Selected Bibliography

GENERAL INFORMATION

Arberry, A. J. *The Legacy of Persia.* Oxford: Oxford University Press, 1953.

Banani, Amin. *The Modernization of Iran, 1921–1941.* Stanford: Stanford University Press, 1961.

Bassett, James. *Persia: The Land of the Imams, a Narrative of Travel and Residence 1871–1885.* New York: C. Scribner's Sons, 1886.

Bausani, Alessandro. *The Persians from the Earliest Days to the Twentieth Century.* Translated by J. B. Donne. New York: St. Martin's, 1971.

Cottam, Richard. *Nationalism in Iran.* Pittsburgh: University of Pittsburgh Press, 1964.

Curzon, George Nathaniel. *Persia and the Persian Question.* 2 vols. London: Longmans, Green, 1892.

Farmanfarmaian, Manucher, and Roxane Farmanfarmaian. *Blood and Oil: Memoirs of a Persian Prince.* New York: Random House, 1997.

Lambton, Ann K. S. *Landlord and Peasant in Persia: A Study of Land Tenure and Land Revenue Administration.* Oxford: Oxford University Press, 1953.

Mackey, Sandra. *The Iranians: Persia, Islam, and the Soul of a Nation.* New York: Dutton, 1996.

Massé, Henri. *Persian Beliefs and Customs.* Translated by C. A. Messner. New Haven, CT: Human Relations Area Files, 1954.

Molavi, Afshin. *Persian Pilgrimages: Journeys across Iran.* New York: Norton, 2002.

Sciolino, Elaine. *Persian Mirrors: The Elusive Faces of Iran.* New York: Touchstone, 2000.

Stevens, Roger. *The Land of the Great Sophy.* London: Methuen, 1971.

Wilber, Donald N. *Iran: Past and Present.* 9th ed. Princeton: Princeton University Press, 1981.

Wilson, Samuel Graham. *Persian Life and Customs.* New York: F. H. Revell, 1895.

Yarshater, Ehsan, ed. *Encyclopaedia Iranica.* London, Costa Mesa, CA, and New York: Routledge, Mazda Publishers, Bibliotheca Persica, 1985–.

HISTORY AND POLITICS

Abrahamian, Ervand. *Iran between Two Revolutions.* Princeton, NJ: Princeton University Press, 1982.

Afary, Janet. *The Iranian Constitutional Revolution, 1906–1911: Grassroots Democracy, Social Democracy, and the Origin of Feminism.* New York: Columbia University Press, 1996.

Avery, Peter. *Modern Iran.* New York: Praeger, 1965.

Bakhash, Shaul. *The Reign of the Ayatollahs.* New York: Basic Books, 1984.

Bill, James. *The Eagle and the Lion: The Tragedy of American-Iranian Relations.* New Haven, CT: Yale University Press, 1988.

Cambridge University Press. *Cambridge History of Iran* (8 vols.). Cambridge: Cambridge University Press, 1968–1991.

Daniel, Elton L. *The History of Iran.* Westport, CT: Greenwood, 2001.

Ghirshman, R. *Iran from the Earliest Times to the Islamic Conquest.* New York: Penguin Books, 1954.

Hairi, Abdul-Hadi. *Shi'ism and Constitutionalism in Iran: A Study of the Role Played by the Persian Residents of Iraq in Iranian Politics.* Leiden, Netherlands: E. J. Brill, 1977.

Hooglund, Eric. *Land and Revolution in Iran, 1960–1980.* Austin: University of Texas Press, 1982.

Kazemi, Farhad. *Poverty and Revolution in Iran.* New York: New York University Press, 1980.

Keddie, Nikki R. *Religion and Rebellion in Iran: The Tobacco Protest of 1891–1892.* London: Frank Cass, 1966.

Lockhart, Laurence. *The Fall of the Safavi Dynasty and the Afghan Occupation of Persia.* Cambridge: Cambridge University Press, 1958.

Olmstead, Albert T. E. *The History of the Persian Empire: Achaemenid Period.* Chicago: University of Chicago Press, 1948.

Poulson, Stephen C. *Social Movements in Twentieth-Century Iran: Culture, Ideology, and Mobilizing Frameworks.* Lanham, MD: Lexington Books, 2005.

Sykes, Percy. *A History of Persia.* 3rd. ed. 2 vols. London: Macmillan and Co., 1951.

Watson, Robert Grant. *A History of Persia from the Beginning of the Nineteenth Century to the Year 1858.* London: Smith, Elder and Co., 1866.

RELIGION AND RELIGIOUS LIFE

Akhavi, Shahrough. *Religion and Politics in Contemporary Iran.* Albany: State University of New York Press, 1980.

Algar, Hamid. *Religion and State in Iran 1785–1906.* Berkeley and Los Angeles: University of California Press, 1969.

Amanat, Abbas. *Resurrection and Renewal: The Making of the Babi Movement in Iran, 1844–1850.* Ithaca, NY: Cornell University Press, 1989.

Bausani, Alessandro. *Religion in Iran: From Zoroaster to Baha'ullah.* Translated by J. M. Marchesi. New York: Bibliotheca Persica Press, 2000.

Boyce, Mary. *A Persian Stronghold of Zoroastrianism.* Oxford: Clarendon Press, 1977.

———. *Zoroastrians: Their Religious Beliefs and Practices.* London and Boston: Routledge & Kegan Paul, 1979.

Donaldson, Bess A. *The Wild Rue: A Study of Muhammadan Magic and Folklore in Iran.* London: Luzac & Co., 1938.

Donaldson, Dwight M. *The Shi'ite Religion: A History of Islam in Persia and Irak* . London: Luzac & Co., 1933.

Fischer, Michael. *Iran: From Religious Dispute to Revolution.* Cambridge, MA, and London: Harvard University Press, 1980.

Keddie, Nikki R. *Religion and Politics in Iran.* New Haven, CT: Yale University Press, 1983.

Lalani, Arzina R. *Early Shi'i Thought: The Teachings of Imam Muhammad al-Baqir.* London: I. B. Tauris, 2000.

Loeffler, Reinhold. *Islam in Practice: Religious Beliefs in a Persian Village.* Albany: State University of New York Press, 1988.

Modarressi, Hossein. *Crisis and Consolidation in the Formative Period of Shi'ites Islam: Abu Ja'far ibn Qiba al-Razi and His Contribution to Imamite Shi'ites Thought.* Princeton, NJ: Darwin Press, 1993.

Momen, Moojan. *An Introduction to Shi'i Islam: The History and Doctrines of Twelver Shi'ism.* New Haven, CT: Yale University Press, 1987.

Mottahedeh, Roy. *The Mantle of the Prophet: Religion and Politics in Iran.* New York: Simon and Schuster, 1985.

Moussavi, Ahmad Kazemi. *Religious Authority in Shi'ite Islam: From the Office of Mufti to the Institution of Marja'.* Kuala Lumpur: International Institute of Islamic Thought and Civilization, 1996.

Richard, Yann. *Shi'ite Islam.* Translated by Antonia Nevill. Oxford: Blackwell, 1995.

Sachedina, Abdulaziz Abdulhussein. *Islamic Messianism: The Idea of the Mahdi in Twelver Shi'ism.* Albany: State University of New York, 1981.

———. *The Just Ruler (al-Sultan al-Adil) in Shi'ite Islam: The Comprehensive Authority of the Jurist in Imamite Jurisprudence.* Oxford: Oxford University Press, 1998.

Shani, Raya. *A Monumental Manifestation of the Shi'ite Faith in Late Twelfth-Century Iran: The Case of the Gunbad-i 'Alawiyan, Hamadan.* Oxford: Oxford University Press, 1996.

Sykes, P. M., and Khan Bahadur Ahmad Din Khan. *The Glory of the Shia World: The Tale of a Pilgrimage.* London: Macmillan, 1910.

Tabataba'i S. Mohammad Hussein. *Shi'ite Islam.* 2nd ed. Albany: State University of New York Press, 1977.

von Grunebaum, Gustave E. *Muhammadan Festivals.* London and New York: Abelard-Schuman, 1958.

LITERATURE

Akbar, Fatollah. *The Eye of an Ant: Persian Proverbs and Poems.* Bethesda, MD: Iran Books, 1995.

Browne, E. G. *A Literary History of Persia.* 4 vols. Cambridge: Cambridge University Press, 1928.

———. *The Press and Poetry of Modern Persia.* Cambridge: Cambridge University Press, 1914.

Christensen, Arthur. *Persian Folktales.* Translated by Alfred Kurti. London: G. Bell & Sons, 1971.

Chubak, Sadeq. *The Patient Stone (Sang-e Sabur).* Translated by M. R. Ghanoonparvar. Costa Mesa, CA: Mazda Publishers, 1989.

Davis, Dick. *Epic and Sedition: The Case of Ferdowsi's Shahnameh.* Fayetteville: University of Arkansas Press, 1992.

Ferdowsi. *The Epic of the Kings.* Prose translated by Reuben Levy. London and Boston: Routledge & Kegan Paul, 1967.

———. *The Tragedy of Sohrab and Rostam: From the Persian National Epic, the Shahname of Abol-Qasem Ferdowsi.* Translated by Jerome W. Clinton. Seattle: University of Washington Press, 1987.

Ghanoonparvar, Mohammad R. *Prophets of Doom: Literature as a Socio-Political Phenomenon in Modern Iran.* Lanham, MD: University Press of America, 1984.

———. *Reading Chubak.* Costa Mesa, CA: Mazda Publishers, 2005.

Hedayat, Sadeq. *The Blind Owl.* Translated by D. P. Costello. New York: Grove Press, 1957.

Hillmann, Michael C. *Iranian Society: An Anthology of Writings by Jalal Al-e Ahmad.* Lexington, KY: Mazda Publishers, 1982.

Javadi, Hasan. *Satire in Persian Literature.* Rutherford, NJ: Fairleigh Dickinson University Press, 1988.

Kamshad, H. *Modern Persian Prose Literature.* Cambridge: Cambridge University Press, 1966.

Levy, Reuben. *Introduction to Persian Literature.* New York: Columbia University Press, 1969.

Meisami, Julie Scott. *Medieval Persian Court Poetry.* Princeton, NJ: Princeton University Press, 1987.

Milani, Farzaneh. *Veils and Words: The Emerging Voices of Iranian Women Writers.* Syracuse, NY: Syracuse University Press, 1992.

Mozaffari, Nahid, and Ahmad Karimi Hakkak, eds. *Strange Times, My Dear: The PEN Anthology of Contemporary Iranian Literature.* New York: Arcade Publications, 2005.

Radhayrapetian, Juliet. *Iranian Folk Narrative: A Survey of Scholarship.* New York and London: Garland Publishing, 1990.

Rahimieh, Nasrin. *Missing Persians: Discovering Voices in Iranian Cultural History.* Syracuse, NY: Syracuse University Press, 2001.

Ravanipur, Moniru. *Satan's Stones.* Edited and translated by M. R. Ghanoonparvar. Austin: University of Texas Press, 1996.

Sprachman, Paul. *Language and Culture in Persian.* Costa Mesa, CA: Mazda Publishers, 2002.

Talattof, Kamran. *Politics of Writing in Iran.* Syacuse, NY: Syracuse University Press, 2000.

Yarshater, Ehsan, ed. *Persian Literature.* Albany, NY: Bibliotheca Persica, 1988.

LIFESTYLE

Barth, Fredrik. *Nomads of South Persia: The Basseri Tribe of the Khamseh Confederacy.* London: Allen and Unwin, 1961.

Beck, Lois. *Nomad: A Year in the Life of a Qashqa'i Tribesman in Iran.* Berkeley and Los Angeles: University of California Press, 1991.

Beeman, William O. *Language, Status, and Power in Iran.* Bloomington: Indiana University Press, 1986.

Browne, E. G. *A Year Amongst the Persians.* Cambridge: Cambridge University Press, 1927.

Garthwaite, Gene. *Khans and Shahs: A Documentary Analysis of the Bakhtiyari in Iran.* Cambridge: Cambridge University Press, 1983.

Harnack, Curtis. *Persian Lions, Persian Lambs: An American's Odyssey in Iran.* New York: Holt, Rinehart and Winston, 1965.

Oberling, Pierre. *The Qashqa'i Nomads of Fars.* The Hague, Netherlands: Mouton, 1974.

Smith, Anthony. *Blind White Fish in Persia.* New York: Dutton, 1953.

Ullens de Schotten, Marie-Therese. *Lords of the Mountains: Southern Persia and the Kashkai Tribe.* London: Chatto and Windus, 1956.

WOMEN AND GENDER RELATIONS

Esfandiari, Haleh. *Reconstructed Lives: Women and Iran's Islamic Revolution.* Baltimore, MD: Johns Hopkins University Press, 1997.

Farman Farmaian, Sattareh. *Daughter of Persia: A Woman's Journey from Her Father's Harem through the Islamic Revolution.* New York: Crown, 1992.

Fathi, Asghar, ed. *Women and the Family in Iran.* Leiden, Netherlands: Brill, 1985.

Friedl, Erika. *Women of Deh Koh: Lives in an Iranian Village.* Washington, DC: Smithsonian Institution Press, 1989.

Haeri, Shahla. *Islam and Feminism: An Iranian Case-Study.* London: Macmillan Press, 1998.

———. *Law of Desire: Temporary Marriage in Shi'i Islam.* Syracuse, NY: Syracuse University Press, 1989.

Keddie, Nikki. "Women in Iran Since 1979." *Social Research* 67, no. 2 (Summer 2000): 405–438.

Kousha, Mahnaz. *Voices from Iran: The Changing Lives of Iranian Women.* Syracuse, NY: Syracuse University Press, 2002.

Lewis, Franklin, and Farzin Yazdanfar, comps. and trans., *In a Voice of Their Own: A Collection of Stories by Iranian Women Written Since the Revolution of 1979.* Costa Mesa, CA: Mazda Publishers, 1996.

Milani, Farzaneh. *Veils and Words: The Emerging Voices of Iranian Women Writers.* London: I. B. Tauris, 1992.

Mir-Hosseini, Ziba. *Marriage on Trial: A Study of Islamic Family Law in Iran and Morocco* (rev. ed.). London: I.B. Tauris, 2000.

———. *Islam and Gender: The Religious Debate in Contemporary Iran* Princeton, NJ: Princeton University Press, 1999.

Paidar, Parvin. *Women and the Political Process in Twentieth-Century Iran.* Cambridge: Cambridge University Press, 1995.

Saney, Parviz. *Law and Population Growth in Iran.* Medford, MA: Law and Population Programme, Fletcher School of Law and Diplomacy, Tufts University, 1974.

CINEMA AND DRAMA

Beyza'i, Bahram, Gowhar-e Morad, and Abbas Nalbandian. *Modern Persian Drama: An Anthology.* Translated and introduced by Gise'le Kapuscinski. Lanham, MD: University Press of America, 1987.

Chelowski, Peter. "Narrative Painting and Painting Recitation in Qajar Iran." In *Muqarnas VI: An Annual on Islamic Art and Architecture*, ed. Oleg Grabar. Leiden, Netherlands: E. J. Brill, 1989.

Chelkowski, Peter, ed. *Ta'ziyeh: Ritual and Drama in Iran.* New York: New York University Press, 1979.

Chelkowski, Peter, and Hamid Dabashi. *Staging a Revolution: The Art of Persuasion in the Islamic Republic of Iran.* New York: New York University Press, 2002.

Dabashi, Hamid. *Close Up: Iranian Cinema, Past, Present, and Future.* New York: Verso, 2001.

Floor, Willem M. *The History of Theater in Iran.* Washington, DC: Mage, 2005.

Ghanoonparvar, Mohammad R., and John Green. *Iranian Drama: An Anthology.* Costa Mesa, CA: Mazda Publishers, 1989.

Maghsoudlou, Bahman. *Iranian Cinema.* New York: Hagop Kevorkian Center for Near Eastern Studies, New York University, 1987.

Malekpour, Jamshid,. *The Islamic Drama.* London: Frank Cass, 2004.

Pelly, Lewis. *The Miracle Plays of Hasan and Husain.* London: W. H. Alden, 1879.

Tapper, Richard, ed. *The New Iranian Cinema: Politics, Representation and Identity.* London: I. B. Tauris, 2002.

CRAFTS AND FINE ARTS

Bier, Carol, ed. *Woven from the Soul, Spun from the Heart: Textile Arts of Safavid and Qajar Iran, Sixteenth–Nineteenth Centuries.* Washington, DC: The Textile Museum, 1987.

Brend, Barbara. *Perspectives on Persian Painting: Illustrations to Amir Khusrau's Khamsah.* New York: Routledge, 2002.

Canby, Sheila. *The Golden Age of Persian Art, 1501–1722.* New York: Harry N. Abrams, 2000.

Diba, Layla S. "Persian Painting in the Eighteenth Century: Tradition and Transmission." In *Muqarnas VI: An Annual on Islamic Art and Architecture,* ed. Oleg Grabar. Leiden, Netherlands: E. J. Brill,1989.

Diba, Layla S. and Maryam Ekhtiar, eds. *Royal Persian Painting: The Qajar Epoch,* 1785–1925. Brooklyn, NV: Brooklyn Museum of Art, 1998.

Edwards, A. Cecil. *The Persian Carpet; A Survey of the Carpet-Weaving Industry of Persia.* London: Duckworth, 1975.

Floor, Willem M. *Traditional Crafts in Qajar Iran (1800–1925).* Costa Mesa, CA: Mazda Publishers, 2003.

Gluck, Jay, and Sumi Hiramoto Gluck, eds. *A Survey of Persian Handicraft: A Pictorial Introduction to the Contemporary Folk Arts and Art Crafts of Modern Iran.* Tehran and New York: Survey of Persian Art, 1977.

Hillmann, Michael. *Persian Carpets.* Austin: University of Texas Press, 1984.

Khatibi, Abdelkebir, and Mohammed Sijelmassi. *The Splendor of Islamic Calligraphy.* New York: Thames and Hudson, 1996.

Pope, Arthur Upham. *A Survey of Persian Art from Prehistoric Times to the Present.* London and New York: Oxford University Press, 1938–39.

Schimmel, Annemarie. *Calligraphy and Islamic Culture.* New York: New York University Press, 1984.

Wulff, Hans. *The Traditional Crafts of Persia: Their Development, Technology, and Influence on Eastern and Western Civilizations.* Cambridge, MA: M.I.T. Press, 1966.

MUSIC AND DANCE

Caton, Margaret. "The Classical 'Tasnif': A Genre of Persian Vocal Music." PhD diss., University of California, Los Angeles, 1983.

During, Jean, Zia Mirabdolbaghi, and Dariush Safvat. *The Art of Persian Music.* Washington, DC: Mage Publishers, 1991.

Farhat, Hormoz. *The Dastgah Concept in Persian Music.* Cambridge: Cambridge University Press, 1990.

Miller, Lloyd. *Music and Song in Persia: The Art of Avaz.* Salt Lake City: University of Utah Press, 1999.

Netti, Bruno. *Daramad of Chahargah: A Study in the Performance Practice of Persian Music.* Detroit, MI: Information Coordinators, 1972.

———. *The Radif of Persian Music: Studies of Structure and Cultural Context in the Classical Music of Iran.* Champaign, IL: Elephant and Cat, 1992.

Nooshin, Laudan. "The Processes of Creation and Recreation in Persian Classical Music." PhD diss., University of London, 1996.

Sawa, George Dimitri. *Music Performance Practice in the Early 'Abbasid Era 132–320* AH / *750–932* A.D. Toronto, Canada: Pontifical Institute, 1989.

Shay, Anthony. *Choreophobia: Solo Improvised Dance in the Iranian World.* Costa Mesa, CA: Mazda Publishers, 1999.

Tsuge, Genichi. "Avaz: A Study of the Rhythmic Aspects in Classical Iranian Music." PhD diss., Wesleyan University, 1974.

Wright, Owen. *The Modal System of Arab and Persian Music,* A.D *1250–1300.* Oxford and New York: Oxford University Press, 1978.

Zonis, Ella. *Classical Persian Music: An Introduction.* Cambridge, MA: Harvard University Press, 1973.

CUISINE

Batmanglij, Najmieh. *Food of Life: A Book of Ancient Persian and Modern Iranian Cooking and Ceremonies.* Washington, DC: Mage Publishers, 1990.

———. *Silk Road Cooking: A Vegetarian Journey.* Washington, DC: Mage Publishers, 2002.

———. *A Taste of Persia: An Introduction to Persian Cooking.* Washington, DC: Mage Publishers, 1999.

Ghanoonparvar, Mohammad R. *Persian Cuisine: Regional and Modern Foods.* Lexington, KY: Mazda Publishers, 1984.

Mazda, Maideh. *In a Persian Kitchen.* Rutland, VT: C. Tuttle: 1960.

SPORTS AND ENTERTAINMENT

Amanat, Mehrdad. "Zurkhaneh." In *The Oxford Encyclopedia of the Modern Islamic World,* vol. 4, 378–79. New York: Oxford University Press, 1995.

Bland, N. "On the Persian Game of Chess." *Journal of the Royal Asiatic Society* 13, no. 1852: 1–70.

Brooks, Geraldine. "Muslim Women's Games." In *Nine Parts of Desire: The Hidden World of Islamic Women,* 201–11. New York: Anchor, 1995.

Chaqueri, Cosroe. *Beginning Politics: The Reproductive Cycle of Children's Tales and Games in Iran; Historical Inquiry.* New York: Lewiston, 1992.

Chehabi, Houchang E. "A Political History of Football in Iran." *Iranian Studies* 35, no. 4 (Fall 2002): 275–294.

———. "The Juggernaut of Globalization: Sport and Modernization in Iran." In *Sport in Asian Society: Past and Present,* ed. J.A. Mangan and Hong Fan. London: Frank Cass Publishers, 2002.

Daryaee, Touraj. "Mind, Body, and Cosmos: Chess and Backgammon in Ancient Persian (Transcription, Translation, and Text of the Wizarisn-I Catrang ud Nihisn I New-Ardaxsir)." *Iranian Studies* 35, no. 4 (Fall 2002): 281–312.

Floor, Willem. "The Art of Smoking in Iran and Other Uses of Tobacco." *Iranian Studies* 35, nos. 1–3 (Winter–Summer 2002): 47–85.

Matthee, Rudi. *The Pursuit of Pleasure: Drugs and Stimulants in Iranian History, 1500–1900.* Princeton, NJ: Princeton University Press, 2005.

Rochard, Philippe. "The Identities of the Iranian Zurkhanah." Translated by H. E. Chehabi. *Iranian Studies* 35, no. 4 (Fall 2002): 313–340.

Thackston Jr., Wheeler M., and Hossein Ziai, eds. and trans. *The Ball and Polo Stick or The Book of Ecstasy: A Parallel Persian-English Text.* Costa Mesa, CA: Mazda Publishers, 1999.

Titley, Norah M. *Sports and Pastimes: Scenes from Turkish, Persian and Mughal Paintings.* London: The British Library Board, 1979.

HOUSING AND ARCHITECTURE

Babaie, Sussan. "Shah 'Abbas II, the Conquest of Qandahar, the Chihil Sutun, and Its Wall Paintings." In *Muqarnas XI: An Annual on Islamic Art and Architecture,* ed. Gulru Necipoglu. Leiden, Netherlands: E. J. Brill, 1994.

Bahadori, Mehdi. "Passive Cooling Systems in Iranian Architecture." *Scientific American* 238, no. 2 (February 1978): 144.

Blair, Sheila S. "The Madrasa at Zuzan: Islamic Architecture in Eastern Iran on the Eve of the Mongol Invasions." In *Muqarnas III: An Annual on Islamic Art and Architecture,* ed. Oleg Grabar. Leiden, Netherlands: E. J. Brill, 1985.

Blake, Stephen P. *Half the World: The Social Architecture of Safavid Isfahan, 1590–1722.* Costa Mesa, CA: Mazda Publishers, 1999.

Gaube, Heinz. *Iranian Cities.* New York: New York University Press, 1979.

Golombek, Lisa, and Donald Wilber. *The Timurid Architecture of Iran and Turan.* Princeton, NJ: Princeton University Press, 1988.

Hejazi, Mehrdad M. *Historical Buildings of Iran: Their Architecture and Structure.* Southampton, UK, and Boston: Computational Mechanics Publications, 1997.

Khansari, Mehdi, M. Reza Moghtader, and Minouch Yavari. *The Persian Garden: Echoes of Paradise.* Washington, DC: Mage Publishers, 1998.

Khansari, Mehdi, and Minouch Yavari. *The Persian Bazaar: Veiled Space of Desire,* Foreword authored by Oleg Grabar, Preface authored by Gérard Grandval, and Introduction authored by Marcel Bazin. Washington, DC: Mage Publishers, 1993.

Lockhardt, Laurence. *Famous Cities of Iran.* London: Luzac & Company, 1960.

Micara, Ludovico. "Contemporary Iranian Architecture in Search for a New Identity." *Environmental Design: Journal of the Islamic Environmental Design Research Centre* no. 1 (1996): 52–91.

O'Kane, Bernard. *Studies in Persian Art and Architecture.* Cairo, Egypt: American University in Cairo Press, 1995.

Pope, Arthur Upham. *Persian Architecture: The Triumph of Form and Color.* New York: G. Braziller, 1965.

Porter, Yves. *Palais et jardins de Perse.* Photographs by Arthur Thévenart. Paris: Flammarion, 2002.

Tadgell, Christopher. *Imperial Form: From Achaemenid Iran to Augustan Rome.* London: Ellipsis, 1998.

Wilber, Donald. *The Architecture of Islamic Iran.* Westport, CT: Greenwood Press, 1969.

———. *Persian Gardens and Garden Pavilions.* Rutland, VT: C. Tuttle, 1962.

Index

Âb-anbârs (water reservoirs), 119, 120–21
'Abbâs the Great, 22
Abbasid Dynasty, 16, 197
'Abdollâh, Mirzâ, 199
Achaemenid period. *See* Persian (Achaemenid) Empire
Afghan invasion and siege of Isfahan, 22
Âghâ Mohammad Shah, 24–25
Ahmadinejâd, Mahmud, 35, 92
Akhavân-Sâles, Mahdi, 81
'Alavi, Bozorg, 87
Alcoholic beverages, 150
Alexander the Great, 10, 14, 126
American embassy hostages (1979), 33
Amir Kabir, 27
Ancient Iran, 8–9
Anglo-Iranian Oil Company, 29, 30
Anglo-Persian Agreement of 1919, 28
Anglo-Persian Oil Company, 26, 99
Anthropomorphized gods and goddesses, 61–62
Anvari, 78
Apostasy, 59
'Aqd ceremony (marriage), 170–71, 172
Arabic script and the New Persian language, 4–5, 67, 68
Arberry, Arthur J., 76
Architecture, 119–36; cities, 123, 134–35; and climate, 119–20; cultural variables,
121; design elements, 121; government regulation and, 136; high-rise housing, 133; home design, 122–23, 133; interactions between men and women, 121–22; Islamic, 124, 127–31; and the Islamic Revolution (1979), 134; and natural resources, 119; neoclassical style, 131, 133; postmodernist styles of hybridized cultural forms, 134–35; prehistoric and pre-Islamic, 124–27; and religion, 121–22; roads, 133; styles of, 123–24; techniques in, 119; twentieth century, 131–36; Western influences, 132–33
Ardashir, 13, 14
Arg-e Bam, 136
Armenian Christianity in Iran, 61
Armenian churches, 130
Arms deals with United States, 33–34
Arsaces, king of Parthia, 10
Arts Festival in Shiraz, 116
Âshurâ music, 191–92
Asian Young Film Festival, 106
Âsieh, 96
Assyrians, 61
'Attâr, Farid-od-Din, 78, 191
Avedisiân, Yelenâ, 208
"Axis of evil," 35
Âyatollâh Khomeini, 31, 32, 33, 34: death of, 109; holidays for, 179, 180; and

Shi'ite hierarchy, 51; tomb of, 56; and women's dress, 161
Âzâdi (Freedom) Square (Shâhyâd Tower), 132
Azalis, 59
A'zm, Hamid-Rezâ, 117

Babism, 59
Babylonian captivity of the Jews, 60
Bâdgirs (wind-catcher towers), 119, 120
Bahaism, 58–60
Bahâollâh, 59
Bakhshis, 195–96
Bakhtiâr, Shâhpur, 32
Bani Sadr, Abo'l-Hasan, 34
Barkeshli, Mahdi, 200
Bathhouses, 123, 129
Bâtmângariân, Ardashir Khân, 95
Bayzâi, Bahram, 117, 118
Bazaars, 123, 129, 135
Bâzargân, Mahdi, 32, 33
Beauxian model of architecture, 131
Behbahâni, Simin, 82
Behjat-Tabrizi, Mohammad-Hosayn (Shahriâr), 80
Behrangi, Samad, 87
Bernadotte (Mme.), 95
Bibi Shahrbânu shrine, 56–57
Brecht, Bertolt, 115
Bridge-dams, 120, 130
Bridges, 120, 126, 130, 192
Bush, George W., 35
Buyid Dynasty, 17, 197

Calligraphy, 68; in architecture, 127–28, 129, 132
Cannes Film Festival, 113
Caravanserais, 123, 129
Carl von Ossietzky Medal, 82
Carpet of the Spring Garden, 143
Carpets, 137–47; ban on import of Iranian carpet to the United States, 146; carpet-weaving centers, 141–42; "carpets" versus "rugs," 138–39; designs in, 137, 139–42; Gabbeh (film), 139; history of carpet weaving in Iran, 142–47; as investments, 137; in Iranian households, 139; knots in, 138; mass-produced and

nonartistic carpets, 147; names of, 140; Persian (Senna) knots, 138; prayer rugs, 138; rise and fall of the carpet industry, 143–47; sizes of, 138–39; structure of, 138; synthetic aniline dyes, 145, 146; tribal and nomadic carpets, 140–41; Turkish (Ghiordes) knots, 138, 143; warp in, 138; weft in, 138; women and children as weavers, 141, Zilu, 139
Carter administration, 32
Caspian Sea, 2
Catholic Church, 61
Censorship: in cinema, 100, 104, 110–11, 113; in drama, 115, 116; of the media, 90; of modern Persian prose literature, 84, 86, 87, 90
Châdor (veil), 158, 159, 161, 172
Chahârshanbehsuri, 186
Chaldeans, 61
Chamber ensembles, 195
Changiziân, Hâydeh, 208
Chehel Sotun (palace in Isfahan), 129
Chemical weapons, 33
Child labor, 141
Children: career choices of, 174; custody laws, 175; father-daughter relations, 174; main characters in cinema, 112; mother-daughter bond, 174; socialization of, 172–74. See also Family
Chogâ Zanbil temple, 125
Christianity in Iran, 58, 60–61
Churches, 130–31
Cinema, 94–113, 200, 210: censorship, 100, 104, 110–11, 113; children as main characters, 112; domestic films, 101, 103, 106, 111; dubbing foreign films, 100–101; during reign of Rezâ Shah, 95–100; early development of, 94–96; Farrokhzâd's documentary film on leprosy ("The House Is Black"), 82; Film Fârsi, 101–3, 112–13, 205; international awards, 104, 113; Islamic cinema, 107–8, 110; Ministry of Culture and Islamic Guidance, 107, 109–10, 118; New Wave cinema, 103–6, 112–13; passion plays, 184; post revolution, 106–13; "Sacred Defense" cinema, 108, 109; sociological challenges, 96–98; theater

burning, 106; translation and presentation of foreign films, 97; women and, 96, 97–98, 107, 108–9, 110; women filmmakers, 111–12

Cities, 7–8, 20; architecture and design of, 123, 134–35; walled, 121

Civil holidays, 179–80

Classical Persian literature, 68–83; court patronage in Persian poetry, 69–70, 71, 78; *ghazal* genre of poetry, 75; influences on, 69–71; *naqqâli* recitations in collective settings, 73; the "new poetry" (*she'r-e now*), 79–83; poetry, 69–83; prose literature, 68–69; religious literature, 78; Sufism and poetry, 70–71, 74, 75

Climate, 3, 119–20

Collectivist culture, 122, 172

College of Television, 105

Communist (Tudeh) Party in Iran, 30, 31, 34, 114–15

Constitutional Revolution, 27-28, 59, 178

Cook, Nilla Cram, 208

Council of Nicaea, 61

Court patronage: and cinema, 94, 96; in music, 192, 196, 197; in Persian poetry, 69–70, 71, 78

Crime, 134

Curzon, George Nathaniel, 132

Custody of children, 165, 175

Cyrus the Great, 9, 60, 125

Damâvand (Mount), 2, 12

Dams, 120, 126, 129

Dance, 118, 202–10; aerobic forms, 209–10; ballet, 208, 209; as collective, 203, 204–5; controversial status of in Islam, 202–3, 206, 209; defining, 202; folk/ethnic dance, 196, 202, 203–4, 208, 209; forms of in Iran, 202; in Iranian history, 206–10; recreational dance in Iran, 202, 203, 204–6; schools of, 203, 206, 208; *Tehrâni* dance, 202, 204; Western dance in Iran, 210

"Dance of rice," 203

Dâr-ol-Fonun, 199

D'Arcy concession for petroleum and gas, 26

Darius the Great, 10, 14, 125

Dating, 167–68, 170

Dehkhodâ, 'Ali-Akbar, 83, 91

Divorce, 174–75; custody of children, 165; personality incompatibility in, 169; *Shari'a*, 175; stigma on women, 175; women's right to, 160. *See also* Marriage

Dowlâtabâdi, Mahmud, 89

Drama: censorship, 115, 116; early history of, 93–94; government development of, 116, 118; Islamic Republic's propaganda tool, 117; modern, 113–18; musical productions, 83; *naqqâli* recitations in collective settings, 73; political-protest, 114–15; secular works, 117–18; stage productions, 102; web site for Iranian theater, 118; women in, 118. *See also* Passion-plays

Dramatic Arts Center, 118

Dualism, 62

Earthquakes, 127, 135, 136

Eastern Catholics, 61

Educational system, 159

Edwards, A. Cecil, 138

Eisenhower administration, 30

Elamite Kingdom, 8–9

Emamzadehs (shrines and tombs), 55–57

Esfandiâri, 'Ali (Nimâ Yushij), 79–80, 82

Esmâ'il, 21, 45

Ethical values, 172

Extended family, 157

Fajr Festival of Music, 118, 201

Fâl (taking an omen), 77

Family, 157. *See also* Children

Family honor, 158, 163

Family law, 52–53

Family Protection Act, 160, 161, 162, 165

Fârâbi Cinema Foundation, 111

Farhat, Hormoz, 200

Farmanfarmaian, Manuchehr, 77–78

Farrokhi (poet), 71

Farrokhzâd, Forugh, 81–82, 103–4

Fârsi, 67

Fâtemeh (Mohammad's daughter), 40, 59

Father-daughter relations, 174

Ferdowsi, Abo'l-Qâsem, *Shâh-nâmeh* ("Book of Kings"), 71–73, 78, 96

Ferdowsi Theater in Tehran, 114
Fiction. *See* Modern Persian prose literature
Fire-temples, 125, 127
Fisher, Michael, 50
Fitzgerald, Robert, 78
Folk beliefs, 53–54
Folk drama, 93, 118
Folk/ethnic dance, 196, 202, 203–4, 208, 209
Folk literature, 66, 83
Folk music (regional music), 193, 195–96
Food and dining, 149–55; appetizers and snack foods, 154; beverages, 155; cuisine and culture, 149–151; fast-food shops, 150; full Iranian dinner, 153–54; Islamic dietary law, 150; rice, 152–53; stews and soups, 153, 154–55; traditional dining habits, 152; wheat and breads, 151–52
Foroughi, Mohsen, 132
Foundation for the Oppressed, 91
Free Cinema Film Festival, 106
Free Cinema of Iran, 106
Free verse, 79, 80, 82
Free will, 54
Freedom of the press, 91
Friday noon prayer, 181
Friend, Robyn C., 209

Ganji, Akbar, 92
"Garden-reading," 54
Gardens, 129
Gathas (hymns), 62
Gender relations, 158–64; anti-shah demonstrations, 161; chaperoning by male relatives, 158; cross-gender socialization, 168; Family Protection Act, 160, 161, 162, 165; in the Islamic Republic, 161–63; modern sector, 160–61; morality police, 161, 163; segregation by gender, 158–59, 161, 162, 168; sex-segregated dancing, 205; traditional sector, 160; Women's Organization of Iran (WOI), 160. *See also* Divorce; Marriage; Women
General Islamic holidays, 180–82
Geography, 1–3; aridity, 2; deserts, 1; lakes, 3; mountain chains, 2; rivers, 2; size of country, 1

Ghaffâri, Farrokh, 102, 103
Ghaznavid Dynasty, 17
Ghostantin, Asia, 96
Godard, Andre, 32
Gogoosh, 192
Golshiri, Hushang, 87
Greek plays, 93
Gregorian calendar, 177, 179

Hâfez, Shams-od-Din, 73, 75–78, 191
Hamidi, H.M. (Hosaynqoli Most'ân), 83
Hârun-or-Rashid, 206
*Hayât*s (courtyards of houses), 122
Healing dances, 204
Hedâyat, Sâdeq, 80, 25–86
Hegira, 178, 179
Hejâb (veil), 158, 159, 161, 162
History outline, 8–35
Holidays, 177, 179–88; civil, 179–80; Muslim religious holidays, 180–85; national holidays, 185–88
Homosexuality, 77, 167
Hosayn, death at Karbalâ, 54, 183, 184, 196
House of Theatre, 118
Huan Tsang, 143

Idiomatic expressions, 67
Il-Khanid Dynasty, 18, 128
Imam Rezâ Shrine, 128, 139
Improvisation in music, 194, 200
Institute of Musicology, 200
International Festival of Films for Children and Young Adults, 106
Iran Carpet Company, 146
Iran-Iraq War, 33–34
Iran-Now Film, 100
Iranian Ballet Company, 208
Iranian-British Cultural Center, 95
Iranian calendars, 177–79
Iranian Center for Preservation and Dissemination of National Music, 200
Iranian Cultural Heritage Organization, 134
Iranian Folk Society, 208
Iranian National Ballet, 208
"Iranian National History," 11–15, 72
Iranian National Television, 116
Iranian News Agency, 91
Iranian pop music, 193

Iranian Society of Architects, 132
Iranian solar calendar (*shamsi*), 177, 178–79
Isfahan, architecture in, 120, 129–30
Islam, 4, 37–44; "clergy" in, 48–49; doctrines of, 38; ritual aspects of, 39, 52. *See also* Shi'ite Islam
Islamic conquest, 15–16
Islamic lunar calendar (*qamari*), 177, 178, 179
Islamic Republic of Iran, 33, 35; and Jews, 60; religion in the constitution of, 37, 51
Islamic Republican Party (IRP), 34

Jalâli calendar, 178, 179
Jamâlzâdeh, Mohammad-Ali, 83–85
Jâmi, Nur-od-Din, 78
Jamileh, 209
Jones, Sir William, 77
Judaism in Iran, 58, 60

Kamâl-oz-Zamân, 197
Karbalâ, 54, 183, 184–85
Karim Khân, 23-24
Kendi, 198
Kennedy administration, 31
Khamenei, 'Ali, 34, 51
Khâqâni, 78
Khâtami, Mohammad, 35, 91, 110
Khayyâm, 'Omar, 71, 78
Khoi, Esmâ'il, 81
Khomeini. *See* Ayatollah Khomeini
Khorâsâni school of music, 197, 198
Khordâdiân, Mohammad, 209–10
Khostrow I Anushirvan, 11
Kiârostami, 'Abbâs, 112, 113, 117, 184
Knots in carpets, 138
Koran, 38, 39, 40; and calligraphy, 68; and music, 191
Kushân, Esmâ'il, 100, 101–2

Languages, 4–5; Persian language, 4, 66–68
Lemaire, Alfred Jean-Baptiste, 199
Literacy, 66, 89, 90
Literary languages, 4
Literature, 65–92. *See also* Classical Persian literature; Media; Modern Persian prose literature; Persian language

Luster tile panels, 128–29
Lyrics in music, 194

Mahmud, Ahmad, 89
Mahmud, Parviz, 199
Majidi, Majid, *Rang-e khodâ* ("Color of Paradise"), 56
Makhmalbâf, Mohsen, 89, 139
Malkom Khân, 90
Manichaenism, 62
Mansur I, 67
Marriage, 160–61, 164–72; arranged, 167, 168, 170; bride price (*mahriyeh*), 165–66, 170; and children, 168, 169; civil laws, 164–65; between close relatives, 63; dowry (*jahiziyeh*), 166; extramarital affairs, 169; Islamic Shi'ite laws on, 164–65; legal age for, 160, 166; legal contract of, 165, 170; polygamy, 167; premarital sex, 167; requests for, 168, 170; rituals and ceremonies, 169–72; temporary, 160; women's surnames, 168. *See also* Divorce
Martial music, 191
Ma'rufi, 'Abbâs, 88
Mashhad, 53, 56
Mecca, 55, 56, 139
Media, 90–92; censorship and state control, 90; freedom of the press, 91; investigative journalism, 92; newspapers, 90–92; types of, 90
Median Kingdom, 9, 125, 142
Meter and rhyme, 69
Mil-e Ajdahâ tower, 126
Miniature painting, 141, 143
Ministry of Culture and Arts, 116
Ministry of Culture and Islamic Guidance: on cinema, 107, 109–10, 118; on music, 200–201
Minority religions in Iran, 58–63. *See also* Bahaism; Christianity; Judaism; Zoroastrianism
Mitrâ Film, 101
Modern Persian prose literature, 83–89: censorship and repression, 84, 86, 87, 90; debate between modernists and traditionalists, 83; female novelists, 89; Islamic Revolution era, 88; nonfiction and

scholarly writing, 83; politics and social criticism in fiction, 86–87; post revolution literature, 88-89; romantic writings, 83; satire, 83–85; story-telling, 83; structuralism, 87–88; war literature (Iran-Iraq War), 88; writers living abroad, 89
Mohâjerâni, 'Atâollah, 110–11
Mohammad, Prophet of God, 38, 39, 57: the Hegira, 178, 179
Moharram, first 10 days of, 54, 183, 196, 202
Mohseni, Majid, 102, 103
Mongol invasion, 17–18
Monophonic music, 200
Monotheism, 38, 62
Montazeri, Hosayn-'Ali, 51
Moqarnas, 127
Morâdi, Ebrâhim, 96
Moraqqa' (mosaic design), 128
Morier, James, The Adventures of Hajji Baba of Isfahan, 84
Mosaddeq, Mohammad 30–31
Moshiri, Fereydun, 80
Mosques, 123, 127–30
Mo'tazedi, Bâbâ Khân, 95, 98
Mother-daughter bond, 174
Mowseli, Ebrâhim, 197
Music, 118, 189–202; controversial status of in Islam, 190–91, 192, 197; as entertainment, 192; folk music (regional music), 195–96; history of Persian music, 196–200; instruments, 192, 195, 196, 197, 199; Iranian pop music, 200, 201; performing for Western audiences, 196; Persian music in contemporary Iran, 200–202; religious influences on Persian music, 190–93; schools of in Iran, 194; structure of, 192–94; Western music, 199, 200, 201
Mystical music, 191
Mystical or Sufi dance, 204

Nâder Shah, 23
Nafisi, Sa'id, 96
Naqqâli recitations in collective settings, 73, 93, 117
Nâser-od-Din Shah, 27
Nasiriân, 'Ali, 116

National Academy of Music, 199
National Folkloric Music, Song and Dance, 208
National Front, 30
National holidays, 185–88
National Iranian Film Society, 102
National Iranian Oil Company, 77
National Iranian Radio and Television, 105
National Music Department, 199
National style of architecture, 131–32
Nationalization of oil, 30–31
Nestorians, 61
New Avestan Calendar, 178
New Film Group, 106
New Year's holiday, 186–88, 207; Nowruz (New Year's Day), 186
Newspapers. See Media
Nezâmi, 78
Nightclubs, 205, 208, 209
Nimâ Yushij ('Ali Esfandiâri), 79–80, 82
Nixon administration, 31
Non-Muslims in Iran, 58–63
Nowruz (New Year's Day), 186, 207
Nuclear technology, 35
Nursing homes, 157
Nushin, 'Abd-ol-Hosayn, 114

'Obayd-e Zâkâni, 78
Ohanian, Hovhannes, 95–96
OPEC, 31
Opera, 208
Orally-transmitted folktales, 83
Ornamentation in music, 194
Osuli school of Imami Shi'ism, 48–49

Pagan Aryans, 61–62
Pahlavi Iran, 28–32, 37; architecture, 131; religion, 40, 58
Panegyric ode (qasideh), 69–70, 71
Pârs Film studio, 101–2
Pârs National Ballet, 208
Parthians, 10–11; architecture of, 126; dance and, 106
Passion-plays (ta'ziyeh), 93, 183, 184–85, 191
Patriarchal culture, 158, 168, 172, 174
Pazyrk carpet, 142
Performing arts, 118

Persecution, religious, 59–60, 61
Persepolis: architecture at, 125–26; celebration of 2500 years of monarchy, 32
Persian (Achaemenid) Empire, 9–10, 60; architecture in, 125–26; dance in, 206
Persian carpets. *See* Carpets
Persian Gulf, 2
Persian language, 4–5, 66–68
Persian literature, 65. *See also* Persian language; Classical Persian literature; Modern Persian prose literature
Pezeshkzâd, Iraj, 87
Pile of carpets, 138, 139
Pilgrimages, 53, 55–56
Poetry, 66. *See also* Classical Persian literature
Polygamy, 167
Polyphonic music pieces, 199
Pope, Arthur, 142
Population, 4, 133–34, 135
Prayer music, 191
Predestination, 54
Processions on holidays, 183
Prose literature. *See* Modern Persian prose literature
Prosody, 69
Prostitution, 163
Protestantism, 61
Public facilities, 123
Public services, 134, 135, 136
Puppet plays, 93, 94

Qâ'âni, 79
Qâjâr period, 24–27, 59; architecture in, 130, 131; carpet industry in, 145; cinema in the, 94–95; classical Persian music in, 198–99; dance in, 205
Qanâts (underground water channels), 119, 120
Qasideh (panegyric ode), 69–70, 71
Qodsi Partovi, 96
Qorrat-ol-'Ayn, 59

Râdi, Akbar, 118
Radif (repertoire), 194–95, 199
Radio, 192, 199, 200
Rafsanjâni, 'Ali-Akbar Hâshemi, 34, 53, 109
Rahbar, Mahmud, 116

Ramazân, 180–81
Rang-e khodâ ("Color of Paradise"), 56
Ravânipur, Moniru, 89
Reagan administration, 33–34
Regional dynasties, 16–17
Regions and provinces, 5–7
Religions in Iran, 4, 37–64. *See also* Islam; Minority religions in Iran; Shi'ism; Sunnism
Religious holidays, 180–85
Religious rituals, 93. *See also* Islam
Revolution of the Shah and the People (White Revolution), 31
Revolutionary Iran, 32–35
Rezâ Khân, 28, 29, 30
Rezâ Shah, Mohammad-, 30, 31, 32; and the carpet industry, 145–46; and the cinema, 95–100; dance and, 207–9; and music, 199–200; national style of architecture, 131–32; return to Iran, 115; and women, 159–60
Roman/Byzantine empire, 61
Rudenko, Sergi, 142
Rumi, Jalâl-od-Din, *Masnavi-e Ma'navi*, 65, 71, 78, 191
Rushdie, Salman, 35
Rusi Khân, Mahdi, 95
Russo-Persian Wars, 25

Sabâh Dance Company in Los Angeles, 209
Saddam Hussein, 33
Sa'di, Mosharref-od-Din, 73–75
Sa'di Theater, 114
Safavids, 20–24; architecture, 129; carpets of, 143; music, 198; Shi'ite Islam, 45–47
Sahhâfbâshi, Mirzâ Ebrâhim Khan, 94
Saljuq Empire, 17, 197
Samanid Dynasty, 17, 197
Sasanids, 11, 13, 14, 15; architecture of, 126–27; carpets of, 143; dance and, 206; music of, 196–97
Self-flagellation, 183, 191, 202
Selucids, 10, 126
Sepantâ, 'Abd-ol-Hosayn, 96
Sepehri, Sohrâb, 82–83
Seyhun, Hushang, 132
Shaif'i Kadkani, Mohammad-Rezâ, 81
Shahâdeh (profession of faith), 38

Shahriâr (Behjat-Tabrizi, Mohammad-
    Hosayn), 80
Shâhyâd Tower (Âzâdi Square), 132
Shâmlu, Ahmad, 81
Shari'a (Islam rules and regulations), 39,
    162, 165
Shi'ite holidays, 182–85
Shi'ite Islam, 4, 44–58; "clergy" in, 48–49;
    emamzadehs (shrines and tombs),
    55–57; family law, 52–53; history of,
    44–48; law, 52; mourning ceremonies,
    54; as official religion of Iran, 37; Osuli
    school of Imami Shi'ism, 48–49; pil-
    grimages, 53, 55–56; religious colleges
    or seminaries, 49–51; religious culture
    of, 52–58; rituals, 52; and Sunnism,
    39–44; taqiyeh (prudent dissimulation),
    57–58; temporary marriages, 53. See
    also Islam
Shirâzi, Sayyid 'Ali-Mohammad, 59
Shirâzi, Qutb-od-Din, 198
Shiraz Art Festival, 106
Shopping malls, 135
Shrines, 128
Shuster, Morgan, 27
Sinemâ Tamaddon, 99
Sizdah Bedar, 186, 188
Social life, 157
Socialization of children, 172–74
Sofreh (holiday tableau), 187
Soltânpur, Sa'id, 116–17
Song and Dance Ensemble, 208
Spiritual dancing, 204
Stone carving, 125, 126–27, 129
Storytelling, 118
Stucco art, 126, 129
Subways, 134
Sufism, 20, 39, 47; classical Persian music
    in, 191, 195, 198; classical Persian po-
    etry in, 70–71, 74, 75; dance in, 202,
    204, 205, 207
Suicide rate among women, 163
Sunna (instructions of Mohammad), 39, 40
Sunnism, 4, 57, 185; family law, 52–53;
    religious culture of, 52; and Shi'ism,
    39–44. See also Islam
Sur-e Esrâfil ("Esrafel's Trumpet"), 90–91
Synthetic aniline dyes, 145, 146

Tâbatabâi, Sayyid Ziâ-od-Din, 28
Takiyeh Dowlat, 198–99
Tâlebi, Farâmarz, 116
Tanâvoli, Parviz, 68
Taqiyeh (prudent dissimulation), 57–58
Taqvâ'i, Nâser, 184
Tehran Carpet Museum, 146
Tehran Declaration, 30
Tehran International Film Festival, 106
Tehran Metro, 134
Tehran Symphony Orchestra, 199
Tehran University: Faculty of Dramatic
    Arts and Faculty of Fine Arts, 106, 116;
    music department, 200
Telefilm, 105, 106
Television, 192, 200, 209, 210
Temporary marriage (sigheh), 53, 160
Tepe Hasanlu, 124
Tepe Sialk, 124
Theodore of Mopsuestia, 61
Three Wise Men visiting Bethlehem, 60
Tile work, 128, 130, 141
Timur Lang (Tamerlane), 18–19, 20, 78,
    207
Tobacco Protest, 26
Tripartite Treaty (1942), 30
Turko-Mongol era, 17–20
Tusi, Nâser-od-Din, 198

United States Information Service (USIS)
    in Iran, 101
Universal House of Justice in Haifa, Israel, 59
Urban railways, 134

Vâ'ez Kâshefi, Hosayn, "Garden of the
    Martyrs," 54
Vahdat Hall, 208
Vakili, 'Ali, 95, 98
Vaziri, 'Ali-Naqi, 199, 200
Veil (châdor or hejâb), 158, 159, 161, 162,
    208
Vishtaspa, 62

Wall paintings, 126
Walled cities, 121
Walled houses, 122
Weddings, dancing in, 202, 205, 209. See
    also Marriage

Western pop music, 192, 200

White Revolution (Revolution of the Shah and the People), 31, 160

White Sheep, 19, 20, 21

Women: Behbahâni, Simin, 82; with children, 164, 172; in cinema and in theaters, 96, 97–98, 107, 108–9, 110; and dancing, 206, 208; Dâneshvar, Simin, 87; in drama, 118; education of, 159, 162; Farrokhzâd, Forugh, 81–82; as filmmakers, 111–12; freed from wearing the veil, 98; history of women's status, 158–64; musicians, 192–93; novelists, 89; in Persian society, 82; poets, 82; Qorrat-ol-'Ayn, 59; Ravânipur, Moniru, 89; *Shari'a*, 162, 165; suicide rate, 163; unveiled in films, 94; veil (châdor or hejâb), 158, 159, 161, 162; in the workforce, 162–64. *See also* Divorce; Gender relations; Marriage

Women's Organization of Iran (WOI), 160

World War I, 28

World War II, 29–30

Writing. *See* Classical Persian literature; Modern Persian prose literature

Yaldâ, 186, 188

Ya'qub Lays, 67

Yâsami, Siâmak, 103

Yazd, city walls of, 121

Zâgheh Tepe, 124

Zenon, 206

Ziaggurats, 125

Zoroastrianism, 46, 48, 58, 61–63; and architecture, 121; cultural influence on Iran, 61, 186, 188, 196; dance in, 204, 206; exposure of the dead in open structures (*dakhmas*), 63; and Iranian cuisine, 150–51; marriage between close relatives, 63; Mazda worshipping, 63; nationalistic aspect of, 62–63; rituals of, 63

Zurvanism, 62

About the Authors

ELTON L. DANIEL is Professor of History at the University of Hawaii, author of *The History of Iran* (Greenwood, 2000), and Associate Editor of *Encyclopaedica Iranica*.

ALI AKBAR MAHDI is a Professor in the Department of Sociology and Anthropology, Ohio Wesleyan University, author of several books on Iran, and editor of *Teen Life in the Middle East* (Greenwood, 2003).

Recent Titles in
Culture and Customs of the Middle East

Culture and Customs of Israel
Rebecca L. Torstrick

Culture and Customs of the Palestinians
Samih K. Farsoun

Culture and Customs of Saudi Arabia
David E. Long